JOSEPH CONRAD
and the
ANXIETY OF KNOWLEDGE

JOSEPH CONRAD
and the
ANXIETY OF KNOWLEDGE

WILLIAM FREEDMAN

The University of South Carolina Press

© 2014 University of South Carolina

Published by the University of South Carolina Press
Columbia, South Carolina 29208

www.sc.edu/uscpress

Manufactured in the United States of America

22 21 20 19 18 17 16 15 14 13   10 9 8 7 6 5 4 3 2 1

LIBRARY OF CONGRESS CATALOGING-IN-PUBLICATION DATA

Freedman, William, 1938–
Joseph Conrad and the anxiety of knowledge / William Freedman.
pages cm
Includes bibliographical references and index.
ISBN 978-1-61117-306-2 (hardbound : alk. paper)—ISBN 978-1-61117-307-9 (ebook)
1. Conrad, Joseph, 1857–1924—Criticism and interpretation. I. Title.
PR6005.O4Z7235 2014
823'.912—DC23   2013022870

Frontispiece: Cartoon by Charles Barsotti, from the *New Yorker,* April 24, 2006. Copyright Charles Barsotti. The New Yorker Collection, The Cartoon Bank, www.cartoonbank.com

To my dearly loved wife, daughter, and son
To the memory of my mother, my father, and my stepfather
And to all those, far too many, whose truth it would have been better not to know

With the truth man cannot live. To be able to live one needs illusions.

OTTO RANK
Will Therapy and Truth and Reality

What makes mankind tragic is not that they are the victims of nature,
it is that they are conscious of it.

JOSEPH CONRAD
Letter to Cunninghame Graham, January 31, 1898

CONTENTS

Abbreviations   viii

    Prologue: Ambivalent Fabulist, Indeterminate Fables   *1*

  1   Forbidden Knowledge and the Saving Illusion   *5*

  2   The Lie of Fiction: *Heart of Darkness*   *36*

  3   The Soft Spot: *Lord Jim*   *61*

  4   A More Dangerous Revolution: *Under Western Eyes*   *88*

  5   Drowning in the Romance of the Shallows: *The Rescue*   *105*

  Epilogue   *129*

Appendix: Woman and Truth, the History of an Association   *133*

Notes   *141*

Works Cited   *165*

Index   *173*

ABBREVIATIONS

All references to Conrad's novels, short stories, and essays are to the Uniform Edition of *The Works of Joseph Conrad* (1923). The following abbreviations are used:

CL: *The Collected Letters of Joseph Conrad*
HD: *Heart of Darkness*
LE: *Last Essays*
LJ: *Lord Jim*
NLL: *Notes on Life and Letters*
NN: *The Nigger of the "Narcissus"*
PR: *A Personal Record*
R: *The Rescue*
UWE: *Under Western Eyes*

PROLOGUE

Ambivalent Fabulist, Indeterminate Fables

The insistent haziness and evasiveness of many of Conrad's novels and shorter tales has provoked readers at least as far back as E. M. Forster and H. L. Mencken and generated much comment and complaint. For Mencken there flows through all Conrad's stories "a kind of tempered melancholy, a sense of seeking and not finding." Quoting Wilson Follett on Conrad's fascination with "the profound meaninglessness of life," Mencken maintains that the author "grounds his work upon this sense of cosmic implacability, this confession of unintelligibility." Mencken was perhaps the first to note what has lately become a sophisticated commonplace: that "the exact point of the story of Kurtz in 'Heart of Darkness' is that it is pointless."[1] Less contentedly Forster complained that "the secret casket of [Conrad's] genius contains a vapor rather than a jewel." "What is so elusive about [him]," remarks Forster, ". . . is that he is always promising to make some general philosophical statement about the universe and then refraining in a gruff disclaimer. . . . There is a central obscurity" in Conrad: something noble, heroic, and inspiring "but obscure! Obscure! Misty in the middle as well as at the edges."[2]

More recent criticism has kept to this path with varying degrees of approval or dismay. The narrative voice in *The Secret Agent* confesses that "true wisdom . . . is not certain of anything in this world of contradictions" (84), and many of Conrad's novels are read, with increasing frequency, as self-contradictory, evasive by habit, compulsion, or design, or otherwise resistant to coherent understanding or interpretation. Edward Said remarks that the subject of Conrad's narratives "is illusory, or shadowy, or dark" and that "what the tale usually reveals is the exact contours of this obscurity."[3]

In what follows I argue that many of Conrad's novels and shorter tales are the elusive and contradictory entities they are not principally for the reasons usually proffered but as an expression of destabilizing ambivalence about the revelation and content of the knowledge they ostensibly seek or glancingly recover. Where the threat of knowledge is especially chilling, the balance tips, weighted to one side by the conviction that, as Jocasta warned, there is much it is better not to know. The reasons typically offered to explain the evasive obscurity or indeterminacy of Conrad's narratives—the inherent inadequacy of language, the multiplicity or elusiveness of truth, a philosophical skepticism or nihilism that negates it, or commitment to an aesthetic of romantic vagueness, among others—are at best incomplete. They must be complemented, I believe, by a reading that recognizes textual inconsistencies as reflective of attitudinal ambivalence, and obfuscation and evasion as marks of a calculated refusal of dangerous knowledge or a defensive recoil from it.

As Andrew Michael Roberts observes, "There is general agreement . . . that Conrad's fiction emphasizes the problematic nature of questions of what we can know, how we can know it and what degree of certainty is possible. These questions are raised in particular in terms of the relationship of language to truth and reality and in this form locate Conrad's work within literary modernism"[4] My point in this study is that while these questions may often be raised *in* these fictions in terms of that relationship, they are as often raised *by* these texts in terms that make of Conrad's modernism in no small measure a defense against powerful forces working beneath the safer epistemological surface and finally destabilizing it. A principal source of the evasions and obfuscations in Conrad's works, as we will see, are threatened assaults on the self-possession—the narrator's, the protagonist's, finally the writer's—on which one's sense of honor, integrity, and personal worth depend. H. M. Daleski rightly emphasizes the determinate importance of Conrad's famous admission that "I have a positive horror of losing even for one moving moment that full possession of myself which is the first condition of good service. And I have carried my notion of good service from my earlier into my later existence" (*PR* xvii), which is to say, from his early life as a merchant seaman to his later life as a writer, the demands of which he often analogized to those required by the successful seaman. For Daleski the four principal threats to the loss of self depicted in the novels are "the surrender of self in passion," the loss "of one's head in a situation which demands physical self-possession," "the loss of self that is a concomitant of spiritual disintegration," and "suicide, the deliberate destruction of self."[5] But these threats are not confined to or safely contained within the narratives. Rather they endanger the writer and his fictions no less than the protagonists they describe, and they are responsible for many of the imposed obscurities and defensive evasions that pervade the writing.

A FEW WORDS about the claims and organization of this study. The first chapter, on dangerous or forbidden knowledge, is divided into two parts. The first section lays the ideational foundation for what follows by situating the key concept—

dangerous and forbidden knowledge—in the history of ideas. The point is that Conrad's subscription to this notion is by no means idiosyncratic. The concept occupies a substantial cross-cultural space in the history of human thought, broad and enduring enough to suggest a deeply rooted, perhaps archetypal foundation not unrelated, perhaps, to the power of its rendering in these narratives. The discussion is brief because the notion is, I believe, familiar to us all, in need therefore of only limited elaboration and emphasis. The considerably longer second part is a study of Conrad's perplexed relationship with truth and knowledge, particularly his dedication to the saving illusion, his conviction, iterated frequently and in a variety of forms in his letters, essays, tales, and novels, that because many truths are too dark altogether, there is much it is better not to know.

The four chapters that follow are intensive text-based studies of four of Conrad's novels: *Heart of Darkness, Lord Jim, Under Western Eyes,* and *The Rescue*. The first three adhere closely to the study's overarching claim that the obscurities of these narratives and the consequent difficulties of interpretation are owed largely to a wrenching ambivalence toward confrontation with threatening knowledge marked, typically, by a recoil from it. All three novels, in addition to much else that Conrad wrote, are dramatized explorations of the question that troubled him throughout his writing career: whether it is wisdom or folly to pursue knowledge that threatens not only our peace of mind but also our will and capacity to function honorably in the time we are allotted on this planet. The answer is implicit in the performance. In all three novels, though the impetus to obfuscation and retreat varies, there is more obscurity, finally, than revelation.

The treatments of this subject, tied to the inevitable differences between the novels, are not identical. In the Marlow tales, *Heart of Darkness* and *Lord Jim,* where the veilings and evasions that obscure meaning are owed to the narrator's glaring, often acknowledged reluctance to discover what he ostensibly so vigorously pursues, attention will be principally on the repeated occlusions and evasions where impending knowledge looms most threateningly and on Marlow's admissions, explicit or inferable, that the better part of wisdom is avoidance. The study of *Under Western Eyes* differs principally in the ways its narrator differs from Marlow. The source or strategy of evasion here is not the narrator's habitual construction of obstacles in the way of his own presumably eager wish to see, but Conrad's imposition of a narrator whose antipathies, remoteness, and obtuseness are themselves a virtually impenetrable obstruction to clear sight. The localized obscurities of *Heart of Darkness* and *Lord Jim* are replaced in this novel by a gauzy, wind-blown curtain readers strain with limited confidence or success to see through. The critical question with regard to *Under Western Eyes* is why Conrad elected to interpose such a baffled and baffling narrator. The answer, I maintain, is the centrality of Russia—a highly charged and extremely problematic subject for Conrad, given his family history and Polish nationality—and the stridently emotional, impulsive, and volatile character of its people, antithetical and threatening to the narrator's and the writer's preciously and precariously guarded self-possession. The threat is compounded by the principally ("passionate" and "hysterical") female composition of the forces of rebellion in the novel.

The struggle between the ostensibly nobler claims of revelation and confession and the fearful inclination to deny, retreat from, or conceal is also dramatized differently in these novels: in *Heart of Darkness* and *Lord Jim*—which constitute, in this regard, a single continuous exploration—in the distinctly different but readily comparable ways Marlow, Kurtz, and Jim deal with the question of dangerous (self-) knowledge or revelation; in *Under Western Eyes* in the contrast between Razumov's hesitantly confessional journal and the overarching opaque narrative of the language teacher. All five texts, in effect, are fictionalized incarnations of the artist tossed into the ring with this dilemma.

It is just this problem of endangering revelation, I believe, that accounts in important measure for Conrad's tormented twenty-year struggle with *The Rescue*, and my reading of that novel will concentrate on this more radical flight or evasion. This reading differs from the others in that it focuses not, as in *Heart of Darkness* and *Lord Jim*, on purposive evasions and avoidances within the novel and not, as in *Under Western Eyes*, on the blanketing opacity of the narration, but on the writer's fitful struggle with and abandonment of the novel itself. Flight in *The Rescue* is from the devouring and debilitating vision of despair Conrad deemed inadmissible in a work of fiction: still more from the dangerously enthralling woman as both body and mirror, other and reflected self, the urgency intensified by a sense of intolerable self-exposure that could be sufficiently obscured or distanced only by abandonment of the project.

I have added an appendix on the ancient and complex history of the identification of woman with (typically dangerous) Truth. It is of use, I think, as background, partial source, and validation of Conrad's frequent if perhaps surprising association of woman with Truth itself and the defensive evasion of knowledge its threat dictates and commends. I have not placed this discussion earlier, as part of the preliminary segment on forbidden knowledge, for fear its length might encourage the misleading impression that woman is the principal repository of dangerous knowledge rather than one important form among many. Readers who feel they may find my arguments for this linkage and its consequences in the tales and novels more persuasive if they are familiar with its history may wish to begin with the appendix. Others, I hope, will, until they get to it, accept my assurance that Conrad's practice is rooted in an ancient, expansive, and authoritative, if at times objectionable, tradition.

1

FORBIDDEN KNOWLEDGE AND THE SAVING ILLUSION

The idea that there are forms of knowledge too threatening to be encountered or acknowledged or otherwise proscribed has many voices and a long, venerable, and variegated history.[1] Psychologically it is at the heart of the psychoanalytic theories of repression and denial, the mechanisms with which we protect ourselves from knowledge that menaces our well-being or sense of self-esteem. "With the truth," as Otto Rank remarked, "man cannot live. To be able to live one needs illusions."[2] And for Freud all of civilization, including its unavoidable discontents, survives the savage waters of human nature in the raft of this necessary avoidance. Ernest Becker, whose *The Denial of Death* is a comprehensive treatise on denial—its rich and ancient history, its philosophical advocacy, its psychological origins, explanations, and justifications—summarily declares, "If repression makes an untenable life livable, self-knowledge can entirely destroy it for some people."[3] Ego psychology complemented psychoanalysis' early claims about repression with the observation that many activities of the ego are summoned to defend against more than the internal threats and conflicts Freud had emphasized. The function of these mechanisms, variously labeled denial, avoidance, or ego restriction, is, Anna Freud argued, "to avoid unpleasure by directly resisting external impressions."[4] Heinz Hartmann went further. In certain circumstances, he maintained, when we are faced with particularly threatening forms of knowledge or experience, turning away from reality is "a positive value for health"; self-preservation itself, in fact, depends to a substantial degree on various forms of neutralization.[5]

Scripturally the danger and prohibition are vividly dramatized in the narratives of the Garden of Eden and the Tree of Knowledge (Gen. 2:17), the Tower of Babel (Gen. 11:1–9), and the flight from Sodom (Gen. 19:17–26), in all of which prohibited seeing, seeking, or knowing meets with fatal retribution. "For in much wisdom," sayeth the Preacher, "*is* much grief: and he that increaseth knowledge increaseth sorrow" (Eccles. 1:18). In Greek mythology the cost is grimly realized in the punishment of Prometheus for his theft; in the ironic "gifts" of grief and evil released with the forbidden opening of Pandora's jar or box; in the story of Orpheus, who shares the fate of Lot's wife for violating, as she did, an injunction not to see; in the tale of Cupid and Psyche, likewise punished for "seeing" what should not be seen;[6] and in the paradigmatic fate of Oedipus, who, ignoring Jocasta's warning to "look no further," is agonizingly self-blinded by (self-)knowledge.

"Christians," Montaigne observed, "have a special knowledge of the degree to which curiosity is a natural and original evil," for which reason "ignorance is so strongly recommended to us by our religion as the appropriate path to belief and obedience."[7] Whether or not one subscribes to Montaigne's elevation of Christianity on this scale—it has much eager competition—Christian thought, particularly in its treatment of Original Sin, is rife with this warning and prohibition. It pervades the writings of Tertullian and the church fathers but is perhaps most famously and influentially present in the work of St. Augustine, who condemns what he memorably calls "libido sciendi," the (sexual) lust for knowledge that explains and justifies the generational transfer of Original Sin through semen.[8] It is prominent, too, in Dante's *Divine Comedy* and in John Milton's Augustinian elaboration of the origin and consequences of the Fall;[9] no less so, as Shattuck makes clear, in folktales such as "Bluebeard" and in literary productions such as Johann Wolfgang von Goethe's *Faust,* Mary Shelley's *Frankenstein,* Robert Louis Stevenson's *Dr. Jekyll and Mr. Hyde,* Oscar Wilde's *The Picture of Dorian Gray,* and a spate of tales by Nathaniel Hawthorne. Jean-Jacques Rousseau, too, sounded a warning about the dangers of knowledge. Sounding, all ironies expunged, like the putative author of Jonathan Swift's "Digression on Madness" in *A Tale of a Tub,* Rousseau scorned the pride on whose back we would "emerge from that happy state of ignorance, in which the wisdom of providence had placed us. That thick veil with which it hath covered all its operations," he continues,

> seems to be a sufficient proof that it never designed us for such fruitless researches. But is there, indeed, one lesson it hath taught us, that we have rightly profited by, or have not with impunity neglected? Be rightly instructed, however, for once, ye people, and know that nature would have preserved you from science, as a tender mother snatches a dangerous weapon out of the hands of her child. Know that all the secrets she hides from you, are so many evils from which she protects you; the very difficulty you experience in acquiring knowledge being a distinguishing mark of her benevolence towards you. Mankind are naturally perverse; but how much more so would they be, if they had the misfortune to be also born learned.[10]

Most pertinent to Conrad's practice is Michel Foucault's contention that from the late seventeenth century until Freud the discourse of sex, that most forbidden of all subjects, "never ceased to hide the thing it was speaking about." Virtually the entire discourse consisted of procedures "meant to evade the unbearable, too hazardous truth of sex."[11] Although the encounter with the dangerous woman is one of the principal sources of textual anxiety, recoil, and obscurity in these fictions, woman in this sense and role includes all she is traditionally and intimidatingly associated with in anxious masculine discourse: not only sex but passion and unreason, corporeality and engulfment, mortality and death, mystery and enigma—truth itself, in fact, in its most feral, "jungular," and mysterious dark-continent forms.[12]

Woman is repeatedly identified with dangerous, enigmatic, and elusive truth in Conrad. In "The Return" (collected in *Tales of Unrest*) woman is explicitly identified as a form of the world's impenetrable and unutterable secret. Groping at the feet of the wife who has betrayed him (as woman, the sea, the wilderness, and other objects of hungering curiosity habitually do), Alvan Hervey was "penetrated by an irresistible belief in an enigma, by the conviction that within his reach and passing away from him was the very secret of existence—its certitude, immaterial and precious" (176). Similarly the smitten narrator of *The Arrow of Gold* identifies the exotic Dona Rita as the unattainable embodiment of that eternally elusive truth. "She listened to me," he reports, "unreadable, unmoved, narrowed eyes, closed lips, slightly flushed face, as if carved six thousand years ago in order to fix for ever that something secret and obscure which is in all women" (146). In *Under Western Eyes*, Razumov, as Terence Cave observes, regards Natalie Haldin "not as an individual, but as the symbol of transcendent value"; his desire for her, therefore, "is transposed metonymically into desire for the truth, the removal of the last obstacle to full utterance."[13] And in "Falk," as in "The Planter of Malata," the link is literal and explicit. The narrator of "Falk," gazing at Hermann's niece, gifted with a bewitching "profusion of sensuous charms," identifies her as "the eternal truth of an unerring principle" (*NN* 236).

In "The Planter of Malata" (collected in *Within the Tides*), Felicia Moorsom's punctuating declarations—"I have an instinct for truth"; "I stand for truth here"; "It's I who stand for truth here!"; and "Here I stand for truth itself" (43, 47, 75, 78)—are especially suggestive because at least two of them are unprovoked, their relevance to context tenuous. Quite uncalled for and surprisingly incongruous with their surroundings, like Conrad's intrusive digression on betrayal in *Lord Jim* (277), they seem less dictated by the exigencies of character or fictional situation than forced to the surface from a concealed subtext where woman is profoundly if elusively identified with truth.[14] It is more than incidental that on almost every occasion that woman is identified with truth, her image blurs and understanding of her is declared impossible and denied, clouded over by the insistence that she is indeed a "mystery" or "enigma." And like truth, she destroys whoever would possess her.

Woman in Conrad's narratives is a palpable reality and a complex symbol. She is out of touch with reality, as Marlow remarks in *Heart of Darkness*, because, identified with the wilderness in that novel, she is, symbolically, the very truth she as literal woman cannot face. But even this woman, the ostensibly fragile member of the cowardly sex, is emblematic. She represents the brittle self in all of us, in men no less than women, that would break apart if exposed too utterly and glaringly to the truths that threaten our self-possession. For it is this alone that maintains, in both senses, our integrity: our sense of honor and our wholeness. And to compound the complicated, the most terrifying truth that the anxious, weak, and fearful woman within us cannot face is precisely that there is an anxious, weak, and fearful female element within man, a principle of unreasoning passion and desire, held in check by self-possession or an "inborn strength" but vulnerable: to the lure of the seductive woman, the whisper of the wilderness, the hollow message of the void.

Broadened in these ways, Foucault's observations about the protectively obscurantist discourse of sex, beginning in the late seventeenth century and culminating in Conrad's Victorian England, is vividly descriptive of the chronically obfuscating discourse of truth and knowledge in Conrad's narratives. Sex—which, unsurprisingly, was, like woman, identified as "a problem of truth"—was expelled, silenced, and denied.[15] Like coherent and definable knowledge in these indeterminate texts, sex, driven behind a thickening curtain of defenses, censorships, and denials, operated under what Foucault called "an injunction to silence, an affirmation of non-existence and, by implication, an admission that there was nothing to say about such things, nothing to see, and nothing to know." The aim of this discourse—as of the defensive discourse of many of Conrad's narratives—was not to state the truth but to prevent its revelation.[16] As August Tardieu, a member of the mid-nineteenth-century medical establishment, remarked in recoil, "The darkness that envelops these facts, the shame and disgust they inspire, have always repelled the observer's gaze."[17] Those who took upon themselves the intimidating task of discussing sex, then, habitually retreated from the menacing truth they ostensibly pursued. Like these fictions, "they constructed . . . an immense apparatus for producing truth [that] . . . was to be masked at the last moment."[18]

Foucault ascribes to this anxious inhibition a metamorphosis in our literature—from one centered on heroic bravery and trials to one devoted to the task of extracting from the depths of the self a hidden truth that assumes the form of a shimmering mirage. What emerges in such a desert is a discourse that spreads this burning and chilling truth over the surface of things, summons it, and "enjoins it to tell the truth," though all in the end is an illusion, "a hasty impression behind which a more discerning gaze will surely discover the same great machinery of repression."[19]

One could expand this survey of forbidden knowledge almost indefinitely, but it seems unnecessary. If there is anything at all to the psychoanalytic notions of repression and denial; if the history of Western religion, mythology, and literature offers even partially reliable testimony; indeed if we are courageous enough to acknowledge our own all-but-instinctive inclination (is anyone exempt from this?) to close at least one eye to intimidating revelations about ourselves, others, and our condition, to the looming inescapability of death perhaps most prominently,[20] denial of the historic and daily influence on human behavior of what is at the least a hesitant, conflict-laden, and potentially clouding ambivalence toward forbidden or threatening knowledge is itself a form of denial. Authoring, surely, is but another expression of our natures, more susceptible than most for the greater concentration and intensity of its probing.

THE SAVING ILLUSION

Although he often claimed he knew little else, Conrad knew there were some things it was better not to know. Driven by a deep if at times conflicted conviction, he affirmed in his letters and essays or dramatized in his tales his belief in the desirability of protective illusion, self-censorship, and avoidance almost as routinely and insistently as his readers, with no bow toward their possible connection, argue for the contradictory, evasive, and enigmatic nature of his tales.

Underlying the question of the desirability of knowledge, which we will come to, is that of its possibility; and the question of truth—whether such a sprite exists or can be known and, if yes to both of these, whether art and language can recover it—preoccupied Conrad as it does the study of his work. Conrad often wrote as though he did believe in the existence and communicability of truth and of its importance to him as man and writer. In a letter to Hugh Clifford, he spoke of the importance of a meticulous care for words, "lest the picture, the image of truth abiding in facts should become distorted—or blurred"(*CL* 2:200)."Fiction," he wrote in his *Personal Record* more than a decade later, is "after all . . . but truth often dragged out of a well and clothed in the painted robe of imaged phrases"(*PR* 93). It was essential, therefore, that the robe fit so as to reveal accurately the shape of the living truth it dressed. For Conrad, Stephen Crane's gift of discovery was more than felicity of language. It was a "penetrating force that seemed to reach, within life's appearances and forms, the very spirit of life's truth" (*NLL* 50). And toward the end of his relentlessly pained and perplexed life, Conrad declared that to envelop unfamiliar things "in their proper atmosphere of actuality . . . was the hardest of all [undertakings] and the most important, in view of that conscientious rendering of truth in thought and fact which has always been my aim" (*Within the Tides*, vi).

But occasional claims for the accessibility of truth and meaning are outnumbered and all but driven from the field by complaints—within the novels and outside them—about the inadequacies of language as a vehicle of meaning; by lamentations over the ultimate elusiveness of truth, if indeed it exists at all; and by the pervasive aura of mystery, uncertainty, and irresolvable enigma that haunts the fiction. Fiction, it turns out, is a painted robe thrown over a truth that may long ago have drowned in the well it was dragged from. And Crane's force, on closer scrutiny, only "seemed" to reach life's truth, even then only to its spirit, which may be a ghost of the same drowned form. Principally in the subtler tales of the early and middle periods but in the later works as well, mystery and uncertainty cloud every straining quest for truth. To such an extent that Marlow's oft-quoted lament in *Heart of Darkness* might serve as a logo for the canon. "Do you see the story?" he asks his listeners hopelessly. "Do you see anything? . . . No, it is impossible; it is impossible to convey the life-sensation of any given epoch of one's existence—that which makes its truth, its meaning—its subtle and penetrating essence. It is impossible. We live, as we dream—alone" (*HD* 82).

Conrad's fiction, letters, reviews, essays, and autobiographical writings are shot through with (usually frustrated or embittered) stabs at the abysmal implacability of heaven, the illusoriness of truth, and the cosmic meaninglessness of human life. "A world," Conrad observed sardonically, "has not been supplied with an obvious meaning." Life is "only a film of unsteady appearances stretched over regions deep indeed but which have nothing to do with the half-truths, half-thoughts, and whole illusions of existence" ("Alphonse Daudet," in *NLL* 21–22). "The only indisputable truth of life is our ignorance," Conrad wrote to the *New York Times*. "Beside this there is nothing absolute, nothing uncontradicted."[21] As the paradox of an absolute truth of unabated ignorance suggests, there is little in Conrad more mysterious than his own sense of mystery, his philosophy, if such it may be called, of truth's nature, status, and relationship to illusion. It is not merely that life has not been supplied with obvious meaning. Rather we cannot be certain whether it has been supplied with any meaning at all or, if it has been, if we can even occasionally glimpse its shadow.

Conrad eased our burden somewhat when he confessed with admirable self-understanding that "my thinking is always multiple" (*CL* 3:492), a view confirmed by Richard Curle's observation that Conrad "never said all he thought about any one subject at any one time, and thus he often appeared to contradict himself."[22] At times Conrad speaks as though nothing at all may be known, perhaps—at least perhaps—because there is nothing finally to be known, no truth at the bottom of the sea of illusion: for once, then, nothing. "There is no morality, no knowledge and no hope," he wrote to Cunninghame Graham; "there is only the consciousness of ourselves which drives us about a world that whether seen in a convex or a concave mirror is always but a vain and floating appearance" (*CL* 2:30). The term *appearance* suggests a "reality" that, as J. L. Austin was fond of putting it, wears the pants, even if they cannot be found in Conrad's closet. And the implicit claim that there is a world to be driven about in and to be perceived through distorting mirrors suggests likewise. But Conrad obscures this implication. Is truth around the corner? he asks. "I can't tell. No one can tell. It is impossible to know. It is impossible to know anything tho' it is possible to believe a thing or two" (*CL* 1:370). At least three readings suggest themselves: Truth may be around the corner, waiting scornfully for a discovery that will never take place; there may be nothing at all around a corner that may itself be pure illusion; or truth may be waiting and discoverable. Although this last seems least compatible with the prevailing skepticism of Conrad's thought, it is, I believe, the most tenable of these hypotheses, the only one, in fact, consistent with Conrad's urgently repeated recommendations and habitual practice of protective denial, obfuscation, and avoidance. There is little logic in urging ignorance or avoidance of truths one is convinced do not exist or of knowledge that cannot conceivably be acquired.

The perhaps deliberate muddling of distinctions that might clarify at least the nature of unclarity finds expression in another letter to Graham. Writing of the elusive beckoning of a safe destiny for himself and humanity, he interjects: "But what business have you O! Man! coming with your uncomprehended truth—a thing less than mist but black—to make me sniff at?" (*CL* 2:88).Truth is there, it seems, and summoning, but its modifiers progressively obscure its signals and sift away its substance. For truth is at once uncomprehended—and what does it mean to speak of such a truth?—less than mist, and finally black, more absence than mystery, more void than being. If the truth is black or, as *Heart of Darkness* suggests, the blackened core of darkness, there may be truth concealed in darkness, or blackness may be a metonymic image of the void, of the appalling absence of anything that may be knowable or known. James Guetti has explained this elegantly in his illuminating reading of the paradoxical title of *Heart of Darkness*.[23] The darkness may in the end have a heart where truth and meaning, however dark, await discovery; or the heart of darkness may be the essence of darkness, the final truth that we are condemned to vacancy and ignorance.

Conrad's mysteriousness on the question of mystery serves as an icon of its subject, thriving on such ambiguities and erased distinctions. The mists and darkness that permeate his fiction and much of his other writing about an alleged reality play a perpetual triple role: as that which obscures an elusive truth behind or within them; as that which is itself the only truth; and in this latter role, as that which denies the existence of all truth, including the dubious refuge of mist or darkness as a palpable entity or form. The sought-for truth in Conrad's fiction is so habitually obscured by mists or buried in darkness that these become the only truths. Yet even their dubious substantiality may be deceptive, for they are truth and illusion at once and this in two ways: as the illusory surface that, concealing all else, becomes the only truth and as mere metaphor for the claim that there is no truth at all. Is the darkness real, reality, or is it a necessarily befuddling device for expressing the absence even of itself? "Our illusions," as Marlow speculates in *Lord Jim,* are "visions of remote unattainable truth, seen dimly" (323).But the momentary clarity of this hypothesis evaporates like so much else—like Jim himself from Marlow's vision and like the novel as an interpretable text from our own. For the unattainable truth that illusions somehow bring to light may be the truth that illusions, as Conrad frequently affirmed, are all we are given and possibly all there is. And what, we may ask in passing, does the syntax and punctuation of this sentence ascribe "seen dimly" to? To truth that, if unattainable, should not be visible at all? To visions that, if they are visions, may only imagine rather than perceive truth? Or to illusions that we had thought blindingly bright? Conrad, to put it plainly, seems to be obscuring his own sense of obscurity.

Earlier in the novel, Marlow confesses that he does not know how much Jim understood of the saving power of land and human rootedness. "But I know how he felt, he felt confusedly but powerfully, the demand of some such truth or some such illusion—I don't care how you call it, there is so little difference, and the difference means so little" (*LJ* 222). Clearly—if one may use that word—Conrad wishes us to believe there is little difference, for truth and illusion in his writing melt into one another like sea and sky, past and present, dark and light, good and evil, all the governing dichotomies. Like the other sources of indeterminacy in Conrad's fiction, the blurring of boundaries Lacan identifies with woman is an averting of the gaze from her (or truth's) more palpable and intimidating shape. The muddle that surrounds Conrad's analyses of the muddle we find ourselves in, the impenetrability of his discussions of impenetrability, are themselves reflections of an ambivalence toward knowledge, truth, and discovery. Contradictions in Conrad, whether in his fiction or in his fitful discourses upon them, may on occasion be calculated images of the contradictory universe he lucidly perceived or signs of his own befuddlement. More often and more tellingly, however, they are images of his own ambivalent dance with truth, an alternating attraction and revulsion, eagerness and failure of will that urge him toward and then away from what he anticipates or glimpses.

Critical opinions about truth in Conrad, or Conrad's conception of truth and knowledge, are as variegated as his own often contradictory pronouncements. Perhaps more so, since they ground themselves, often convincingly, not only in the author's extrafictional assertions but also in their dramatic and narrative realizations in the tales and novels.

Although it is a minority view, several writers adhere to the notion that Conrad "portray[s] the truths of experience, however terrifying they may be, and [that] this honesty will reveal to his readers the common lot of humanity."[24] Or more commonly, if less daringly, that for all his hesitations about the efficacy of language, Conrad was committed to the conviction that it could provide a glimpse of the truth behind the visible world.[25] By making us "see," wrote H. M. Daleski, the goal he set for his work in the famous preface to *The Nigger of the "Narcissus,"* he leads the reader beyond the surface, beyond the "encouragement, consolation, fear [and] charm" the reader looks for and expects, to "that glimpse of truth" for which he has "forgotten to ask."[26]

A more common conviction is that while Conrad may have believed in the existence of something reasonably identified as truth, he doubted the capacity of language to convey it. For Ted Billy he viewed language "as a pseudo-reality, an irresistibly ensnaring illusion that dictates rather than interprets human action."[27] And as Edward Said remarked, while Conrad may have committed himself to the task of making the reader see, "with few exceptions what the reader remembers is a sustained effort to make words tell, even as it is frequently evident that words are ultimately inadequate, so special and eccentric is the experience."[28]

J. Hillis Miller and Royal Roussel each offer a darker (in both senses) view of the notion that truth for Conrad was real, in some sense "out there" yet defiant of expression. For Miller the aim of Conrad's fiction is to lift the veil of illusion and provide a glimpse of truth, however dark and ominous it may be. The obstacle to this noble ambition is that truth is nothing more than this: an ominous darkness, amorphous and opaque, the primal chaos out of which the world was formed and to which it rushes, annihilatingly, to return. Undoing Milton's oxymoron, it is darkness invisible, resistant not only to expression but also to apprehension.[29] Similarly for Roussel this darkness from which all being emerges "is an image of matter stripped of all attributes but existence. It *is,* but nothing more can be said about it." Devoid of accessory qualities and inaccessible to apprehension, it is experienced by Conrad's characters "not as a sensation, but as the absence of sensation, an absence which is like 'a foretaste of annihilation.'"[30]

Another widely held perspective on the author's slippery wrestle with the question of truth is that Conrad was a literary impressionist who shared his painterly compatriots' conviction that objective truth, less eel than phantom, less elusive than illusory, is irreducibly multiple, insubstantial, and subjective. There is, in short, no "object" at all to be clearly seen, only subjective perception and experience to be gropingly and imperfectly rendered. Given the fogged, unsteady nature of that perception, the haziness of Conrad's image "is not an accidental atmospheric interference" standing between the perceiver and the "real" object; "the difficulty and the obscurity are essential parts of what the artist is trying to convey."[31] There are, then, no facts to be garnered, no definable truths or realities to be apprehended and conveyed. As another reader renders it, "to suggest that the intellections, the causes and categories and explanations" one finds in Conrad's fiction "are somehow the 'truth' encoded in the original sensation is to ignore an important aspect of the impressionist impulse and movement" and of Conrad's praxis and belief.[32]

If anything at all unites these varied, contrary, at times contradictory insights into Conrad's notions of truth and knowledge, it is their exclusivity. Each selects a color from the spectrum of radically shifting attitudes and convictions Conrad expressed in his prefaces, essays, and letters, placed in the mouths of his characters or rendered in sunlight, haze, or darkness in his fictions. Relatively unique in this regard is the view that Conrad's texts dramatize the author's vacillation between a belief in the existence and accessibility of truth and a radical skepticism that stops just short of nihilism. Robert Penn Warren found an "apparent discrepancy between his professions of skepticism and his professions of faith."[33] For Mark Wollaeger, until the more comprehensive skepticism of *The Secret Agent,* Conrad's appeals to transcendence are at war with his skeptical empiricism. Reluctant "to abandon his faith in transcendent truths," his fictions betray "an impatience with the limitations of empiricism and a desire to pierce through material fact to an absolute real beyond."[34] And John Peters likewise sees Conrad "moving between a radical skepticism and a desire to find some point of belief."[35]

There is much validity in this position, strength in the reasoned elaborations of its adherents. But this bilateral epistemological figure requires, I believe, another side. The opposing planes of skepticism and discovery or belief meet with a wavering third line marking textual apprehensions about the wisdom and desirability of certain kinds of knowledge and the retreat, deliberate or instinctive, from it. Both writers recognize Conrad's need for what Wollaeger calls a "sheltered retreat." But the shelter, as they perceive it, is provided by the discovery of whatever redeeming knowledge, certainty, or truth can be salvaged from an extreme and paralyzing skepticism.[36]

Although Peters produces an imposing litany of quotations from Conrad's letters, essays, and stories detailing the writer's forcefully explicit reservations about the desirability of certain kinds of knowledge and his belief in the saving wisdom of avoidance or illusion, he seems to set aside the possible, perhaps the humanly likely, implications of such apprehension in his conclusions. Like Wollaeger he identifies the roof and walls of Conrad's "shelter . . . from such potentially withering knowledge" not in its avoidance or obfuscation but exclusively in whatever small or larger truths one can retrieve from the shell-cratered field.[37] I believe, rather, that like most nervous mortals, Conrad often sought refuge from withering or dangerous knowledge not in small or larger truths but in the evasion, avoidance, and obscurity that mark so many of his stories; that these withdrawals and obfuscations, together with the contradictions arising from their alternation with seeming affirmation, are responsible for much of the notorious elusiveness—at times the indeterminacy—of his narratives; and that the knowledge from which his characters and narratives recoil is frequently associated with woman, whether as a literal, often highly sexualized presence or as any of a variety of more metaphoric but equally intimidating guises.[38] Such ambivalence and reluctance is of course most likely to appear in tales preoccupied with the quest for hidden knowledge of a distinctly dark and ominous cast. But the phenomenon is especially salient in a number of narratives in which the engulfing feminized landscape, the sexually enthralling and possessive woman, or the danger of enervating feminization of the vulnerably masculine hero in fact plays a significant role.

The mist, mystery, and muddle of Conrad's fiction that make it resistant to coherent interpretation are routinely explained as reflections of an impressionistic aesthetic that replicates the mystery and evanescence of experience;[39] as evidence of the writer's skepticism about the communicative efficacy of language and fiction;[40] or as signs of a deeper philosophical skepticism that had lost all faith in knowable truth.[41] A recent reader conflates them succinctly: "Suspicious of the power of language to transmit truth, skeptical of the value of fiction as a mirror of existence, and doubtful that life could ever be fathomed by the human mind, what other kind of fiction could Conrad create but narratives of indeterminacy?"[42]

Claims that the evasiveness and indeterminacy of Conrad's narratives are the product of his alleged conviction that nothing could be known are at least partially weakened by the writer's frequent claims to know terrible truths about the world and our pathetically ephemeral passage through it. Explanations in terms of an alleged distrust in the adequacy of language to convey reality are likewise undermined by the writer's forceful elaboration of a very different view of the representational power of language in the letter to Clifford cited earlier.[43] There is reason, then, to suspect these familiar explanations, in part because Conrad was of more than one mind on these issues, and more warily, perhaps, because they reflect a too deliberate and controlled conception of creation and the writer's enterprise and a reductively narrow view of Conrad's lifelong subscription to the need for saving illusion. Conrad's fictions are overdetermined, but more so and more fractiously than these ultimately quite tidy packagings suggest. Accounts of evasiveness and indeterminacy that restrict causation to a calculated reflection of certain beliefs about the limitations of language or human comprehension overlook the darkly serious play of reluctance, aversion, self-deception, and recoil. More important, perhaps, they overlook Conrad's more consistently held and oft-repeated conviction that there were many things it was better not to know. And the two are related in that these withdrawals may be the reactive expression of that conviction.

Speaking, significantly, of Stein's aphoristic exhortation in *Lord Jim* that each man follow his dream, Marlow reflects that "the whisper of his conviction seemed to open before me a vast and uncertain expanse, as of a crepuscular horizon on a plain at dawn—or was it, perchance, at the coming of the night? One had not the courage to decide; but it was a charming and deceptive light, throwing the impalpable poesy of its dimness over pitfalls—over graves" (*LJ* 215).

The passage is rich with the qualifications, withdrawals, and blurrings characteristic of Conrad's prose. There is no conviction, despite Stein's seeming confidence, but a "whisper" of conviction. That whisper does not open an expanse to Marlow's ken but seems to open a "vast and uncertain" expanse that may herald the coming either of morning or of night. The distinction is critical, of course; all the world of hope or despair hangs upon it. And it is for just that reason, that and the plaguing belief that night is a likelier prospect than dawn, that the courage to decide is shaken. Note that one lacks not—as we might have expected, given the epistemological haze that permeates Conrad's world—the wherewithal or acuity to decide. Rather one lacks the courage, and with that we arrive at another, less controllable but, I believe, more fundamental cause of the mystifying haze that permeates the fiction: namely reluctance in the face of a truth the author falteringly because ambivalently pursues. J. Hillis Miller correctly labeled knowledge as the darkness in Conrad's world that makes "ordinary human life impossible."[44] And it is naive to think that such a belief has no ramifications for the fiction, only within it, that it tells us much about what motivates the characters in Conrad's novels and tales and little or nothing about the origins of the contradictions, avoidances, and uncertainties that characterize the works themselves. The claim that it is "impossible to know anything" becomes at once less surprising and more suspect when convictions about the mortifying danger of knowledge peer from behind it.

There is in fact little in Conrad to suggest the attractiveness of truth or the desirability of knowledge. The truth about the nature and destiny of the human animal is, for him, quite terrible to behold. The heart of darkness that may be the rotten core of evil or the obscuring essence of unknowability may be the latter as a defense against the former, for whatever else we know or are prevented from knowing about "The horror!," we know it is as near to truth as the novel or human knowledge can approach. "Dark powers" is a phrase that haunts Conrad's fiction, and while they are sometimes agents of a merciless destiny, they are as often expressions of our own venal natures.[45]

That destiny is grimly worthy of the species. Marlow's hatred of the lie, as he admits, flows from his loathing for the taint of death that stains it. What he despises about it, in other words, is its core of truth, its connection with the consciousness of death that, whatever else we may deny, insists on our attention. The Congo in *Heart of Darkness* contains "invincible truths" and "overwhelming realities" that, while inaccessible to traditional modes of cognition, are unmistakably menacing and horrific, as unappetizing as they are indefinable—undigested, perhaps, precisely because they are unpalatable. "The last word is not said," remarks Marlow in *Lord Jim*, speaking quite transparently for Conrad. "Are not our lives too short for that full utterance which through all our stammerings is of course our only and abiding intention? I have given up expecting those last words," he declares, "whose ring, if they could only be pronounced, would shake both heaven and earth.... [and] heaven and the earth must not be shaken" (225). What begins as a submission to indomitable mystery and ignorance moves through the implicit acknowledgment of a truth too terrible to bear and culminates in a protective refusal to expose it. The world, then, does indeed contain its truths, and our problem, writhing painfully through the existence it so grudgingly allows, is not their inherent inaccessibility but the danger of importunate eruption into consciousness. One gives up expecting those last words not because they cannot be pronounced but because their pronunciation would shake a heaven and earth that deserve the mercy of our silence. Fortunately, in Conrad's view, man is preserved by a wisely self-protective inclination to stop his ears against such sounds or drown them in a finer music. "Every age is fed on illusions," remarks the narrator of *Victory*, "lest men should renounce life early and the human race come to an end" (94). And in his author's note to that novel, Conrad spoke in his own voice of the saving adaptability of the species' capacity for an avoidant detachment. The play of man's destiny, he wrote, "is too great for his fears and too mysterious for his understanding. Were the trump of the Last Judgment to sound suddenly on a working day the musician at his piano would go on with his performance of Beethoven's Sonata and the cobbler at his stall stick to his last in undisturbed confidence in the virtues of the leather. And with perfect propriety. For what are we to let ourselves be disturbed by an angel's vengeful music too mighty for our ears and too awful for our terrors?" (ix–x).

In his personal correspondence, Conrad hinted at or was quite unforgivingly explicit about what those last words might sound like, and they ring with the chilling resonance of meaningless life and the vacant totality of its obliteration. In a letter to John Galsworthy, he posited "a mere declaration not of the vanity of things (that would be a too optimistic view) but of the utter futility of existence. ... Pessimism can no further go" (*CL* 4:116). We are nothing, he wrote still more bleakly to Cunninghame Graham. "Words fly away; and nothing remains—but a clot of mud, of cold mud, of dead mud cast into black space, rolling around an extinguished sun. Nothing. Neither thought, nor sound, nor soul. Nothing" (*CL* 2:70). Conrad's letters are pocked with such expressions, and this is not the language of one for whom truth is beyond language, illusory or an illusion. Unsurprisingly the avoidance of such vision is preferable to recognition and, therefore, an all-but-universal habit. "I had become awake," the narrator of "The Warrior

Soul" (collected in *Tales of Hearsay and Last Essays*) relates, "with an exaggerated mental consciousness of existence extending beyond my immediate surroundings. Those are but exceptional moments with mankind, I am glad to say" (20).

When we are told that the silent wilderness struck Marlow "as something great and invincible, like evil or truth," we recognize the interchangeability of the disjunctive terms and perceive more than dismissive contempt in his observation that "the majority of us . . . want to be left alone with our illusions," more acknowledgement than mere resignation in his "Perhaps it's just as well" (*LJ* 143). Conrad's "Youth" (collected in *Youth, Heart of Darkness, and The End of the Tether*) is dedicated thematically to the cementing of the synonymy of the life worth living and illusion. All the transcendent drive and splendor of that incomparable period derives from the "romance of illusions" that spares us the paralyzing revelations of our maturity, if we are foolish or self-loathing enough to pursue them. Looking back with an irreparable sense of loss, the disillusioned speaker recounts, in rhapsodic rhetoric that does not discredit it, the glorious and energizing feeling that will never return, "the feeling that I could last for ever, outlast the sea, the earth, and all men." It is this admittedly "deceitful feeling" that "lures us on" to all that is joyful, heightened, and worthy in this life: "the triumphant conviction of strength . . . the glow in the heart that with every year grows dim, grows cold, grows small, and expires—and expires, too soon, too soon—before life itself" (36–37). When he remarks that he lived his youth "in ignorance and hope" (18), he offers a juxtaposition that, as Conrad's often do, conceals a causal bond. Only in deceit can there be joy, only in ignorance the hope Conrad posited among the guiding moral obligations the writer of fiction assumes with his profession.

The guarded secrets that pervade Conrad's stories are always terrible secrets, and Terence Cave is right to observe that for him secrecy is "the means by which ordinary life sustains itself" and that "not wanting to probe . . . is in normal circumstances the only tolerable solution."[46] Typically these secrets are violations of the cardinal principle of fidelity: secrets of betrayal, treacherous deception, or abandonment, often of one's precious but fragile masculine self-possession as it yields to the temptations of untrammeled vice, the dread of mortality and obliteration, the summons of despair, the lure of indulgent, unconsidered impulse, or the all-but-irresistible seductions of the sensuous woman without and the seditious feminine element within. All are seen and not seen, glimpsed and turned from, illuminated and obscured, acknowledged and denied, and all assault and mortally threaten the treasured self-possession that alone sustains us.

In the city, less covertly than in the jungle, citizens flee these truths. "Outside the big doorway of the street," writes Conrad in "The Return," "they scattered in all directions, walking away fast from one another with the hurried air of men fleeing from something compromising; from familiarity or confidences, from something suspected and concealed—like truth or pestilence" (119). Like evil or truth, like truth or pestilence. The juxtapositions are not incidental, the disjunctions not exclusive but indices of interchangeability. Truth is evil, a pestilence, and "that ugliness of truth [must] . . . be kept out of daily life by unremitting care for appearances" (167). Alvan Hervey and his wife, then, are two skaters on the surface of the ice, disdainfully ignoring the dark, restless, hidden stream that runs beneath (123). Like the consort and the Intended in *Heart of Darkness*, who raise their hands to ward off darkness, Alvan "put both his hands out as if to ward off the approach of a defiling truth" (130).[47] That is the nature of truth glimpsed, evaded, and obscured in Conrad's narratives and, since the actions of the novels are frequently reflections of their technique, by them as well. Truth is a "dark and restless stream," a "terrible and annihilating knowledge," a "taint of death," evil, a pestilence, an ugliness, or a defilement. Those who glimpse the truth are privy to the "dark heart" of the universe, "the mysterious universe of moral suffering," the blackness, or the horror.

Given this paralyzing view of reality, it is no surprise that Conrad sustained throughout his life a profound and inhibiting ambivalence toward the desirability of knowledge, vacillating uncertainly between a respect for the courage of the unblurred vision and a mortal dread of its consequences. Working against the outward drive toward revelation is the equally or more powerful pull of a saving thoughtlessness, most urgently, perhaps, when the risk is of mortifying knowledge of oneself. We will see pervasive evidence of this in the studies that follow, but we should note here briefly that Conrad closes in on this idea from both sides: in the devastating consequences of recognition and the blessed relief of avoidance. The narrator of "A Smile of Fortune" (collected in *'Twixt Land and Sea*) who has reason not to probe too deeply into his own motives and the roots of his dubious good fortune, congratulates himself for sharing "in the blessed forgetfulness of sailors, that forgetfulness natural and invincible [these adjectives are to be dwelt on], which resembles innocence in so far that it prevents self-examination" (82). Peter Willems, in *An Outcast of the Islands*, is one of many less fortunate victims in these fictions who, lacking this blessed forgetfulness or the alternative protections of self-deception, evasion, or illusion, pay full price. "He had a sudden moment of lucidity—of that cruel lucidity that comes once in life to the most benighted. He seemed to see what went on within him, and was horrified at the strange sight" (80).[48]

The preferred and paradigmatic refuge from menacing truth in any of its forms is the "saving illusion" Marlow interposes between the Intended and an intolerable confrontation with a truth identified, quite typically for Conrad, with horror. The narrator of *The Nigger of the "Narcissus"* betrays a comparable preference when he laments the passing, with Jimmy's death, of the binding faith "we had put in his delusions." What they have lost, regrettably, is a "common bond . . . the strong, effective and respectable bond of a sentimental lie" (155). The affinity for such saving deceptions is pervasive and strikingly explicit in his letters and essays as well as his fiction.[49] "What makes mankind tragic," he wrote to Cunninghame Graham, "is not that they are the victims of nature, it is that they are conscious of it" (*CL* 2:30).[50] For this reason, he declared, "thinking is the great enemy of perfection. The habit of profound reflection ... is the most pernicious of all the habits formed by the civilized man" (*Victory* x–xi). "Of course reason is hateful," he wrote again, "—but why? Because it demonstrates (to those who have the courage) that we, living, are out of life—utterly out of it" (*CL* 2:16).

"There are often in men's affairs," observes the narrator of "Falk," "... moments when an otherwise insignificant sound, perhaps only some perfectly commonplace gesture, suffices to reveal to us all the unreason, all the fatuous unreason, of our complacency" (*NN* 169). One of our fatuous assumptions, as Miller sees, is the assumption that our world is organically unified (*Poets of Reality*, 20). But it is only one of many, and like the sentimental lie it must be maintained, not because complacency is heroic but because the alternative is destructive to our common bond and more unnerving than our fragile nerves can bear. To hear these otherwise insignificant sounds too keenly or note such perfectly commonplace gestures too sharply is to risk too much. For Conrad it is to put oneself in the situation of the tightrope dancer "who in the midst of his performance should suddenly discover that he knows nothing about tight-rope dancing." A "broken neck is the result of such untimely wisdom."[51]

Where knowledge menaces, threatens its agent with a debilitating paralysis or worse, consciousness and reason are not unequivocal virtues but instruments of awareness better dulled than sharpened. The aim of art, whatever we may have thought of Conrad's dedication to discovery at any cost, "is not in the unveiling of one of those heartless secrets which are called the Laws of Nature" (*NN* xi–xii) but in the offering of hope in compassionate deference to man's fragility. Conrad's models of efficiency and good sense, therefore, are characters such as Singleton of *The Nigger of the "Narcissus,"* Captain Beard of "Youth," and—with a larger dollop of ambivalence—Captain MacWhirr of *Typhoon*, men who are protectively unconscious, whose unflinching strength and fortitude derive from an obliviousness to the ultimate meaninglessness of their actions and of the world in which they are performed. The most admirable of them all is old Singleton, the all-but-wordless and unthinking hero of *The Nigger of the 'Narcissus,'* who functions effectively because unaware of the paralyzing subtleties and complex implications of Wait's refusal. As the narrator reports with undisguised admiration, "Singleton lived untouched by human emotions.... We were disturbed and cowardly. That we knew. Singleton seemed to know nothing, understand nothing" (41–42). When Cunninghame Graham, troubled by so much unqualified admiration for so little thought and understanding, asked Conrad to create a "Singleton with an education," Conrad responded with revealing vehemence:

I think Singleton with an education is impossible. But first of all—what education? If it is the knowledge how to live my man essentially possessed it. He was in perfect accord with his life. . . . Would you seriously, of malice prepense cultivate in that unconscious man the power to think. Then he would become conscious—and much smaller—and very unhappy. Now he is simple and great like an elemental force. Nothing can touch him but the curse of decay—the eternal decree that will extinguish the sun, the stars one by one, and in another instant shall spread a frozen darkness over the whole universe. Nothing else can touch him—he does not think. Would you seriously wish to tell such a man: 'Know thyself'. Understand that thou art nothing, less than a shadow, more insignificant than a drop of water in the ocean, more fleeting than the illusion of a dream. Would you? (*CL* 1:423).[52]

As with so much more, Conrad's attitude toward these thoughtlessly effective or effectively thoughtless figures is fraught with ambivalence. In his fine introduction to *Nostromo*, Robert Penn Warren situated Conrad's characteristic narratives under three basic headings: "the story of the MacWhirr or the Don Pepe or the Captain Mitchell, the man who lacks imagination and cannot see the 'true horror behind the appalling face of things,' and who can cling to fidelity and the job; the story of the Kurtz or Decoud, the sinner against human solidarity and the human mission; the story of the redemption, of Lord Jim, Heyst, Dr. Nonygham, Flora deBarral, Captain Anthony, Razumov."[53]

For Warren while Conrad admires the simple, narrowly devoted men of natural virtue, their unawareness mitigates their appeal to the more insistently curious and probing author, and it is the last type of story, the tale of the relentless if suffering, imperfect, and thwarted searcher, that engages him most profoundly.[54] But what engages most profoundly is not always what one can live with or follow to its faith- and spirit-destroying conclusion. Conrad's searchers are indeed suffering and imperfect, but they are also pointedly thwarted and, like the fictions that contain them, often notably less than relentless in pursuit. Their efforts are hesitant, their journeys clouded and obscured; revelations are withheld, meanings are elusive and contradictory, interpretation baffled by Conrad's equal and opposite attraction to whatever it is that blurs or conceals that true horror behind the appalling face of things. Put another way, it is the educated Singleton in Conrad and his fictions that prevents their Marlow from heeding the siren that lures Kurtz and Decoud into the epistemological and moral maelstrom that destroys them. Not the lack of imagination, surely, but envy of its failure and a refusal to submit utterly to its beckoning allow the writer to remain faithful to the humanely self-limiting job of writing as he conceived and committed himself to it.

Nothing is simple or univocal in Conrad, no attraction uncountered or unqualified. He is markedly ambivalent toward his unthinking captains and steerers who, at the price of imagination and reflection, remain faithful to their task. Singleton, with his "spectacles and a venerable white beard[,] ... resembled a learned and savage patriarch, the incarnation of barbarian wisdom serene in the blasphemous turmoil of the world" (*NN* 6). Venerable, wise, learned, and serene. Also strong, silent, faithful, uncomplaining, and enduring (*NN* 25). But at the same time, troublingly savage and barbarian. And as the narrative elsewhere makes clear, unthinking, simple of mind, childishly impulsive, and "untouched by human emotions" (*NN* 6, 24, 41). There is little doubt, I think, as to where the weight of Conrad's favor rests. Warren cites Conrad's frequently quoted "conviction that the world, the temporal world, rests on a few very simple ideas. . . . It rests notably, among others, on the idea of Fidelity ("A Familiar Preface" to *PR*, xix). And he turns to Conrad's tribute to the Merchant Service in his 1918 essay "Well Done," where the author declares: "For the great mass of mankind the only saving grace that is needed is steady fidelity to what is nearest to hand and heart in the short moment of each human effort."[55] "Fidelity and the sense of the job,"[56] as Warren encapsulates it, and in these terms Singleton is impeccable. "He steer[s] with care" (*NN* 89). He gets the ship through. He saves them. The balance of power and limitation always leans toward the former; the ambivalent descriptions tilt in that direction and typically end there. And the deficiencies, such as they are—the simplicity, the absence of thought and imagination—are themselves essential virtues; they are what make fidelity and successful devotion to the undertaking possible.

The lack of emotion, ascribed to Singleton, MacWhirr, and others of this stripe, is of special interest. Like the other gaps and limitations, it enables the saving action, but it also holds, I think, a special appeal for the painfully overwrought, often paralyzingly tormented and depressed author of these tales. Their lack of curiosity and emotion is often cited as evidence that Jonathan Swift could not, after all, have truly favored the rational Houyhnhnms, could not possibly be commending them to us, offering them if not as models for emulation—they are beyond our reach—then as supremely fortunate paragons. And yet, for the same reason that Swift finds these seeming deficiencies powerfully if somewhat shamingly appealing, similar privations commend Conrad's unthinking heroes to their author. Where the light at the end of the tunnel of probing intellect and thought is the searing fire of decadence, failure, horror, or annihilation, the inability or disinclination to think is a saving refuge. And where *emotion* is a collective term for anxiety, frustration, torment, and depression, as it was with painful regularity for both Swift and Conrad, to be "untouched by human emotions" is to be touched by the gentle hand of mercy.

And yet, of course, particularly to driven, complex, and self-reflective minds such as Conrad's (and Swift's), there is something demeaning, even somewhat contemptible about these absences. We see this quite glaringly in the more negatively weighted, even mocking ambivalence Conrad brings to the character of MacWhirr. In his author's note to *Typhoon*, he commends MacWhirr as the figure he requires "to bring out [the story's] . . . deeper significance," the "leading motive that would harmonize all these violent noises, and a point of view that would put all that elemental fury into its proper place." That MacWhirr is gifted with a "literal mind and . . . dauntless temperament"; that he is "irresponsive, and unruffled," possessed of "just enough imagination to carry him through each successive day, and no more"; that he is "tranquilly sure of himself" and "unperturbed" not only bring out the deeper significance of the tale and harmonize its noises. They also explain why "every ship Captain MacWhirr commanded was the floating abode of harmony and peace" (vi, 4, 8), and why he is a calming, ordering, and reassuring influence during the monstrous storm that gives the tale its name and nearly wrecks the ship. But the placid spirit that "gets his ship along all right without worrying anybody" (17) is achieved at a substantial price. If Singleton is unthinking, MacWhirr "hasn't brains enough to enjoy kicking up a row." He is "too dense to trouble about" (17, 18). And he is literal-minded to the point of ludicrousness, unevolved, it seems, beyond Jean Piaget's early childhood stage of concrete thinking. Captain MacWhirr, as the narrator sums him up, "had sailed over the surface of the oceans as some men go skimming over the years of existence to sink gently into a placid grave, ignorant of life to the last, without ever having been made to see all it may contain of perfidy, of violence, and of terror. There are on sea and land such men thus fortunate—or thus disdained by destiny or by the sea" (19). Thus fortunate and thus disdained. The ambivalence is manifest. It is a blessing to be spared such vision, such understanding, but deserving at the same time of contempt, for, stealing from man his bravely defiant determination to see, however horrific the vision, it reduces him to the less-than-venerable ignorance and innocence of prelapsarian Eden.

What we witness, I believe, in the occasionally degrading delineations of Singleton and the often blatantly contemptuous portrait of MacWhirr is the writer's admirable if undoubtedly self-punishing—admirable because so costly—contempt for his own unlaudable but necessary defenses. Conrad envies the lack of curiosity and strong emotion, but he is not proud of the impulse or the retreat it often impels. He praises in his essays and letters the rejection of reason and reflection, but the proud seeker in him recoils from that judgment. Unable finally to gaze unflinching at the horror, he turns repeatedly, at the last moment or before, away from terrifying revelation, from the utterance that would shake him and the rest of us to the core. But he despises that lack of courage and occasionally leaks that condescension into his portraits of the unthinking and unfeeling semi-heroes who remain faithful to the job and get it done. The ambivalences within these characterizations, then, are internal reflections of the broader ambivalence that pulls the quester back from final knowledge, the fictions, often, from clarity, coherence, and definable meaning.

Kindest, perhaps, is the gift of thoughtlessness, the "unthinking and blessed stiffness before the outward and inward terrors" (*LJ* 43) whose absence is Jim's undoing. But where one is not blessed with this saving mindlessness, evocatively equated, it seems, with a phallic stiffness, a deliberate avoidance of the depths or a self-deceiving denial of their contents is the recommended recourse. Like Marlow, Charles Gould recognizes that action offers saving respite from useless and tormenting thought. "That irreparable change a death makes in the course of our daily thoughts," observes the narrator in *Nostromo*, "can be felt in a vague and poignant discomfort of mind. It hurt Charles Gould to feel that never more, by no effort of will, would he be able to think of his father in the same way he used to think of him when the poor man was alive. His breathing image was no longer in his power. This consideration, closely affecting his own identity, filled his breast with a mournful and angry desire for action. In this his instinct was unerring. Action is consolatory. It is the enemy of thought and the friend of flattering illusions. Only in the conduct of our action can we find the sense of mastery over the Fates" (66). There is not a trace of irony in this assessment.

When late in life Conrad declared to his friend Lenormand, "Je vie veux pas aller au fond. Je veux considerer le réalité comme un chose rude et rugueuse sur laquelle je prom, ene mis doigts—rien de plus" (I have no wish to probe the depths. I like to regard reality as a rough and rugged thing over which I can run my fingers—nothing more),[57] he was not speaking with mere modesty or exclusively for the later writings that stiffened in the cold shadow of his breakdown. He was confessing, as he did often and unashamedly, to an instinctive refusal of "the depths." "It is my belief," Marlow observes of Jim's attempt to escape the truth of his failure, that "no man ever understands quite his own artful dodges to escape from the grim shadow of self-knowledge" (*LJ* 80). Conrad himself said much the same thing, with emphatic self-reference, in a letter to Charles Chasse. "Men have but very little self-knowledge," he wrote, "and authors especially are victims of many illusions about themselves."[58]

Many of these illusions are what Conrad was fond of calling saving illusions, the self-deceptions that make life endurable. The writer's habit of willful self-deception is perhaps least consequentially evident in his tendency to falsify autobiographical data. Conrad cultivated his own "family romance," a favorable correction of personal history designed to replace the deprivations of early childhood with compensating fantasies. He offers a false claim of rescue by a native African woman, a probably spurious history of a smuggling enterprise aboard the *Tremolino* and its subsequent wreckage, an unlikely self-heroizing tale of gunrunning for the Carlist cause, and an almost certainly false account of his wounding in a duel—probably a bungled suicide attempt—and he habitually glosses over the traumas of his early childhood. In this last, wrote Meyer, "Conrad was displaying a formula for dealing with insupportable realities which he had undoubtedly begun to employ at a very early age and would continue to use throughout his life: the denial of intolerable 'truths' and their replacement by 'memories,' perceptions and actions designed to create an illusion of invulnerability."[59]

These relatively superficial but revealing flights from painful self-awareness are early signs of a characteristic recoil from defiling truths of self and other, from the inner and outer terrors the thinking man is shatteringly exposed to. Conrad vacillated between a vigorous drive toward discovery and exposure on one hand and a weakening dread of knowledge on the other. He sometimes had the courage to let "hateful" reason show him what it would but as often lacked or defensively renounced it. The ramifications of this ambivalence are multiple: among them Conrad's fitful vacillation between a belief in truth and its disavowal, the often disingenuous lamentations about the failure of language to retrieve what is safer left untouched, the dynamic of approach and withdrawal, and the contradictoriness, obscurity, and evasiveness of his writing.[60] Where knowledge is of human fragility, insignificance, or worse, ignorance, evasion, confusion, and concealment are redemptive acquisitions.

Conrad betrays his apprehensive ambivalence toward terrible knowledge in the curious apposition in his letter to Cunninghame Graham, suggesting that Graham help Roger Casement in his noble campaign to expose the atrocities of the Belgian colonizers in the Congo. "I would help him," Conrad pleads (meaning "I would help him myself if I could"), "but it is not in me. I am only a wretched novelist inventing wretched stories and not even up to that miserable game.... [But Casement] could tell you things! Things I've tried to forget; things I never did know" (CL 3:102).[61] Conrad pleads a helpless ignorance here, but trumping "things I've tried to forget" with "things I never did know" strongly suggests an attempt to deny awareness of what he actually seeks to suppress. The surprising substitution may in this instance be an unconscious if revealing lapse of attention, but it speaks broadly and vividly to a pervasive feature of Conrad's writing. Like this remark and, perhaps, like his attitude toward what he had witnessed in his voyage up the Congo, his indeterminate tales deny knowledge of what, behind a variety of techniques of obfuscation and concealment, they anxiously strive to forget. Beneath the impenetrable surface crouches an anxious unwillingness to know. In the darkness of a ship at night, remarks the narrator of *Nostromo*, when sky, land, and sea disappear out of the world, "the eye of God Himself ... could not find out what work a man's hand is doing in there; and you would be free to call the devil to your aid with impunity if even his malice were not defeated by such a blind darkness" (pt. 1:7). Where evil and truth are equated, the darkness that obscures it is a blessing quite literally in disguise. Conrad knew with Alvan

Hervey that "truth would be of no use to him. Some kind of concealment seemed a necessity" (131).[62]

Donkin, the contemptible seaman of *The Nigger of the "Narcissus"* and one of the most reprehensible figures in all of Conrad, is excoriated for his relentless urge "to tear the veil, unmask, expose, leave no refuge—a perfidious desire of truthfulness!" (*NN* 150). Kurtz, driven by that perfidious desire, is a vivid object lesson in the price of the unaverted gaze, and Jim, fleeing a knowledge and reality that have become insufferable, takes refuge on an island repeatedly analogized to the world of art. Like Jim, Flora, the dubious heroine of *Chance*, rebels against unpalatable knowledge. Although frequently scathing in his responses to Flora, Marlow is capable of sympathy when her protective ignorance is violated. He speaks wistfully of the "last sleep, I won't say of innocence . . . but I will say: of that ignorance, or better still, of that unconsciousness of the world's ways, the unconsciousness of danger, of pain, of humiliation, of bitterness, of falsehood" (*Chance*, 99). Less than fully reliable narrators or dependably moral characters may speak profoundly, and one dismisses too lightly as mere subjective utterances Marlow's observation in *Chance* that "no one . . . is anxious" to take "stock of the wares" of their mind "if it can be avoided" (136); or Winnie Verloc's apprehensive conviction that things do not bear too much looking into. Both resonantly echo sentiments Conrad expressed repeatedly in his essays and letters and more implicitly urged in his fictions. "Winnie's philosophy," readers are told, "consisted in not taking notice of the inside of facts" (154). And why becomes clear two paragraphs later, where the conveyance awaiting Winnie and her mother "would have illustrated the proverb that 'truth can be more cruel than caricature' if such a proverb existed" (155). Whether or not such a proverb predates this writing, it is the proverbial truth behind the protective opacity of much of Conrad's fiction.

THESE ARE THE FACES of truth in Conrad's world, and to seek them out and stare them down holds, for him, only the appeal of distant admiration. "Even a small child lives, plays and suffers in terms of its conception of its own existence," Marlow opines in *Chance*. "Imagine, if you can, a fact coming in suddenly with a force capable of shattering that very conception itself" (117). It is to avoid such shattering that Jim flees to Patusan, that Gould, Hernandez, and Nostromo strive to avoid recognition of their own darker selves, and that Marlow withdraws his foot from the edge of the abyss into which Kurtz has fallen. Marlow praises work for its capacity to distract us from the inner and outer terrors. And while he expresses disdain for the glazed inhabitants of the sepulchral city who have never approached the edge, he himself recoils from it, as does Conrad. The author's obfuscating retreat into evasive language ("unfathomable," "impenetrable," "inconceivable," and the like) and inconclusive or inexplicable action is a textual extension of Marlow's protective lie to the Intended.

Conrad's preoccupation with the theme of threatening and unwanted knowledge and his commitment to the wisdom of selective ignorance are most explosively condensed in the black hole of *The Secret Agent*, a novel from which little light, whether of hope or understanding, escapes. In his author's note, written thirteen years after the publication of the novel, Conrad informs us that "the figures grouped about Mrs. Verloc and related directly or indirectly to her tragic suspicion that 'life doesn't stand much looking into'" are the organizing principles of the narrative (xii–xiii). It is important to note, lest we give way too easily to the bracing hope that the author is disdainfully dismissive of this conviction, that he refers to it not as a cynical or craven simplification but as a "tragic suspicion," which, given the writer's own profoundly tragic view of the human condition, lends it an initial authorial credibility the tale itself substantiates. It is pertinent, too—to step outside this novel for a moment—that the more reliable Heyst, in words that place no apparent distance between himself and either the narrator or the author of his tale, offers as undeniable truth a near replication of Mrs. Verloc's defensive edict. "Man on this earth," he reflects, "is an unforeseen accident which does not stand close investigation" (*Victory* 196).

As Conrad claimed, virtually all the major and several of the minor figures in *The Secret Agent* are grouped around the wary belief that truth is better left unsought and undiscovered. Its principal adherent and purveyor, of course, is Winnie Verloc, whose "maternal [and finally murderous] passion" (xii) Conrad identifies as the novel's driving impetus. In what becomes an almost Homeric epithet, Mrs. Verloc is identified as "incurious" or "uninquiring" on at least six occasions (153, 198, 199, 237, 239, 244). And her conviction that "things do not stand much looking into" is repeated in one of its several permutations on at least five more (177, 178, 180, 241, 267). The purpose of her studious avoidance is evident. It serves, as the narrator relates, as the foundation of her and Mr. Verloc's domestic accord (237) and constitutes "her force and her safeguard in life" (153).

Winnie is not alone in her resort to this sanctuary. She is accompanied in her protective insulation by all the figures systematically clustered around her motto, all the inhabitants of this urban heart of darkness, full knowledge of whose cynically devious and unprincipled workings would be "too dark altogether" (*HD* 162). Chief Inspector Heat and the assistant commissioner on one side of the porous barrier, the anarchists Michaelis, Ossipon, and the Professor on the other, and Mr. Verloc, who wanders precariously between them, all share the narrator's observation and Conrad's elsewhere-repeated acknowledgement that "it may be good for one not to know too much" (169)—particularly about oneself, the wretched world the mangy human insect inhabits for his pathetic rag of time, and the abyss of eternity he drops into when the clock runs out. Heat, who is convinced that "there are things not fit for everybody to know" (132) and that "it would not be good for . . . [the department's] efficiency to know too much"

(91), relieves himself of the burden of doubt and suspicion endemic to his job "by putting unbounded faith in the sporting prophets" of the racing form (206). The assistant commissioner and his whist party turn to their periodic game of cards, we are told, "in the spirit of co-sufferers, as if it were indeed a drug against the secret ills of existence" and "the pangs of moral discontent" (103, 102). Verloc joins his wife in her refusal to go "to the bottom of facts and motives" (245) and nurses the "delusion" that "in a prison there is room for hope" (235). Others turn for comfort and salvation to other, somewhat more exalted, if equally unactualizable illusions. Michaelis, who "never looks at the newspapers . . . [because] they make him too sad," sails free of an intolerable reality with "the idea of a world planned out like an immense and nice hospital, with gardens and flowers, in which the strong are to devote themselves to the weak" (302). The Professor, the great theoretician of the revolution, "averts his eyes from the [indifferent, theory-murdering] multitude of mankind" and finds solace, however meager and preposterous, in "the simplicity of his idea calling madness and despair to the regeneration of the world" (311). Ossipon, crushed in the end by his knowledge of Mrs. Verloc's murder and suicide and stripped by their mystery of the narrowing scientific lens that concealed his "secret fear," takes refuge in a catatonic numbness, "feeling nothing, seeing nothing, hearing not a sound" (311), and begins "to drink with pleasure, with anticipation, with hope" (310).

As if to concentrate our attention on the relative desirability, however unheroic, of delusion, Conrad closes the novel with a compressed iteration of our meager options to an insufferable reality, a "cursed knowledge" that makes preferable even the most wretched forms of escape. At the end readers are left with three, all preferable, presumably, to Mrs. Verloc's suicide: desperate retreat (Ossipon's flight to insensate numbness, aided by alcohol); the saving illusion (the Professor's absurd dream of a world regenerated by the madness and despair that will presumably trigger the essential revolutionary rage); and potbellied ignorance (the mindlessly insouciant multitude, transplants from the Intended's "sepulchral city," from whom the Professor protectively averts his eyes and who, triumphant, ignore him "like a pest in the street full of men" [311]).

Winnie Verloc, then, seems to cry out, if metaphorically, for virtually every inhabitant of the grotesque world of *The Secret Agent* when she pleads desperately with Ossipon to "put out the light" shining menacingly in the apartment in which the murdered corpse of her husband lies exposed. "The light—the light," she cries. "Go in and put it out—or I'll go mad" (283). And earlier, surveying the city's signs of luxury, her husband likewise speaks with expandable application when he reflects, "All these people had to be protected. Protection is the first necessity of opulence and luxury. They had to be protected . . . in the heart of the city and the heart of the country; the whole social order favourable to their hygienic idleness had to be protected against the shallow enviousness of unhygienic labour" (12). Verloc refers, directly, to the need for physical protection for a privileged class. But his "All these people had to be protected," made emphatic by the mantra-like repetition of his revelation, is no less apposite to the emotional and psychological fragility of all the threatened inhabitants of this novel and of Conrad's world.

It is tempting to read the narrator's endorsement of Mrs. Verloc's calculated avoidance—"Obviously it may be good for one not to know too much" (169)—the transparent and unsympathetic shallowness of the novel's characters, and the painful inadequacy of their illusions and escapes as evidence of authorial irony. Conrad admits, after all, in his author's note that only ironic treatment would allow him to say "all I felt I would have to say in scorn as well as in pity" (xiii). The narrative is indeed ironic, principally in its contemptuous detachment from the "squalor and sordidness" of the tale (viii), for which he offers a less than convincing apologia. But the ironic distance, like that achieved in *Under Western Eyes* by the imposition of the uncomprehending narrator, is, like a number of Conrad's other techniques of obfuscation and detachment, less a dissociation from Mrs. Verloc's tragic suspicion than a confirmation that, for the author as well, things do not safely bear too much unfiltered scrutiny.[63]

The nature of this rotting urban jungle and the terrible knowledge it would bring to those who, unlike Winnie and the others, would go "to the bottom of things" testify to the wisdom of a self-induced half blindness. J. Hillis Miller is unquestionably right to suggest that in *The Secret Agent* Conrad sees "all society as rotten at the core, as a vast half-deliberate conspiracy of police, thieves, anarchists, tradesmen, aristocratic blue-stockings, ministers of state, and ambassadors of foreign powers."[64] Winnie Verloc and her mother, as Anthony Winner remarks, "are prototypical in their intuition that direct perception of the world around them would be catastrophic. The intuition is correct."[65]

Indeed it is. In his author's note, Conrad himself referred to the London of the novel as "a monstrous town ... a cruel devourer of the world's light ... [with] darkness enough to bury five millions of lives" (xii). The tale confirms this judgment and, with brutal consistency, the narrator's observation that in such a wasteland "truth can be more cruel than caricature" (155). Here is a "vast and hopeless desert" (179) where the terrorist and policeman come from the same basket (69), where there is no law or certainty, and where everything—art, philosophy, love, virtue, even truth itself—is changed by economic conditions (50). But the condemnation assumes broader dimensions. It seems to encompass all of human life—not only in its adumbration of a vast and hopeless desert surely larger than London, but also in Ossipon's despairing plaint that he will believe in God when he comes to the end of his "scurvy, mangy little bit of time" (306) and in the lonely clock on Winnie's landing that "count[s] off fifteen ticks into the abyss of [an] eternity" (181), which Conrad recognized as the centerpiece in the blackened hall of our condition.

I argue later, principally in reference to other works, the habitual connection between terrible truth often associated with woman or the feminine and the evasiveness, obscurity, and interpretive entanglements of these texts. But it is small wonder, given the grotesque and repugnant nature of the world of *The Secret Agent*, that the novel has often been seen as hovering at the edge of coherent interpretation or falling beyond it. Stevie's "mad art attempting the inconceivable," his scribbled "tangled multitude of intersecting curves" and "confusion of intersecting lines" (45) that wind through, around, and back upon themselves, would seem to function as an internal icon of the novel's social, moral, and political labyrinth of deception and of the novel itself. In effect *The Secret Agent* is bracketed between Stevie's chaotic scribblings and the obsessively repeated and perhaps equally iconic newspaper report that drives Ossipon to a madness that, in another of the novel's coiling circles, recalls Stevie's. "An impenetrable mystery," it reads, "seems destined to hang for ever over this act of madness or despair" (307). Jocelyn Baines believed it might. *The Secret Agent*, he maintained, "lacks . . . a unifying theme, and when it is carefully examined falls apart into a succession of only superficially related scenes."[66] Daniel Schwarz and J. Hillis Miller believe that the narrator's ironic detachment provides enough protection to allow immersion in this slimy, vermin-ridden world and, despite the darkness, occasional glimpses of its meaning.[67] Winner likewise holds somewhat precariously to the belief that the novel's "flat faith and stolid order do finally hold meaninglessness and the horror of primal disorder at a remove." But he puts his own faith at risk with the acknowledgement that both in itself and as a conclusion to the novel, the climactic scene between Ossipon and Mrs. Verloc "balks any meaning other than its own offensiveness." While he remarks that "faith and fact, fiction and falsity, meaning and absurdity" are subject in the novel to a dizzying array of "doublings, overlappings, and contortions,"[68] William Bysshe Stein is unequivocal and insistent. In his view, "The flow of action in *The Secret Agent* erodes in meaning under the insidious counter flow of language." The "sordid and squalid [are transformed] into sublime nonsense."[69] Conrad's publishers at Athenaeum seem to have had a few doubts and questions of their own. Anxious that the novel's complicated time shifts and perhaps irresolvable ironies would befuddle readers, they chided his refusal to "show some regard for the simple reader."[70]

In the world of *The Secret Agent*, as in Conrad's world generally, knowledge is a demonic curse, trenchant and focused thought an invitation to agony, madness, or suicide. And all who unwisely seek or are unluckily invaded or overwhelmed by it pay this price. Winnie's profoundly "queer" and precariously balanced brother, whose "intelligence was very alert" and who, unlike Winnie, does wish "to go to the bottom" of things, disintegrates under the pressure of his perception. Suffering a morbid dread of the pain of others so intense that "the mere names of certain transgressions filled him with horror" (173), Stevie, if this does not already signal his imbalance, is driven to an anguished madness that ends in his destruction. Contemplating the resistant sludgy mediocrity of the multitudes, the Professor is crushed "under a load of doubt and uneasiness" that he escapes through self-imposed "seclusion in the room with the large cupboard closed by an enormous padlock" (305). The syntax leaves unclear whether it is the room or the cupboard that is padlocked (or in which compartment he secludes himself). But we are encouraged to infer that having seen too much, he avoids confinement in a padded cell by retreating to one of his own. Winnie, who finds safety behind her practiced devotion to the idea that things do not stand too much inquiring into, is driven to murder, nerve-rattling terror, and suicide when she loses her grip on this shield. Assaulted by the realization that her husband has in effect murdered her brother, her "whole being was racked by that inconclusive and maddening thought" (246). The result is the consummating act of "maternal passion" Conrad identifies as the driving force of the novel, the brutal stabbing of her husband. The consequences are horrific and tragically inevitable, largely because Winnie loses, with this act, her protective capacity for unthinking recoil from reality. The narration is explicit and detailed in its description of the agony of concentrated thought and its unraveling consequences for one who, until now, had survived on the hoarded wisdom of unknowing. Vividly dramatizing Dr. Johnson's famous proclamation that nothing concentrates one's attention like an imminent hanging, "Mrs. Verloc, who always refrained from looking deep into things, was compelled to look into the very bottom of this horrific prospect. She saw there no haunting face, no reproachful shade, no vision of remorse, no sort of ideal conception. She saw there an object. That object was the gallows. Mrs. Verloc was afraid of the gallows. She was terrified of them ideally" (267). Her mind fixed on reality in a way it has never been, she thinks about the gallows, pictures them sharply in her imagination, and imagines herself being brought to execution, and snared by one horrific detail she recalls from newspaper reports, she is driven past the limits of her endurance to the determination to end her own life by drowning before it is taken from her in this insufferably mortifying way. "'The drop given was fourteen feet.' No! that must never be. She could not stand *that*. The thought of it even was not bearable. She could not stand thinking of it. Therefore, Mrs. Verloc formed the resolution to go at once and throw herself into the river off one of the bridges" (268).

As with little else in this tangled and resistant novel, Conrad is unequivocal and relentless on this point. That things bear looking into only at an unconscionable price is not accessible to argument, ironic detachment, or dismissal. And it is drilled deep into our own defensive armor by the experience of Ossipon.

As comfortingly protected by a gridlike scientific view as Winnie is by her veil of incuriosity, Ossipon, like many of Conrad's protectively self-possessed male characters, is undone by a woman's seductively warm allure and consuming passion. Encountering Winnie after the still-unrevealed murder of her husband and attracted by the imagined prospect of a sexual liaison, Ossipon is drawn to her flame. Sent back to her apartment to "turn out the light," his own is fatally turned on. His rationalizing defense begins to break down, and reality in the form of the "savage," manipulative, and entrapping woman swarms through. Ossipon's first line of retreat, common to those invaded by an intolerable reality, is denial and a protectively imposed confusion.

> He did not believe the woman, or rather he was incapable by now of judging what could be true, possible, or even probable on this astounding universe. He was terrified out of all capacity for belief or disbelief in regard to this extraordinary affair, which began with police inspectors and Embassies and would end goodness knows where—on the scaffold for someone. He was terrified at the thought that he could not prove the use he made of his time ever since seven o'clock, for he had been skulking about Brett Street. He was terrified at this savage woman who had brought him in there, and would probably saddle him with complicity, at least if he were not careful. He was terrified at the rapidity with which he had been involved in such danger—decoyed into it. (288–89)

When he learns, later, of Mrs. Verloc's suicide, induced finally by her realization that he will not assist her, Ossipon is as maddeningly obsessed with a newspaper headline as Winnie was by the fourteen-foot drop of the gallows. The phrase, repeated italically in his own unprotected imagination—"*An impenetrable mystery seems destined to hang for ever over this act of madness or despair*"—becomes, for him, "an obsession, a torture." And he is tormented above all by the thought of mercilessly unremitting thought, by the dread of knowledge, by the fear that "he alone of all men [might] never get rid of the cursed knowledge" (307). Like Stevie and Winnie, the once-insulated scientist is driven mad by cursed, forbidden knowledge. Broken by the unbearable weight of obsessive thought, he retreats, as noted earlier, into an unfeeling and unthinking numbness. And though he can "neither think, work, sleep, nor eat . . . [he begins] to drink with pleasure, with anticipation, with hope" (310).

However foolish and shallow she is, however brutal in the end her maternal passion, Winnie Verloc is right. *The Secret Agent* offers full-length narrative confirmation of what Conrad affirms repeatedly in his letters and essays and suggests dramatically in as many stories: Given the cruel, potentially destructive nature of suspected truth, often it is better not to know.

Conrad's late novel *The Arrow of Gold* brings the issue to the surface, reframed, as though summarily, in the personal terms of art. Rita remembers longingly a time when she was "inconceivably young—still beautifully unthinking" (8); and there is much in the novel to suggest her identity with the obscure, retreating, and impenetrable work of art. It is the intolerable "hard truths" to which Allegre brutally exposes her that drive her to a self-protective inaccessibility and obscurity analogous to a work of art. Like the novel itself, she is alternately familiar and cold, approachable and resistant, knowable and unfathomable. And in her vacillation she is "manifest and mysterious, like an object of art from some unknown period" (36). Since Rita describes herself as "a precious object in a collection, an ivory carving or a piece of Chinese porcelain," her observation that "greatness in art is a protection" (84), though directed elsewhere, speaks of her own defensive distance from threatening reality. It also defines Conrad's view of the proper positioning of art in relation to that reality, a view he refines in Rita's response to the discovery that "having to do with men" is "like taking the lids off boxes and seeing ugly toads staring at you" (100). "My instinct may have told me," she explains, "that my only protection was obscurity" (85).

The slide from terrible revelation or near revelation to obscurity is a signature feature of Conrad's narratives. In *The Shadow Line*, the narrator informs us that "the impenetrable blackness beset the ship so close that it seemed that by thrusting one's hand over the side one could touch some unearthly substance. There was in it an effect of inconceivable terror and of inexpressible mystery" (108). What seems here, deceptively, I think, a mere interchangeability of terror and mystery is elsewhere more obviously a progression. I discuss in chapter 3 a number of such passages in which woman or the man's debilitating desire for her is the source and object of obfuscation, where the dread of the feminine generates the dissolution into mystery. But we may note here the revealing ending of "The Tale" (collected in *Tales of Hearsay and Last Essays*), where the commanding officer's uncompromising passion for truth, his need to put to a fatal test the reliability of a ship's crew's explanation of their presence, precipitates their demise. Pondering the event, he reflects: "At the time I was certain. They all went down; and I don't know whether I have done stern retribution—or murder; whether I have added to the corpses that litter the bed of the unreadable sea the bodies of men completely innocent or basely guilty. I don't know. I shall never know" (80). What begins as a declaration of unalterable uncertainty, already manifestly self-protective, reappears as a stern and distancing insistence:

> He rose. The woman on the couch got up and threw her arms around his neck. Her eyes put two gleams in the deep shadow of the room. She knew his passion for truth, his horror of deceit, his humanity.
>
> "Oh, my poor, poor—"

"I shall never know," he repeated, sternly, disengaged himself, pressed her hands to his lips, and went out. (80–81)

One must, as Marlow does and Kurtz does not, step back from the abyss: the narratives themselves no less than their protagonists, the writer no less essentially or preservingly than his creations. "Words," remarks the professor of linguistics who narrates *Under Western Eyes*, "... are the great foes of reality" (3). "Because of the imperfection of language, there is always something ungracious (and even disgraceful) in the exhibition of naked truth" (293). Conrad, like his narrators, takes frequent refuge in language as the enemy of truth, an inadequate instrument that, hovering between vagueness and rigidity, cannot capture the living core of human experience the novelist or storyteller would convey. Marlow and other narrators frequently complain of the enfeebling inadequacies of their instrument. But there is something disingenuous in blaming the medium for its failure to delineate a truth we are repeatedly encouraged to abjure. Where concealment is necessary to sustain sanity, morality, and life, authorship is neither exempt from the obligation nor immune to the appeal of a saving obfuscation. For all his evident distance from the fearful Hervey and the emotionally intimidated linguist of *Under Western Eyes*, there is a seminal core of Conrad in both. Faithful to the demanding responsibilities of authorship, assiduously attentive to the writer's job of work and to the details and the surface facts of life that enable us to "see," he raises his creations against the darkness, and with a subtler haze that seems like light, he wards it off.

For Conrad truth was a pestilence, knowledge equatable with terror. Denouncing thinking as the enemy of perfection and profound reflection as the most pernicious habit of civilized man (*Victory* x–xi), he openly advocated the adoption of saving illusions when other defenses prove inadequate and repeatedly dramatized the benefits of denial, self-deception, and repression. To separate these attitudes, urges, and beliefs from the obscurity of Conrad's texts, from the evasiveness with which he is alternately credited and charged, is, I believe, itself a form of denial. Radically slighting the complexity of the creative act, such a separation is an inversion of the early Freudian view of literature as a kind of dream. Where members of the Vienna circle and their successors saw in literature chiefly unconscious processes, paying little or no attention to deliberate choice and craft, criticism of Conrad typically views the creative enterprise as quite masterfully calculated and controlled, leaving too little room for the psychological, emotional, and other unruly forces that influence literary choice and production.

Although Conrad is both explicit and emphatic about the undesirability of certain forms of knowledge and the wisdom of denial, I do not claim that every instance of textual obfuscation or evasion is a deliberate turning away. Although it would be no less futile than fruitless to attempt to distinguish deliberate from unwitting or reflexive recoil, both are common and pervasive. That Conrad was convinced of the undesirability of certain forms of knowledge and often explicitly advised against discovery by no means assures that conscious intent motivates every instance of avoidance. Since he was, after all, perplexingly ambivalent about the wisdom, virtue, or profit of such revelation, the urge to obscure, retreat from, or turn from what he glimpsed or more glaringly perceived may have taken over even when he believed he was in hot and determined pursuit. In any event, although I believe this biographical and textual evidence serves as a helpful guide to the sources of obscurity and aporia in Conrad's writing, the question of ambivalence and avoidance and their connection to dangerous knowledge must finally be tested in the tales themselves.[71]

2

THE LIE OF FICTION

Heart of Darkness

Conrad began writing *Lord Jim* in May or June 1898, set it aside in December to write *Heart of Darkness*, and returned to *Lord Jim* in February 1899, when he had finished the shorter novel. Their overlapping composition, together with their shared use of Marlow as both narrator and character, led one reader to the persuasive hypothesis that *Heart of Darkness* and *Lord Jim* are "connected acts of imagination, that the two novels are joined together in a common impulse and project."[1] For Glassman the impulse is autobiographical, an attempt to define and sustain the personality of its author. But while that may indeed be one of the bones at which the twinned novels are joined, they are bound more tanglingly and pervasively at the aesthetic joint. Continuously composed, *Heart of Darkness* and *Lord Jim* constitute a complex exploration of the writer's problematic relationship to the dark and potentially dangerous knowledge these narratives fitfully and conflictedly pursue. It is because the novel is so intimately, if perhaps covertly, concerned with this ambivalent enterprise, I believe, that *Heart of Darkness* is the most notoriously evasive, contradictory, perhaps finally indeterminate of all Conrad's fictions.

In Kurtz, Jim, and Marlow, Conrad offers three quite divergent approaches of the artist to the truths of self and other, the terrors within and without that account for much of the tantalizing obscurity and elusiveness of this and a number of other of his enigmatic fictions. For Otto Rank the artist, like the neurotic, experiences an excruciatingly sharp and therefore threatened perception of a reality with which none of us can comfortably live. Deprived of the mechanisms that conceal reality from the rest of us, they are robbed of the "illusions important for living,"[2] another name for Conrad's "saving illusions." The problem of neurosis, which is at least occasionally identical with the problem of the artist, assumes, in Rank's description, two related forms: In one the artist (or neurotic) merges with the world around him and, becoming too much a part of it, loses his own claim to life. In the second, staking his claim for complete autonomy, he cuts himself off from the world and so loses the ability to function in it on its terms.³

The dichotomy provides a frame for the Janus faces of Kurtz and Jim. Both creative acts in a sense apply to Kurtz. Kurtz merges with the wilderness around him, incorporating it even as it swallows him in return, and in so doing forfeits his claim to life. In his act of obliterating inclusion, however, he also "kicks himself loose of the earth" in order to establish his unqualified dominion, thereby losing his ability to function in the world on its own terms. More escapist than confrontational, Jim seeks severance rather than merger. Fleeing to Patusan, he isolates himself from an intolerable reality in order to establish his claim to an imaginable world submissive to his will. The escape serves its purpose, at least temporarily, but at the price of contact with the saving facts of real existence that ground and redeem Marlow's more adaptive enterprise. Viewed from another angle in their mutual intimidation and self-protectiveness, Marlow and Jim carve separate roads away from the wilderness Kurtz's imperial appetite fatally leads him into. Following a brief sally toward the center, Jim cuts a sharp retreating path toward the exits and the refuge of the light. Marlow's route is circuitous and erratic. Testing the darkness from its periphery, entering and leaving like a nervous scout, he obscures his exit in a fog of mystification. Although Marlow, unlike Jim, shares with Kurtz a fascination for the abominable, even when he seems to stare he turns away.

THE ARMORED FOG

E. M. Forster complained of Conrad's habitual retreat from promised revelation to gruff disclaimer. The subtle if often sudden shift from depths to surfaces, from inquiry to image, is more a tacit than a gruff disclaimer, but Forster's charge is not groundless. Periodically and pointedly Marlow drops a curtain, veil, or fog over the narrative, clouds his voyage to the center with shoulder-shrugging claims that what lies before him is inscrutable, ineffable, or beyond one's powers of discernment. The language of mystery and haze is pervasive, as proficient a source of indeterminacy in *Heart of Darkness* as the flight to surfaces or the paradoxes and contradictions that seem to drain coherence from the tale. As in most of Conrad's narratives, however, it is not an arbitrary imposition. The mist that stills the atmosphere of *Heart of Darkness* does not descend haphazardly but, more typically, in order to obscure what has or threatens to become "monstrous, intolerable to thought and odious to the soul" (*HD* 141). Like the reach for surface fact, in other words, the renunciatory claims of inscrutability save the speaker or his narrative from witnessing what Jocasta warns is better left unseen. Deflections to the palpable facts of existence are supplemented by the occlusions of insistent mystification. Both are among the "unostentatious holes" (117) in Conrad's pitted texts in which the contaminating stench of the wilderness is buried.

The harlequin, Kurtz's self-effacing disciple, provides a succinct demonstration of the uses of a surrounding haze. Forced at last to confront the murderous consequences of his savior's obsession, the harlequin is alarmed, defensive, and confused. Viewing the staked skulls around his master's house, he claims ignorance, then attempts to mitigate, but Marlow will not let him off. When the harlequin adds explanation to excuse, Marlow redirects the parry to the speaker, compelling the disciple to consider the fuller implications of his unexamined identification with his mentor. It is more than the harlequin can handle. His dissociating disclaimers yield first to a silence like the elisions in Marlow's own obstructed discourse, then to a saving claim to ignorance equally reminiscent of Marlow's professions of bafflement. "I! I! I am a simple man," he blurts out. "I have no great thoughts. I want nothing from anybody. How can you compare me to . . . ?" Like Marlow tangled in the cord that ties the abomination to the saving idea, himself to Kurtz, the harlequin is silenced by the chilling implications of the bond. "His feelings," Marlow observes, "were too much for speech, and suddenly he broke down. 'I don't understand,' he groaned" (132). As Marlow, shaken earlier by the implications of one of his own self-justifications, "broke off" (51), the harlequin breaks down. But instead of the textual shift to surface imagery, the deflection assumes the form of an insistent noncomprehension Marlow usually reserves for himself.

Shortly before this breakdown, Marlow dropped just such a curtain over a scene whose drama drew him toward a demeaning identification with the harlequin's vulnerability to Kurtz. Having recently read Kurtz's document with its demonic postscriptum ("Exterminate all the brutes"), Marlow is aware that the harlequin's devotion to Kurtz opens a dark path to the wilderness. And yet the clownish acolyte has experienced what Marlow had obsessively dreamed of: he has heard, and at eloquent and expansive length, Kurtz's voice. Having listened all night while the great man talked and talked, the harlequin is ecstatic: "He made me see things—things." Kurtz's disciple is Marlow in extremis and *in potentia*. He is what Marlow might have become had he been a little less prideful, a little less the self-protective survivalist, and, not stumbling on the dazzling call for extermination, a little less fortunate in his reading. There is no sign of such self-awareness as Marlow listens to the harlequin. Rather he looks around and perceives a scene of land, river, jungle, and sky that never before appeared to him "so hopeless and so dark, so impenetrable to human thought, so pitiless to human weakness" (127). Marlow cannot account for this sudden intensification of the darkness, this sudden impenetrability to thought. Nor can we—though our ignorance is the textual point and purpose—except in terms of Marlow's own threatened but unacknowledged weakness. Shaken by the implicit identification with Kurtz's degradation, the harlequin does not know. Less directly menaced, but sensibly addressed by the serpent of his own longing to be taught and shown by Kurtz, Marlow is baffled by the unrelieved opacity of all that includes him. What threatens too unnervingly one's better sense of self is intolerable to thought and so defies it.

Each of the three occasions on which Marlow despairs of his narrative effort is a model of the protective uses of obfuscation. At three quite evenly distanced locations in the narrative, Marlow stops his discourse about the whisperings of the wilderness to lament its futility. The truth of his sensations, he fitfully remembers and reminds us, cannot be conveyed in mere language or to coddled listeners who did not share and therefore cannot comprehend them. On all three occasions, however, it is at a point where Marlow has just acknowledged the dangers of self-knowledge or perception or where that threat is palpable that discourse veers suddenly to the argumentative insistence on its pointlessness. Marlow's progressive retreat from knowledge, magnified as the threat intensifies, replicates Conrad's self-protective impulse in the face of menacing knowledge or awareness in *Heart of Darkness* and elsewhere.

In the first of these sequences, Marlow has been wondering nervously about the wisdom of their having strayed into the darkening wilderness and their capacity to cope with it. He feels "how confoundedly big, was that thing that couldn't talk, and perhaps was deaf as well" (81). And the anxiety has an immediate cause. The dumb thing, if anything, is handling him. For he has approached the lie he loathes by permitting the foolish brick maker to believe whatever he liked about Marlow's influence in Europe. In so doing Marlow has become as much of a pretense as any of the contemptible pilgrims he journeys with. Worse still, he is participating in the lie he detests for its taint of death, its flavor of mortality. Like virtually everything else Marlow loathes or fears, it is also what he wants to forget. And it is here, where the desire to forget meets the crawling sense of contamination, that Marlow drifts, seemingly unaccountably, toward the futility of his telling. Suddenly remembering his auditors, he wonders, without apparent provocation, if they can see Kurtz or anything at all or understand what he now identifies as an incommunicable dream. His familiar conclusion is that his enterprise is without hope or foundation. It is impossible to convey the life sensation that gives to life its truth and meaning: "we live, as we dream—alone."

At this point, following a resonant pause, Marlow has a portentous insight that will dictate further obfuscation and retreat. "Of course," he confesses, "in this you fellows see more than I could then. You see me, whom you know . . ." (83). Little is more certain in Conrad than that uncertainty will descend on such impending knowledge. One's self, especially under threat, is precisely what cannot and must not be clearly seen or intimately known. Marlow's vulnerable invitation is broken by silence, then by another shift to the primary narrator's majestic description of surface fact that adds darkness to deflection. Marlow's suggestion that his auditors see more than he because they see and know the teller gives way to the narrator's observation that "it had become so pitch dark that we listeners could hardly see one another. For a long time already he, sitting apart, had been no more to us than a voice." The auditors, including ourselves, see nothing. And when Marlow resumes, it is to announce, revealingly, that what he really wants is rivets. What he really wants, that is, are palpable objects from the saving surface, "to get on with the work—to stop the hole" (83). When they are not available, the descending dark suffices.

The passage leading up to Marlow's second declaration of narrative futility also begins with his confession of a lie, more direct and inescapable this time, for it is the climactic lie to the Intended he speaks of. Admitting he laid the ghost of Kurtz's gifts with a lie, Marlow launches into a series of defensive protestations whose repetitive urgency suggests self-doubt. More concerned, it seems, to lay his own anxiety to rest than to answer those who have not questioned him, Marlow insists that women "are out of it—should be out of it. We must help them to stay in that beautiful world of their own, lest ours gets worse. Oh, she had to be out of it" (115). Note the progression here, the slippage from the declarative ("are out of it") to the judgmental ("should be out of it") to the self-serving ground of that judgment (we must help them stay out of it for our own sake) to the climactic imperative ("had to be out of it"). The sequence reveals not only the source of Marlow's insistence on woman's exclusion from the truth, but also an important cause of truth's banishment from much of Conrad's work. The simple absence of knowledge gives way to the subjectively grounded desirability of such ignorance and in turn to an insistence on its urgency. Women are out of touch with truth for the same reason Conrad's tales and novels are: to keep men from a confrontation with horror, despair, dread, or uncontrollable sexual desire and all that arouses them—to protect men from every threat, inside us and beyond, to self-possession and control.[4]

Moving associatively from Kurtz's possessive view of "My Intended" to his equally incorporative harvesting of ivory, Marlow subordinates this rapacity to a more terrifying suggestion: that everything that belonged to him was a trifle. "The thing was to know what he belonged to, how many powers of darkness claimed him for their own. That," adds Marlow, "was the reflection that made you creepy all over. It was impossible—it was not good for one either—trying to imagine" (116). The notion of "creepy" reflections occurs on one other occasion in *Heart of Darkness:* when Marlow explains how, attending to the immediate tasks of steering and stoking, neither he nor the fireman "had any time to peer into our creepy thoughts" (98). Those creepy thoughts were of their frightening kinship to the savages howling and leaping on shore; these link him to the related powers of darkness that claimed Kurtz for their own. And in both instances such thoughts are to be avoided. In the earlier episode, they are lost in the writerly occupation of moving one's boat along. Here they will be banished with the aid of a projection from speaker to listener. The juxtaposition is a familiar one in Conrad. The creepy thoughts are first impossible, then unhealthy to imagine; and in Conrad's conceptual syntax, the latter of two explanations is typically the cause of what it ostensibly only supplements. Dread thoughts of the powers of darkness, then, are impossible to conceive because not salutary to imagine. And it is here, where Marlow acknowledges the inadvisability of reflecting further on these powers, that for the second time he accuses his auditors of a pampered inaccessibility to harrowing knowledge. Having recognized the need for his own protective insulation from such thoughts, he imputes with no little disdain a numbing incomprehension to those he speaks to. Stepping delicately between the butcher and the policeman, they cannot imagine the powers of darkness whose banishment from thought he has just identified with wisdom. What is projectively imputed to Marlow's auditors is applicable to the novel's readers, for the same reason. On deck as in our easy chairs, *Heart of Darkness*'s audience cannot comprehend the tale because its tellers are in discretionary retreat from a dark, forbidden knowledge associated here with the jungle, whose female body Kurtz plunders at his peril.

The jungle or wilderness is a multivalent symbol. It is the absence of external restriction and internal restraint; the locus of and human capacity for the savagery made likely by that absence; the hollowness at the core of the soul devoid of "inborn strength" and of a universe or heaven dumbly indifferent to that hollowness, that savagery, that absence. And the melting of this toxic alloy into the eroticized body of the woman magnifies its threat and insures its inscrutability and ineffability. The identification of the wilderness with the sensuous and passionate woman, the "savage and superb" African consort, is explicit and emphatic: "And in the hush that had fallen suddenly upon the whole sorrowful land, the immense wilderness, the colossal body of the fecund and mysterious life seemed to look at her, pensive, as though it had been looking at the image of its own tenebrous and passionate soul.... She stood looking at us without a stir, and like the wilderness itself, with an air of brooding over an inscrutable purpose" (135–36).[5] This complex of menacing associations closes all but inevitably with an insistence on the wilderness's impenertrability, its defiance of rational comprehension, and sends Marlow scurrying behind another of his rationalized insistences that it is equally defiant of communication.

Marlow's final insistence on the futility of his effort returns the responsibility to its initial source. On the first occasion, it is the incommunicable nature of the experience as dream that obviates comprehension. On the second blame shifts to the gap between the overprotected listeners and the brutally exposed speaker. Now it is language again, the unsuitability of words, invented as vehicles for commonplace waking experience, to convey the nightmare and the dream.[6] Like the earlier disclaimers, this one follows the recognition of extraordinary terrors and a warning of the need for their suppression.

Gazing into Kurtz's cabin, Marlow is unnerved by a purely abstract terror he cannot connect with any definable shape or physical danger. What makes the emotions so overpowering, he reflects, is "the moral shock I received, as if something altogether monstrous, intolerable to thought and odious to the soul, had been thrust upon me unexpectedly" (141). The truly monstrous, for Marlow and Conrad, is almost invariably intolerable to thought; and what is intolerable will not be introduced. The phrase, like so many others that resemble it, is a kind of syntactical warning, a presage to the onset of mystery. In this context Marlow's claim that to this day he cannot explain his reluctance to share the peculiar blackness of his experience acquires additional meaning. In the end, of course, he will not share it with the Intended. He will lie to her, not, too simply, because he wished to be loyal to the nightmare of his choice but because the tale he had to tell was horrible, unthinkable, and unutterable. The peculiar blackness of that experience, as he will later explain, would have been "too dark altogether." Marlow's reflections on his loyalty to Kurtz, his jealous hoarding of this experience, are a digression from the narrative. It intrudes and disappears back into the description of his final approach to the elusive Kurtz. But there is a psychological logic to its positioning. Marlow's refusal to share his experience rises out of the moral shock of a perception intolerable to thought. What is unthinkable, as the novel repeatedly attests, will be neither clarified, dwelt upon, nor shared. Here the anxious reluctance to communicate finds expression in Marlow's despair at the hopeless inadequacy of words. The messenger is beaten for the message. One meaning of *unspeakable* displaces another.

Marlow's lament is framed on both sides by revelations of personal relevance and involvement that make welcome sounds of the alleged poverty of language. Marlow has just confessed to finding relief in the replacement of his pure, abstract terror by "the usual sense of commonplace, deadly danger," which, he relates, brings him a welcome sense of peace and composure (141). He will not admit as much of the "common everyday words" he deems useless for the communication of this nightmare, but they are an equally pacifying defense against what is intolerable to speech and thought. As the unthinkable will not be thought, the unspeakable will not be spoken. That Marlow will be served by such deflection is established further by what leads to and away from it. It was at this very moment, he remarks, that the foundations of his intimacy with Kurtz were being laid. And what gave a special terror to his position was the fact that this intimacy was being forged with a creature who, having kicked himself loose of the earth, threatened to detach Marlow from the surface facts that save him.

Immediately after his protective remarks on the failure of language to convey what he had admitted is better left unspoken, Marlow faces the impending likelihood of a direct inspection of Kurtz's blasted spirit. Kurtz's soul had looked within itself and had gone mad, and Marlow speculates that he, for his own sins, will have to endure a similar ordeal of self-scrutiny. He never will, of course—not steadily, not probingly, not revealingly. Instead he will evoke a delphic fog that obscures all vision: "I saw the inconceivable mystery of a soul that knew no restraint"; "I saw a smile, a smile of indefinable meaning, appear on his colourless lips"; "And then that imbecile crowd down on the deck started their little fun, and I could see nothing more for smoke" (145, 146, 147).

In *Lord Jim* the climactic imposition of the veil is the structural shift from the inquiring emphasis of the Patna section to the escapist romance of Patusan. In *Heart of Darkness*, it is the substitution of the Intended for the wilderness-as-consort, the absorption of terrible truth into the protective denial implicit in Marlow's saving lie. Art and truth, for Conrad, are incompatible. As Marlow tells us, all wisdom, truth, and sincerity are compressed into that moment when we step over the edge into the invisible (*HD* 151). To preserve oneself for the restrained moral discipline of literary creation one must step back from the edge where all wisdom, truth, and sincerity reside. It is Marlow's initial failure to grasp either this fact or the length of Kurtz's fall that sends him on his mission to bring Kurtz back with him.

Kurtz and Marlow are two dimensions of the creative imagination and two facets of Conrad's own. Kurtz is the great magician who yields to the seduction of a reckless freedom kicked loose of the saving surface. Surrendering to occult and irresponsible powers, he learns the truth but cannot shape it as narrative art. Marlow, in contrast, is the force of self-possession, the attention to work and craft, the anxious creature who steps back from the truth to save himself for the rigorous task of re-creation. Conrad's expressed horror at the loss of self-possession testifies to the strength of the Kurtz inside him, as Marlow's loyalty to Kurtz and his at least partially acknowledged kinship to the savage uproar testify to the presence of a Kurtz within Marlow. Marlow's mission to bring Kurtz back, then, is an effort to merge the reckless perceiver of truth with the disciplined crafter of tales. There is resonance in Marlow's admonishing entreaty to Kurtz that unless he returns he will be lost (*HD* 143). To bring Kurtz back is to bring to those who will listen the whisper of truth that will otherwise be lost. It is to transport in the steamboat to which he is carried—in Marlow's "craft," if you will—that part of the irresponsible imagination that has descended into the self and passed beyond all borders into the chaotic realm of revelation. Returning Kurtz would give the artist's voice to a lost imagination that has "something to say"; it would carry truth directly into art, a task that cannot, or will not, be performed. Kurtz expires, his message on his lips, and it is left to the figure who has deliberately withdrawn his foot from the edge to bring his message home. It falls to the man who has not clearly seen and who warns us repeatedly of the dangers of intolerable sight to make us see. Finally what is exposed most lucidly—in *Lord Jim,* in *Heart of Darkness,* in most of Conrad's richly obscure fictions—is the tale of the storyteller's fearful ambivalence toward discovery, the contradictory and finally inscrutable narrative of the struggle between fascination with the abomination and the manifold techniques of self-protection that overwhelm it.

Marlow's lie to the Intended, then, is finally the lie of art, the preservation of the protectively delusive Intended at the expense of the truth of the barbarous woman. As Peter Hyland observes, "The magnificent savage, 'barbarous and superb,' is reduced [by this ending] to the Little Woman.... It is precisely the knowledge of this darkness [represented by the passionate woman] that Marlow has to repress with his myth of the pure woman."[7] Like the darkness, the two kinds of women are externalizations of the human interior, two expressions—one protective and unseeing, the other savage and nakedly exposed—of the attitudes toward truth and self-disclosure these narratives embody.

Heart of Darkness is a tangle of identities. The replacement of the African woman by the Intended does not efface the darker woman, because there is much they share. Both in a sense possess and are possessed by Kurtz. Both are noble and tragic, dignified and proud. The Intended shares with the consort a mature capacity for fidelity, belief, and suffering. And in extending her arms as if after a receding figure, the Intended recalls another tragic and familiar shade who, similarly powerless, stretched her arms over the stream of infernal darkness (*HD* 160–61). Since the African woman is a reflection and embodiment of the wilderness that is also Kurtz's soul, Kurtz is an image of the dark woman and, through her, of the Intended—not only through the consort but directly as well or through Marlow's eyes. As the Intended speaks of her loss, the two conflate in Marlow's mind. He sees them "in the same instant of time—his death and her sorrow—I saw her sorrow in the very moment of his death.... I saw them together—I heard them together" (157).[8] Again Marlow hears in the Intended's whisper echoes of Kurtz's gasping declaration. "She had said, with a deep catch of the breath, 'I have survived' while my strained ears seemed to hear distinctly, mingled with her tone of despairing regret, the summing up whisper of his eternal condemnation" (157). And the resemblance reverberates outward, gathering the two radically different environments into a single horror. What Marlow felt in the jungle he feels in the collecting darkness of the Intended's room. Here too he feels he has "blundered into a place of cruel and absurd mysteries not fit for a human being to behold" (157).

That Kurtz is in many ways a doppelgänger, Marlow's libidinal alter ego, is rudimentary; but the identifications mesh and multiply. Marlow is Kurtz, Kurtz is his own primitive consort, and the dark woman is the seemingly opposite Intended who is also identified with Kurtz. But there is one more merging of identities that has received less notice and that speaks to the narrative's finally imperious impulse toward exclusion and denial: Marlow's resonantly echoing resemblance to the Intended. Associatively implied in the Intended's identification with Kurtz, it surfaces emphatically in their encounter. Virtually everything the Intended says during their portentous conversation suggests either the similarity between them or a susceptibility to her influence suggestive of such resemblance. The mature capacity for fidelity, belief, and suffering that Marlow ascribes to the Intended and that survives most securely through denial is a no-less-fitting description of his own painful and convicted dedication to a man who has won, in almost equal measure, the unshakable loyalty of both. When Marlow perceives in her carriage the implicit declaration that only she knows how to mourn for him as he deserves, he reads in her bearing what he believes of himself. Her explicit claims that she has been worthy of him and that she understood Kurtz better than anyone on earth are assertions Marlow might have appropriated for himself with equal right and conviction. And her resonant "I have survived" carries echoes of the retreat from the edge that permits Marlow's equally survivalist "I have a voice."

At times the Intended knowingly includes him, identifies Marlow as a kindred sufferer and disciple. "What a loss to me—to us!" (159), she adds, with more than the mere beautiful generosity Marlow notes in her addendum. "You know what vast plans he had. I know of them too," she remarks (160). Like her, Marlow is aware of the depth of shared experience. "For her he had died only yesterday. And, by Jove! the impression was so powerful that for me, too, he seemed to have died only yesterday" (157). And when neither takes conscious note of these echoes, they reverberate in the dialogue. Repeatedly throughout the pathetic exchange, Marlow reiterates or completes his interlocutor's remarks—so regularly that they begin to sound like a single speaker or an echoing set of twins. When she says that Marlow knew Kurtz well, Marlow answers that he knew him as well as one man may know another. When she remarks that "it was impossible" to know and not admire him, his reply is that "it was impossible not to—," which she completes with "love him." "I knew him best," she claims. "'You knew him best,' I repeated" (158). "You and I—" she begins. "We shall always remember him," Marlow closes. "Something must remain," she says plaintively. "His words, at least, have not died." "His words will remain," Marlow assures her. "And his example" she adds, not yet satisfied. "His example...." "'True,' I said; 'his example too. Yes, his example'" (*HD* 160). When the Intended stands, Marlow rises too, but the "too" is almost redundant; their identities having merged, his repetition of her act, as of her words, might be assumed. There is something faintly ludicrous about all this mimicking repetition, or, viewed more charitably, something suggestive of Marlow's heroic self-effacement, a willful obliteration of self in the interest of the interlocking preservation of the Intended's illusion and his own chosen nightmare. What undermines our ready dismissal of Marlow's echoing reassurances is the realization that none of them violate his own dedication and belief. Marlow did indeed know Kurtz well, think him remarkable and in a way admire him, does indeed believe his words and example will remain. And while all these accessions have, for Marlow, a brace of meanings, only one is ironic; the other is an earnest replication of the Intended's praise. What the Intended does not want to know and will never hear Marlow suppresses in his willing participation in her illusion.

What the repeated merging of their thoughts, expressions, and beliefs evinces is the extent to which Marlow is identified with the Intended as both survivor and symbol. Women, we have been told, must be kept in their unreal worlds lest men's get worse. The Intended is such a woman, perhaps the ultimate exemplar of this gendered need. But the need is projected, a reflection of man's (and Marlow's) own scurrying search for a wall to hide behind, a hole in which to bury rancid truths, a fog to obscure his vision. The Intended's/woman's need for illusion is Marlow's/man's own. Lying to her, he lies chiefly to and for himself. Marlow bows his head "before that great and saving illusion," lies to exclude the darkness from which he understands he could not have defended her and from which, he adds poignantly, "I could not even defend myself" (159). His lie, the novel's conclusion, is no divergence but a culmination. It is the climactic expression of the defensive flight from truth, knowledge, and coherent meaning that steers the floating fiction from the moment it sets sail.

KURTZ AND THE DEVOURING IMAGINATION

That Marlow is no mere narrator but the narrator as creative artist who articulates and exemplifies many of Conrad's own beliefs and anxieties about literary creation is apparent. That Kurtz, who almost voicelessly whispers his brief but telling message, is also an adventuring artist is perhaps less evident, though no less important to an understanding of Conrad's aesthetics and the avoidant instincts of *Heart of Darkness*. It is also perhaps essential to understand the nature and consequences of the Kurtzian artist's illicit relation to forbidden knowledge in order to understand why Marlow, nearer to Conrad's ego-as-artist ideal, recoils from and obscures it.

The writer, for Conrad, though he is always writing about himself, remains like Kurtz "a figure behind the veil; a suspected rather than a seen presence—a movement and a voice behind the draperies of fiction" (*PR* xiii).[9] Conrad's words describe the shimmeringly magnetic effect of the invisible Kurtz upon Marlow and the reader, and the focus on voice deepens our sense of Kurtz, despite his almost unbroken silence, as an instrument of creative speech. Kurtz, we know, is an imaginative genius—a poet, painter, and musician who, as the Russian harlequin excitedly tells Marlow, "enlarge[d] the mind.... He made me see things" (123, 127). He is also the author of a report that Marlow describes as "a beautiful piece of writing," vibrant with "the unbounded power of eloquence" and marked by "the magic current of phrases" (118). But until their long-delayed meeting, for Marlow as well as the reader, Kurtz is above all else a voice. Conrad held that it is in his voice, the sound and ring of his sentences, that the author's personality shapes and presents itself. And it is just this voice that Marlow, the artist as ephebe, pursues with arduous if ambivalent dedication into the jungle.[10]

Kurtz's defect as a voice and as an emblem of verbal eloquence is that he is very little more than a voice and that behind the "burning noble words" igniting his report on the suppression of savage customs there are no practical hints; there is no substance, no saving adherence to the surface facts of life.[11] That his hollowness of language is an expressive revelation of a more fundamental vacancy is particularly dangerous for Kurtz because he at the same time persists at every cost in the task Conrad sets for the writer in the preface to *The Nigger of the 'Narcissus'*: the descent into the dark and unprotected self in pursuit of truth. The honor of a writer, Conrad wrote to Galsworthy, lies not in the fidelity to personages, but in the love of the idea and a scrupulous faithfulness to his conception of life (*CL* 2:359). Kurtz's conception is appalling, unforgiving, and unforgivable, one that Conrad forbids the writer to give his fiction to, as Marlow resists its revelation to the Intended. But it is a temptation and a powerful one—hence its glimpsed incursion into the text and Marlow's often less–than-grudging admiration for Kurtz, his proclaimed preference for this nightmare over the flabbier devils of self-protection, circumlocution, and escape. In this sense Kurtz is a type of Guy de Maupassant, whom Conrad praises for "an unswerving singleness of purpose." If our tender feelings, wrote Conrad in his essay on Maupassant, "happen to be hurt because his talent is not exercised for the praise and consolation of mankind, our intelligence (which is great) should let us see that he is a very splendid sinner, like all those who in this valley of compromises err by over-devotion to the truth that is in them" (*NLL* 26).

Even the splendid sinner, however, is more object lesson than a model for emulation; there is no acceptable approach to the darkest truths, only variously reprehensible stances in relation to them. For Conrad the devouring and self-devouring plunge into the invisible where alone all truth resides may be preferable to the sepulchral oblivion of those who dare not look, but it is mad and venal for all that. Only obfuscation, gesturing ambiguously in the shadows, permits escape and escapes unscathed.

Conrad warns that in the interior world of the artist, where there are no external restraints to keep him in bounds, he has only his conscience to resist the beckoning temptations. He must let "none of the fascinations that beset a writer working in loneliness turn him away from . . . the vouchsafed vision of excellence"(*NLL* 26). Kurtz is a sobering lesson in the consequences of the triumph of those fascinations. One of these is the hollow eloquence Kurtz is prey to,[12] ominous not because it rings untrue but because it lacks the clatter of traffic noise and rivets that mute the echoes resounding with deafening conviction from within. Other fascinations summon with almost equal fervor: the indulgent satisfaction of one's own sentiment, an instinctive effusion of his own emotions, and the negativist inclination to denounce—three of the vices Conrad named as the special bêtes noire of the national English novelist (*LE* 132). All of these, however, are mere carbuncles on the back of the ultimate fascination: the fascination of the abomination, the words the wilderness whispers in Kurtz's too eagerly inclined ear.

No less minatory than the wilderness's message is the means of its pursuit, though finally the two are inseparable. The great danger of the Kurtzian enterprise lies in its abandonment of self-possession in the surrender of all restraint that is at once the method of discovery and what it ultimately exhumes. Kurtz has something to say, has glimpsed his truth, because unlike Marlow and the others, he had stepped over the edge. Perhaps, admits Marlow, "all the wisdom, and all truth, and all sincerity, are just compressed into that inappreciable moment of time in which we step over the threshold of the invisible" (151). Here too Conrad's strained ambivalence is apparent. On the one hand, as he wrote in "A Familiar Preface" to his *A Personal Record,* to achieve greatness the artist-magician must surrender to occult and irresponsible powers outside or within him. On the other hand, such a surrender is a fool's bargain; for as Conrad confesses, "I have a positive horror of losing even for one moving moment that full possession of myself which is the first condition of good service," the sine qua non of successful art (xvii–xviii) and vulnerable prey to the predatory wilderness.

"In order to move others deeply," the Kurtz in Conrad knows, "we must deliberately allow ourselves to be carried away beyond the bounds of our normal sensibility. . . . But the danger," the Marlovian side interjects, "lies in the writer becoming the victim of his own exaggeration"(*PR* xvii–xviii). In this passage the exaggeration leads to a loathing of truth as something too cold. But in *Heart of Darkness* there is an anxious recoil from a truth that is entirely too warm: the truth of the savage wilderness, the engulfing nihilistic abyss, or the passionate hungerer that collapses self-possession. Kurtz, in his abandon, wrestles it to the earth he has kicked loose from, but at the price of morality, sanity, and life. In Blakean terms it is the road of excess that leads to the palace of wisdom, and the means of transport are the same: the breath of the unrestrained imagination. "Only in men's imagination," Conrad avers, "does every truth find an effective and undeniable existence. Imagination, not invention, is the supreme master of art as of life"(*PR* 25). Entering the jungle under the force of his conception of himself and what is possible, Kurtz would be precisely such a man and master of his house. A tragic version of the narcissistic artist who, indifferent to moral constraints, reinvents the world in the image of his own imagination and language, Kurtz would bend the jungle's seductively wild and unbounded reality to his will and make it his own.

The great struggle of the nineteenth- and twentieth-century poets, one might argue, has been for an acceptable balance between the greed of an all-consuming imagination that would distance all reality or subsume it and the demands of an implacable reality whose call for immediacy and recognition threatens the extinction of that imagination.[13] As romantic individualism idealized liberation from religious, social, and ethical norms and institutions, the romantic imagination sacralized comparable freedom from the restraints of literary convention and tradition and from whatever else might restrict its organic stretch. *Heart of Darkness* is a study of the imperialist impulse and appetite that would ingest what it conquers and reconstitute it as an aspect or expression of the self. This view, however, is too narrowly political. It treats the Congo in its literal sense alone, ignoring its metaphoric function as an image of the inner life, more specifically that of the descending artist in search of his truth. Jean-Jacques Mayoux defines the romantic as a "devotee of unreality" most at home "in an unreal and fabulous world where his imaginings precede and create the events instead of being surprised by them."[14] Jim and Kurtz are both romantics in this sense, but the unreality to which they devote themselves is different and unstable. The unreality of Patusan is an escapist fantasy, an inverting flight from the "unreal" vision of the crew laid out for death that is in its way truer than the events of history or the dispensations of destiny. Kurtz's imagination, "unreal" in this latter sense, is an embodiment of the credo of the Romantic movement, about which Conrad expressed a troubled and characteristic ambivalence.

In the author's note to *Within the Tides*, Conrad declared that the romantic sense of reality was inborn in him. But he qualified his gratitude for the gift with an admission that he feared its dangerous evasion of "the hard facts of existence" (v–vi), which are not to be mistaken for the profoundest truths of existence but appreciated as the surface facts that protectively distance us from these depths. His voracious mouth wide open, as if to swallow all the earth and its inhabitants (*HD* 155), Kurtz is the atavistic embodiment of the devouring romantic imagination that cannibalizes reality and incorporates everything into itself.[15] Kurtz's conquest, in this sense, is an extreme form of a condition Rank identifies with artistic creativity. The creative individual, wrote Rank, has difficulty whittling and narrowing reality to controllable forms. More afflicted than blessed with a vivid imagination, he "makes the reality surrounding him a part of his ego. . . . Bound up in a kind of magic unity with the wholeness of life around him much more than the adjusted type . . . [he] has taken into himself potentially the whole of reality."[16]

Like the true romantic and like man in the thralls of a blinding passion, Kurtz, who can compel himself to believe anything (*HD* 154), believes his own fictions. But in the paradoxical logic of the novel, by submitting to the twin fictions of omnipotence and its legitimation, Kurtz arrives not at a supreme fiction but a savage reality of self. Kurtz "has forced life to expand to the pressures of the self."[17] He shapes life to suit his own unrestrained needs and makes it not merely an extension but an expression of himself. The darkness is, after all, Kurtz's darkness, its horror the horror he has cannibalistically made of it.

For all the venal heroism of his acknowledgment, however, even Kurtz is given to self-deception and illusion. That he could make himself believe anything hints at this self-serving inclination. His confrontational integrity is brought again into question by his convenient forgetting of the inculpating postscript ("Exterminate all the brutes!"), more actively by his "contemptibly childish" insistence, almost to the end, that his motives were commendable and right (*HD* 148). Like Jim's fictionalizing self-heroization, Kurtz's monstrous incorporation and the horror it generates represents a flight from the real but demeaning limitations of self and world. Kurtz's totalizing fusion is a circumvention of partiality and constraint, an escape toward demonic godhead from the limitations of the human animal and condition. Ironically Kurtz's confrontation with a terrifying reality derives its impetus from an evasive urge.

The heart of darkness is Kurtz's, not only through ideational association or metaphoric transfer but structurally as well. The way to discovery is identical with its object. Abandoning the restraints disciplined search accepts, Kurtz discovers his own abandon. Like all the male protagonists whose loosed impassioned selves mirror the women who destroy them and who are destroyed because of this reflection,[18] his nature is an image of his quest. Kurtz arrives at the heart of darkness, glimpses its truth and recognizes it for his own, largely because he is "hollow at the core." Lacking the inborn strength required to resist temptation where all external conventions and restraints have been removed, Kurtz steps over the edge and finds his truth, the truth of moral chaos that knows no boundaries. Lacking belief, he finds "some sort of belief." And lacking a guiding conviction, he finds a conviction that bears the appalling face of a glimpsed truth.

In a phrase that all but insists on the identification of the subject and ethic of *Heart of Darkness* with his literary aesthetic, Conrad declares that "the writing of [a book] . . . is an enterprise as much as the conquest of a colony" (*LE* 132). Nor is this an idle analogy. Conrad frequently likened the task of writing with comparable explorations and ordeals, and he did not share the faith of his contemporaries—of Ezra Pound and T. S. Eliot, D. H. Lawrence and James Joyce—that they could subdue in their art the chaos and cruelty of the world they all perceived.[19] Marlow's report that "the silent wilderness surrounding this cleared speck on the earth struck me as something great and invincible like evil or truth, waiting patiently for the passing away of this fantastic invasion" (76), urges the parallel. The artist, descending into the lonely regions of the self in search of truth, necessarily confronts, as one face if not the living body of that truth, his own and the human heart of darkness, an anarchic hunger that does not know restraint.[20] These are the waiting ghosts that frighten the writer's invasion of this inner wilderness and account in part for the characteristic blur and evasiveness of his pursuing style. Truth and evil, of course, survive each incursion and patiently, perhaps scornfully, await the next. The question is the survival not of truth and evil but of the explorer who challenges them. The ominous "dumb thing" that Marlow wonders if he and others are strong enough to handle (81) is reality, dead to our entreaties for meaning, silent in its refusal of revelations. The artist's question is whether, given such intimidating circumstances, he or she can somehow bring that reality to heel or whether, like Kurtz, s/he will be swallowed by the monster s/he seeks vainly to devour. Kurtz, in other words, is an expression of Conrad's doubt that one can tame in art the cruel chaos of the real—"savage" and "wild-eyed," mysterious and teeming, turbulent, furious, and uncontrolled. Marlow's restraint and the equally concealing obscurity and vagueness of the novel are the soaked blankets in which he winds the madman.

The writer's failure to colonize reality may be owed to several causes. For Conrad the one that dooms the halfhearted efforts of the English national novelists is the absence of the "clear conception of . . . craft" requisite to conquest. Descending into the lightless wilderness of self, where there are no restraints but conscience, the imagination must not be allowed the liberty indulged by those novelists who, devoid of artistic dedication, merely satisfy their own sentiments (*LE* 132). As Jim discovers on the deck of the *Patna*, the untethered imagination is a menacing demiurge. Imagination, as the first narrator of *Lord Jim* declares, is man's most terrifying enemy, a judgment later confirmed by Marlow's inference that Jim must have been unconsciously aware that the reality could not be half as terrible or vengeful as the terror created by his imagination (*LJ* 113). Since the ultimate truths, the ones the artist seeks, are those found within, the terrors of the inward-looking imagination are not denials of reality but profounder recognition.

Worthy of admiration, perhaps, such recognition is also an invitation to excess, and it must be tempered, filtered, or averted. It must be tempered by hope, deflected by a saving attention to the often trivial surface facts of our existence, or protectively obscured. The revolutionary spirit, Conrad complained—and Kurtz was in possession of such a spirit—is too convenient, for it releases one from all scruples; its relentless optimism, like that with which Kurtz begins his arrogant mission into the Congo, contains the "menace of fanaticism and intolerance" (*PR* xviii).

Conrad understood himself and others well enough to know that the frustration of such optimism, coupled with the fanaticism that would egoistically remake others into versions of the self, breeds malice and despair. All writerly ambitions are lawful, Conrad argues, "except those which climb upward on the miseries and credulities of mankind" (*PR* xviii). And there is room in the house of fiction for every kind of furniture but dry despair (*PR* 93). In other words and by clear implication, if truth or knowledge, discovery or revelation increases the complement of man's miseries or the magnitude of his despair, as Conrad was convinced they would, it is the writer's duty to avoid them. Again Kurtz appears as the image of the dark, rejected side of his creator, here the denounced nihilist revolutionary in himself. Conrad acts out, through Kurtz, his own ambivalent urge for a devouring freedom from all restraint, which he repudiates through destruction and condemnation. But only partially: Conrad's ambivalence toward Kurtz persists in Marlow's qualified but reverent admiration for one who "had something to say" (151).

If Jim turns away from reality by fleeing to Patusan, Kurtz squats at the heart of darkness and attempts to devour it. His imagination does not so much take up residence outside the world as seek to draw the world within it, to remake it in the image of his needs. Lacking the precise intention and steady mind required to build up a colony or a book, Kurtz, like Galsworthy and W. H. Hudson, as Conrad disapprovingly reads them, ignores the rigorous work and preparation necessary for the colonization of reality and, wanton artist/lover that he is, frees his soul to satisfy his desires. When the manager rejects Kurtz's achievements on the seemingly absurd grounds that his "method is unsound," there is more than callousness in the remark, more than dismissive irony behind it. Initially stunned by the indictment, Marlow reconsiders, recognizing that having no method at all is indeed unconscionable (137–38). What is wanted, in other words, is not truth but method, a method or craft whose primary functions include the evasion of truth when the preservation of self and self-possession requires it.

For Conrad it seems, as for Edgar Allan Poe and Nathaniel Hawthorne, there is an immoral component to the artist's obsessive pursuit of his calling. Art is a form of colonization, an exploitive plundering or devouring assimilation of the real world by the imagination. Like truth or evil, the wilderness waits patiently for the invasion to pass. But for its duration the artist assumes responsibilities that mitigate his offense. The search for a truth that may prove a horror, like the colonizing of darker peoples, "is not a pretty thing when you look into it too much" (*HD* 50–51). Both conquerors, unless restrained by discipline, law, or inborn strength, will stare too fixedly and long; they will breathe dead hippo and be contaminated. What is required is an awareness of the existence and stench of rotting flesh but the preserving ability to dig "unostentatious holes to bury the stuff in" (117). Aware of the risks of breathing too long the air of rotting mortality, one must show a greater concern for survival than for raw experience. The writer must be willing to obscure what cannot be safely observed or taken in. In short he must be prepared to tell the lie of fiction that banishes a reality that is "too dark altogether." The tale of Kurtz is Conrad's portrait of the triumph and failure of an imagination that, like all his defeated lovers, rejects all restraint and falls prey to all temptation. Kicking loose of the earth, one is free to step over the edge into the invisible where truth resides. But to kick loose of earth is also to sever all contact with the moral and physical world and therefore to create the horror the seeker is dubiously privileged to perceive. As we might well expect from the descent into the self in quest of truth, one perceives what one creates. The nature of the descent shapes the object of perception: content and method are indistinguishable.

The same is true of the haze that surrounds the heart of darkness, defying penetration. The darkness at the center of the novel is the product of a technique of obfuscation no more but no less deliberate than Kurtz's abandonment of restraint. When it is fearfully hesitant, no less than when it is rashly determined, the journey mirrors what it finds.

MARLOW AND THE AMBIVALENCE OF PARADOX

For Albert Guerard, "Conrad, like Marlow, had a passion for truth—including the dark truth concerning our human nature—and a hatred of complacent egoism."[21] In fact, however, a destabilizing ambivalence toward both dark truth and complacent egoism rocks *Heart of Darkness, Lord Jim,* and much of the rest of Conrad's fiction. As there is a woman who knows and one who turns away from virulent realities, so there is a Marlow who pursues his own and other truth into the darkness and a Marlow who averts his attention, who withdraws his foot from the abyss, and who lies as much to save himself as the Intended. Marlow vacillates between Kurtz's fascination for the abomination and a revulsion with that abomination that partializes his view or sends him scurrying toward a redeeming hope or the saving facts of the physical surface.[22]

Marlow's double view of Kurtz—revulsion alternating with a reverential fascination—is also expressive of his conflicting attitudes toward forbidden truth and its discovery. He admires the relentless courage of those who hunt the dragon. But he too is repulsed by the slime it trails and driven back by the flames it breathes. Kurtz's sketch of a woman, "draped and blindfolded, carrying a lighted torch" (79), captures not only the doubleness of woman as self-blinding illuminator, but also the ambivalence of both Marlow and Conrad toward full knowledge of the savage wilderness within us and without. The dance of Conrad's fictions between cowardice (or strategic retreat) and courage is on stage in the tendency of the narratives to offer and remove, to give or seem to give and take away. Present too in the remarks of a disgruntled reader Conrad quotes in his author's note to *Mirror of the Sea*. Echoing Forster's annoyance at Conrad's habit of melting away at the burning edge of promised revelation, the reader complained that "in reading these chapters one is always hoping for the revelation; but the personality is never quite revealed" (vii).

Toward whatever secret, Conrad, torch in hand, leads us to the edge, peers over, and, extinguishing his flame, withdraws. Although the pull is in both directions, the stronger forces are centrifugal. Unlike Plato's Leontius, whose craven urge to cast his frightened eyes on carnage finally overwhelms the reluctance of his reason, Marlow's attitudes about reflection, truth, and knowledge are consonant with his natural timidity. Like Conrad's, his fascination for the abomination and for those who confront it is always tempered, filtered, and restrained by his dread of tragic wisdom and his attraction to the refuge of knowing not to know.

"Thinking," Conrad declared, "is the great enemy of perfection. The habit of profound reflection . . . is the most pernicious of all the habits formed by the civilized man" (*Victory* x–xi)—not merely, as he argued earlier in his "Familiar Preface," because nothing humanely great ever comes from reflection (*PR* xi), but because reflection, as it includes reason, leads to paralysis and despair. For Conrad reason, recognizing the void over which we hover so precariously, is pernicious, for it reveals "(to those who have the courage) . . . [the] mysteries of a universe made of drops of fire and clods of mud . . . the fate of a humanity condemned ultimately to perish from cold" (*CL* 2:16–17). Conrad, then, is not an epistemological nihilist. There are what we are in the habit of calling "truths"—more, I am arguing, than he identifies even in his bleakest moments—and they are accessible to those courageous enough to examine them. But because, if revealed, the objects of such inspection may be devastating to the spirit, more particularly to personal identity and pride, the urge that confronts them is more nearly pernicious rashness than commendable courage. The wise, therefore, obscure the percept or avert their gaze. Marlow will not enter territory Conrad cordons off. He too believes in "absurd mysteries not fit for a human being to behold" (157). He detests lies because they carry the "taint of death, a flavour of mortality" (82), which is what he wants and labors to forget. And in lying to the Intended, he is forced to choose between these aversions.

In what may be a revealing slip of Conrad's pen, if it is not cagily deliberate, long before he ever meets up with Kurtz, Marlow indicates his intention to understand nothing of his journey or that meeting. "I would talk openly with Kurtz," he muses; "but before I could come to any conclusion it occurred to me that my speech or my silence, indeed any action of mine, would be a mere futility. What did it matter what any one knew or ignored? . . . One gets sometimes such a flash of insight. The essentials of this affair lay deep under the surface, beyond my reach, and beyond my power of meddling" (100). What Marlow exhibits here,

I believe, and what I am arguing Conrad pervasively betrays, is unwillingness disguised as incapacity. Marlow insists that the affair lay beyond his reach and powers of penetration, but the oddly skewed construction—"What did it matter what any one knew or ignored?"—suggests a determination not to know. As Daphna Erdinast-Vulcan rightly observes, "The structure of the utterance, beginning with the antithesis of speech/silence, calls for a parallel construction of binary oppositional verbs: i.e., 'what did it matter what anyone knew or didn't know?' But by substituting the verb 'ignore,' Marlow indicates not that he does not or cannot know, but that he will suppress what he perhaps too strongly suspects he will discover."[23] Erdinast-Vulcan reads this substitution, evocatively, in the context of Conrad's own peculiarly silenced journey up the Congo River in 1890–91, a voyage conspicuously absent from his Congo diary and letters, perhaps because its own horrors were too dark to confront. As I understand it, it is also a linguistic encapsulation of the habitual inclination of Conrad's fictions to conceal or repress what they appear courageously to seek and helplessly not to know.

The artist is obliged, for Conrad, to sustain an undying hope. For all the importance of liberty of the imagination and for all the putative importance of the artist's fealty to the truth of experience, Conrad, as we have noted, denies the writer the freedom of moral nihilism or despair (*PR* xviii).[24] Insisting, somewhat unpersuasively, that he always approached his writing in a spirit of love for mankind, Conrad argued for a "last utterance" that "will formulate, strange as it may appear, some hope now to us utterly inconceivable" (*NLL* 14). Truth-seeking, then, takes a backseat to the limits of tolerance and the demands of ethics. There are truths that, even if perceivable or perceived, should not be related. To have told the truth to the Intended would have brought to her and to the sepulchral city the heart of a conquering darkness whose pulse Marlow himself dared not take and whose traces he feels obliged to conceal. To tell the truth, in other words, to bring the horror back from the wilderness, would be to climb on the miseries of humankind and betray the hope the artist is obliged to formulate in his last utterance and to sustain for our benefit.

Rejecting that temptation and offering the lie as the final formulation of the artist's descent into himself is an act of compassion essential to the artist's moral enterprise. Because "the sight of human affairs deserves admiration and pity" (*PR* xix), the artist, valuing intellectual humility more than either a relentless truthfulness or the trivial gift of words, must look with forgiveness at men's ideas and prejudices and offer a tender acknowledgement of their obscure virtues (*NLL* 9). If Marlow is less merciful and compassionate toward those who hear him on deck or read his narrative, he is just such an artist in his delicate handling of Kurtz's memory and the Intended's sensibility and needs. The truth, when we apprehend it, is at once too terrible for most of us to bear and less important than the call of compassionate fellowship among creatures worthy of forgiveness.

The compassion that leads Marlow to sacrifice "barren truth" to the merciful preservation of Jim's sense of worth and honor is a guiding motive of Marlow's behavior in both narratives and a principal incentive for the lie. Conrad is reluctantly censorious of Kurtz, yet Marlow, finally, is kind. He shows, surely, a tender recognition for the obscure virtues of both the demonic Kurtz and his pallidly noble Intended. What Marlow offers in the name of hope and compassion is what Stein offers Jim in his suggested passage to Patusan: a great and saving illusion that may be preferable to truth. Patusan, the world of imagination and of art, is, as such, the equivalent of the artful lie Marlow tells to the Intended. Both are refuges from a truth in any case evasive. Both are offered as carriers of hope and buffers against despair. And both reflect the author's pitying admiration for a subject who is also an audience. Marlow's lie, in other words, is Jim's Patusan, an escape from dreaded truth into a realm of art that offers in its place the illusion that sustains life. Unlike Patusan, however, Marlow's lie incorporates a truth. As a deliberate lie, it bears the taint of what Marlow seeks most eagerly to forget: the inescapable truth of mortality.

To offer hope as a mark of one's compassion demands renunciation. Conrad requires of the writer the cherishing of a hope that he is convinced "implies all the piety of effort and renunciation"(*NLL* 8). For Conrad, beset by the horror of the loss of self-possession, renunciation—in man, in the explorer, perhaps above all in the artist—is the cardinal virtue, responsible for all adventure, love, and success, in effect for everything of worth, including the sustaining of hope (*NLL* 16). It is for his gift and treatment of renunciation that he praises Henry James, and Conrad identifies the contained idea with the containing craft. In his admiring essay on the writer, his discussion of renunciation in James's work shifts imperceptibly between character and author. The renunciation of James's men and women is, for Conrad, most saliently demonstrated not in their described behavior but "by the art of the novelist in the only possible way in which the task can be performed: by the independent creation of circumstance and character, achieved against all the difficulties of expression, in an imaginative effort finding its inspiration from the reality of forms and sensations"(*NLL* 15). Writers, as Marlow's navigation down the Congo River suggests, must steer their "tin-pot" steamboat through the shoals (*HD* 97). They must renounce the very human but ultimately paralyzing temptation to go ashore, to participate in or listen attentively to the horror that whispered Kurtz into the abyss. The aim of art, Conrad argues tellingly in the preface to *The Nigger of the "Narcissus,"* "is not in the clear logic of a triumphant conclusion; it is not in the unveiling of one of those heartless secrets which are called the Laws of Nature" (*NN* xi–xii). The heartless secret Conrad strikes from the aims of art in the preface is, in *Heart of Darkness*, the triumphant darkness implicit in Kurtz's utterance and excluded from Marlow's. Fearful of its resonance, Marlow may yet defend the Intended, himself, his audience, and ourselves by offering in its place a lie that preserves the great and saving illusion.

Beyond the need for hope is the simpler fear of what removes it. Marlow follows Kurtz with a driving if satiable curiosity, admires the singleness of purpose that leads Kurtz to his glimpsed truth, and wishes to see. But he knows, to his salvation, that "to keep the eyes so long on one thing was too much for human patience" (100), knows too for all his ostensible eagerness for self-knowledge that "one can't live with one's finger everlastingly on one's pulse" (105). Of a Swede who hanged himself in the Congo, it is said that he may have taken his life because "the sun was too much for him" (63). In Conrad's metaphoric dictionary, that is a way of ascribing the suicide to excessive exposure to a brutal reality. One cannot, as Marlow learns, steadily breathe dead hippo—another incarnation of rotting mortality—without contamination, and one must therefore bury the stuff in inconspicuous holes (HD 103–4, 117). This is not to say that one never breathes dead hippo. Rather one must, for there is something about the abomination, about the luridness of the wilderness and our own irredeemably animal nature that draws us on. But every attraction is matched by an equal (or stronger) and opposite repulsion. The protective need to bury and conceal vies with the heroic urge to know.

Since the ultimate lie or saving illusion is fiction itself, the conflations suggest that while art is an illusion that sustains life and hope, it is also rank with the mortality it would inter. Marlow seems, with some alarm, to recognize this, though in a political context that muffles its resonance. Marlow is speaking, early in his narrative, of the ugliness of colonization and conquest. The wilderness the conqueror enters exerts a fascination, but it is a fascination one must warily resist. The conquest of the earth, which is in fact little more than the confiscation of land from those with darker skin and flatter noses than the conquerors', is an ugly thing when scrutinized too closely (HD 50–51). Viewed honestly, there is little more to it than untrammeled greed, violent robbery, and murder on a massive scale. Colonization, then, which Conrad viewed as an analogue for writing, is another reality that repels scrutiny, another Medusa better veiled from view. Like all such truths, however, it may be tamed or transformed by a justifying fiction, a redeeming idea. But the description of that idea, as Marlow begins to spin it out, draws us back into the savagery it was intended to redeem. What is required, he argues, is "an unselfish belief in the idea—something you can set up, and bow down before, and offer a sacrifice to" (HD 51). Conceptualized in these terms, the saving idea—reminiscent in function and allegiance to the task of art—ominously acquires the features of the abomination, whose fascination he has just acknowledged. Its adoption is tainted with Kurtz's lunatic ascent to godhead; its execution invites practices darkly suggestive of the unspeakable sacrificial rites performed at his behest and in his name. As one may indulge a practice in elaborate repudiation, the abomination may be implicit in the idea or fiction constructed to redeem it. Hounded by fascination, the transformation of the abominable may assume its shape.

Whether that work is the writing of a book or the navigation of a steamboat that is an analogue for the same creative task, redemption lies in attention to the hard facts of existence and to the practical requirements of a demanding and imperiled "craft." The text displays the requisite efficiency when it turns from the implied identification of the saving idea with the abomination it ostensibly redeems to the imagery of the "beautiful world" women inhabit not alone. Stunned perhaps by his ominous portrayal of the idea as an icon you can bow down and offer a sacrifice to, Marlow breaks off. The primary narrator notes the interruptive silence; then, with a narrative gift and devotion to efficiency equal to Marlow's, drifts toward the safe isle of the world as poetic spectacle and fact: "Flames glided in the river, small green flames, red flames, white flames, pursuing, overtaking, joining, crossing each other—then separating slowly or hastily. The traffic of the great city went on in the deepening night upon the sleepless river" (51). It will be a long time before Marlow speaks again about either the fascination of the abomination or the idea that redeems it. He will never again speak of the latter in these terms.

Marlow's contradictory remarks on work are another reflection of his own and Conrad's ambivalence toward self-knowledge and discovery. After an unnerving conversation with the papier-mâché brick maker, Marlow turns for relief to the more substantial world of his steamboat. He has invested enough hard work in his vessel "to make me love her." He appreciates this craft (in both senses) for giving him the chance, as he puts it, to come out a bit—to find out what he could do. And he is led by his musing on this peculiar relationship to the boat toward deeper reflections about the nature and value of work: "No, I don't like work. I had rather laze about and think of all the fine things that can be done. I don't like work—no man does—but I like what is in the work,—the chance to find yourself. Your own reality—for yourself, not for others—what no other man can ever know. They can only see the mere show, and never can tell what it really means" (85). At this stage work is offered as a plumb line to the depths, appreciated as an inducement to the discovery of one's own inner reality. Shortly thereafter, however, as his ship approaches the seductive wilds of the inner station, personal no less than geographical, Marlow articulates what appears to be a quite contrary view of the value and effects of work's vigilant attention to surfaces. Again he is led from random descriptions of the specifics of his task to deeper reflections about the value of such activity. "I had to discover, mostly by inspiration," he recalls, "the signs of hidden banks"; "I watched for sunken stones.... I had to keep a look-out for the signs of dead wood we could cut up in the night for next day's steaming. When you have to attend to things of that sort, to the mere incidents of the surface, the reality—the reality, I tell you—fades. The inner truth is hidden—luckily, luckily. But I felt it all the same; I felt often its mysterious stillness watching me at my monkey tricks, just as it watches you fellows performing on your respective tight-ropes for—what is it? half-a-crown a tumble—" (93–94). Here, clearly, surfaces are valued not as a source of illumination but a place of refuge. Marlow welcomes them because they provide not a revelation of the profoundest realities of the naked self but a busy suit of clothes to cover them. The inner truth rewardingly exposed in the preceding reflections is luckily hidden here, though it is still vaguely palpable. Marlow feels the mysterious stillness of the hidden reality through the surfaces now summoned for avoidance.

But even that awareness will soon diminish or disappear, as need and augmented threat require. Soon after, approaching the very heart of darkness, Marlow hears the "wild and passionate uproar" (96) to which he claims to recognize his kinship. As Conrad's "unmanned" lovers experience in their resonating passion a reflective surge of the woman who enthralls them, so Marlow claims a kinship to this uproar. Unlike Kurtz and these less wise and armored victims, however, Marlow cautiously turns again to the demands of his steamer. He does not, as they do, go ashore "for a howl and a dance" (97) because he has work and hard realities to attend to. And once more they are valued as distractions from inner reality—unalloyed this time—rather than as passages of discovery. "I had no time. I had to mess about with white-lead and strips of woollen blanket helping to put bandages on those leaky steam-pipes—I tell you. I had to watch the steering, and circumvent those snags, and get the tin-pot along by hook or by crook. There was surface-truth enough in these things to save a wiser man" (97).

Again one may discover reason in this seeming arbitrariness of shifting ground. There is psychological sense and artistic method to this progression. When it is the rankling hollowness and unreality of the papier-mâché brick maker Marlow seeks refuge from, work and surface assume the substance lacking in the man; they suggest to Marlow a core of being unknown to such a flimsy devil. But as he approaches the inner station and makes contact first with its stillness, then with its fierce, alluring music, the task of laborious distraction is inverted; its job is no longer to remind him of the inner reality that makes him human but to obscure that reality, now stained by association with an all-too-human, too-unmanning passion. First he tinkers; then he keeps a vital watch; finally he steers and patches for his life.

What psychological and aesthetic point one discovers in the shift, however, cannot obscure the conflicting view of the relationship between work, surfaces, and reality the blurred distinction implies. Surfaces rewardingly reveal one's inner reality; surfaces beneficently obscure or conceal that reality. Shifting his attitudes toward surfaces and depths, knowledge and avoidance, Conrad wavers and eludes us, denies us a synchronic consistency of perspective that would persuade us we have him in our grasp at least for the moment, at least between the covers of a single work of fiction. The impetus, once again, is not the inadequacy of language or the impalpable mysteries of the world it vainly seeks to articulate. The text is pulled to contradiction by a careening ambivalence toward the desirability of self-knowledge identified with passion and desire. When courage is high, curiosity may indulge itself, and one is grateful for what it learns of reality. The nearer one comes to the heart of darkness, the instinctual self that, libidinous, passionate, and uncontrolled, responds unresistingly to the seductive whispers of the savage wilderness it consorts with, the more one welcomes the surface as a refuge from these depths.

Art, for Conrad, has a double function that can only end in contradiction and confusion. Its genetic impetus is a descent into the self in search of one's personal truth. Its saving enactment, contrarily, is a devotion to surface facts that preserve us from these gloomy revelations in the dark. The fascination for the abomination is balanced by intimidation and revulsion, dedication to the darkest truths of self unraveled by the need to sustain hope and contact with the grounding facts of ordinary existence. Like Marlow the texts approach the edge beyond which truth and meaning lie and, in the name of art's redeeming function, step back. The results, unavoidably, are texts riding a magnet whose field forever changes, tales mired in endemic contradiction, given to protective obfuscation when the darkness glares too brightly.[25] More than a philosophic skepticism, a belief in the inadequacies of language, or an aesthetic of romantic vagueness, it is this defensive urge and flight that, squidlike, jets the inky fluid of opacity across these texts.

3

THE SOFT SPOT

Lord Jim

While some earlier readers claimed to find coherent meaning in *Lord Jim*, the novel has become, as one recent critic put it, "famously ambiguous," read with increasing frequency as a paradigmatic postmodernist construction whose only meaning rests in its steadfast refusal to yield it.[1] For J. Hillis Miller, *Lord Jim* is "an admirable example of the tendency . . . to weave a fabric of words which is incapable of being interpreted unambiguously as a fixed pattern of meaning."[2] As the pattern of narrators within narrators deprives the reader of any solid ground to stand on, the temporal structure of times within times creates a whirlpool of unprioritized repetitions that prevent the reader from deciding among alternative possibilities and discovering the "why" behind the events.[3] Paul Armstrong draws a comprehensive conclusion from the example of *Lord Jim*'s apparent incoherence. The hermeneutic aim of Conrad's technique in this novel, writes Armstrong, is "to frustrate the reader's efforts to discover hypotheses that will fit together elements in a coherent pattern" and thereby demonstrate that "contingency is ubiquitous and ineradicable."[4]

Lord Jim has, amid the inevitable and excusable misses, been well read by these and other readers, and there is much to be gleaned from these accounts. But they stop short, I think, of the full integration of indeterminate meaning and evasive subject, do less than full justice to the relationship between novel, principal narrative, and subject that *Lord Jim*, like *Heart of Darkness* and other Conrad fictions, exemplifies. What this and other of Conrad's fictions demonstrate is that the ubiquity and ineradicability of contingency is owed less to the nature of reality or our powers of cognition than to the saving refuge it provides from unpalatable likelihoods or certainties.

Lord Jim is a study in evasion, and that on three causally connected and mutually reflective levels: subject, narration, and total construct. Jim's flight from recognition, responsibility, and the truth of his nature and his act is both assisted and mirrored by Marlow's alternately anxious and principled reluctance to make coherent sense of what he sees. And both, I believe, are interior analogues of the novel's own evasion-based obscurity. As Poe's tales of imaginers, conjurers, and half-concealed artists are often self-reflexive renderings of the writer's perplexed struggle to banish and exclude, *Lord Jim*, as both tale and telling, is an explanatory icon of the novel's notorious elusiveness. Peter Glassman is near the mark when he observes that "no one in the novel consciously wishes to restrict the experiences of the self; they want rather to protect the self—and the community of selves *from* experience." But Glassman, it seems to me, artfully dodges the projective implications of his own observation when he suggests that Conrad wished to establish and legitimize "an intelligible picture" of himself as a defense against his terrifying vision and his mind's irrational forces.[5] The force behind the novel, as so many have remarked, generates not an intelligible picture of the writer but an unintelligible picture of what he only ostensibly wishes us above all else to see. Only through unintelligibility, the palmed joker in Conrad's deck of saving illusions, may the self and others be protected from the forbidden knowledge that saps and destroys.

That Jim is a kind of artist is sufficiently evident to permit a summarizing brevity. Like Kurtz and Marlow, he is preoccupied with language. But while Kurtz's gorgeous eloquence forfeits all allegiance to an abiding substance and is sucked, like reality, into the whirlpool of his imagination, Jim, like Marlow, would make language expressive of a fleeting reality. His Sisyphean effort, he tells the court, is "to interpret for you into slow speech the instantaneous effect of visual impressions" (48). Marlow recognizes Jim as a kindred worker in the narrative fields, a storyteller whose story of the self strives, at least ostensibly, for understanding and explanation. Praised by the host for his subtlety of narration, Marlow demurs. He feels himself hampered in the presentation of his tale, missing innumerable nuances too fine to render in mere words. Unlike himself Jim achieves the requisite subtlety, paradoxically because he "complicated matters by being so simple" (94). Jim, then, is another sort of artist: a "finished artist" (96) in his own uncertain way, who scans his auditors "with satisfaction [at] the undeniable effect of his phraseology" (239). The antithesis of Kurtz in this regard, he is not eloquent. Rather he achieves a dignity in his reticence, a lofty seriousness in his stammering (248). If Kurtz's dubious gift is an ultimately hollow grandiloquence that communicates only (self-)deception, Jim's worthier talent is a directness of expression that, like the whispered "The horror" to which Kurtz is reduced when rhetoric fails, transmits glimpsed meanings almost in spite of the language that coarsens and discolors. A "gifted poor devil with the faculty of swift and forestalling vision" (96), Jim burrowed deep, driven by a gift that cast upon his listeners, despite or rather because of its stammering simplicity, "the spirit of his illusion" (109).

This last is important. It is not the truth that Jim conveys but the spirit of his illusion. For that, ultimately, not discovery either as finding or self-revelation, is the goal of speech and writing, the goal of the artist. The hidden reality Jim would give voice to is his own: evasive, partial, and self-protective. He understands that something invisible dwells within the surface facts and that "only a meticulous precision of statement would bring out the true horror behind the appalling face of things" (30). Pertinently, he never provides that precision. Rather "while his utterance was deliberate, his mind positively flew round and round the serried circle of facts" that separated him from others. Marlow perceives Jim's mind as a desperate creature that, trapped within an enclosure of high stakes, races around in frantic search of "a weak spot, a crevice, a place to scale, some opening through which it may squeeze itself and escape" (31).[6] As it quite typically is, Jim's activity here is an interior image of the novel's, his defensive evasion a replica of narrative and authorial practice. It is in the light of Jim's avoidance that we may understand the labyrinthine circlings of the novel that Miller and others attend to. To inhibit the stark emergence of the true horror behind the face of things, like Jim's defensive fiction, both Marlow's narrative and the work that contains it substitute for meticulous precision a spiraling evasiveness and an obscuring haze.

Jim's verbal evasions are a circumlocutory version of the physical inclination to bolt. The novel's opening depiction of Jim as a charging bull who "advanced straight at you" (3) is quickly replaced by the more accurate and enduring portrait of a man in perpetual and characterological flight. Before we learn anything of causes, we are in the company of a man who conceals his last name in order to conceal an as-yet-unnamed fact and who, "when the fact broke through the incognito," would leave one seaport for another. It was, as the first narrator remarks, anticipating the second half of the narrative, "his keen perception of the Intolerable" that drove him forever from the world of white men to the jungle village, "where he had elected to conceal his deplorable faculty" (4–5).

The keen perception of the intolerable refers specifically to the knowledge of Jim's betrayal, his undutiful abandonment of the *Patna* in the midst of a thunderous squall. But the phrase has extended relevance. If, as the initial narrator has it, Jim's incognito was designed to conceal not his personality but a fact (4), his tendency to recoil from the keen perception of the intolerable describes a personality. It is his perception of an intolerable reality or truth—his stark, prescient, but ultimately unrealized image of "that crowd of bodies, laid out for death, as plain as daylight" (105)—that leads him to jump ship. Like the artist as Conrad describes him, Jim descends into himself for his images of truth. It is when he "goes below," into the body of the vessel that is also the self and is tossed helplessly in the sea, that Jim, betraying his heroic ideal self, recognizes the inescapable imminence of disaster.

The shutting of his eyes and the subsidence of the great cloud upon the ship signal the descent into the lonely region of stress and strife where the creator seeks his reality. And it is here that Jim perceives the vision of extinction that provokes the paradoxically fatal leap to safety. What Jim has seen and fled from is not an achieved reality but a "created terror of his imagination" (113), at once more certain and more terrible than any objectifiable perception. Since it is the imagination, inevitably, that brings fiction into being, we are in the realm of fictions here, and the "awful visions" they contain. Imagination, which the speaker names the enemy of men and the father of all terrors, impels Jim to leap into the "great hole," into the abyss of interminable and indeterminate explanation that is the novel. Jim's abandonment, then, which generates the mystery and vagueness the novel stubbornly fails to dissipate, is, like Marlow's withdrawal from the edge in *Heart of Darkness*, a leap into fiction. It is a plunge from the hidden truth at the hollowed core of darkness into the swirling clouded efforts to render and explain it. The quest for truth, radically avoidant and deceptive, is only apparent. The ultimate goal is not clarity but the obfuscation Jim and *Lord Jim* savingly achieve, for only in vagueness and the averted gaze are the terrors of the imagination allowed to sleep. As Conrad wrote to Cunninghame Graham, "Our refuge is in stupidity, in drunken[n]ess of all kinds, in lies, in beliefs, in murder, thieving, reforming—in negation, in contempt" (*CL* 2:30). But it also lies in turning away and the gift of uncertainty it bestows. When the danger is not seen, the narrator reflects, it acquires "the imperfect vagueness of human thought." At such moments, "the fear grows shadowy; and Imagination, the enemy of men, the father of all terrors, unstimulated, sinks to rest in the dulness of exhausted emotion" (11). It is this exhausted emotion that *Lord Jim* seeks and, the history of its reading attests, creates. The object of fiction, in aesthetic imitation of Jim's progress, is to move from the mortifying certainties of the eidetic imagination through the exhausting labyrinth of perspectives, temporal structures, and unresolvably competing explanations to the remote island of Patusan. In that insulated refuge, a blatant metaphor for the realm of art, one creates, in flight from the truth of his nature and performance, an imaginative construct he can at least temporarily dominate and control.

Jim's flight to Patusan is a continuation of his own and the novel's pervasive pattern of escape. Jim seeks this refuge because, like dead hippo meat, "this thing must be buried" (191). Such things must always be buried, never exhumed. The corpse he refers to here is the victim of his trampled masculine ideal of self, the haunting specter of his desertion. On board the *Patna*, it is the image of the dead seamen that must be interred. Prior to that it is the sense of self as limited, ordinary, unheroic. Jim's fantasies of heroism, his Steinian dream image of the perfected self, is, like all such fantasies, at bottom an escape from the less exhilarating realities of the self. "On the lower deck in the babel of two hundred voices he would forget himself, and beforehand live in his mind the sea-life of light adventure. He saw himself saving people from sinking ships, cutting away masts in a hurricane.... He confronted savages on tropical shores, quelled mutinies on the high seas ... always an example of devotion to duty, and as unflinching as a hero in a book" (6). Much attention has been paid to Jim's author-echoing devotion to an idealized code of conduct whose world-creating word is fidelity, too little to its motivating benefit. Entertaining these fantasies, re-creating himself as a hero out of fiction, Jim "would forget himself," escape from an ordinariness as deadening as the awful vision that impels him overboard at sea or the guilty fear of identification that drives him from seaport to seaport. "Would you seriously wish to tell ... a man: 'Know thyself,'" Conrad asks rhetorically in the letter to Cunninghame Graham quoted earlier. "Understand that thou art nothing, less than a shadow, more insignificant than a drop of water in the ocean, more fleeting than the illusion of a dream. Would you?" The innermost of three concentric circles in this novel, Jim, like its narrator and the man who asked this question, would not.

However admirable it may appear to be, fictionalizing self-idealization is a form of flight, an escape from the stark perception of the intolerable. When the dream of becoming a hero in a book is shattered, Jim attempts to reconstitute it on the "real" island of Patusan. In the work of art, Rank observed, the artist justifies his heroism by objectifying it in concrete creation. Creative work, then, is an act of compensatory self-glorification, an escape from the intolerable truth of mortality and limitation.[7] Rank's claim may be reductive, but Conrad and Jim fall, with the Marlow of both novels, comfortably within its range. Patusan, a metaphor for both fiction and the work of fiction that contains it, serves Jim in this way. "Three hundred miles beyond the end of telegraph cables and mail-boat lines [Marlow muses], the haggard utilitarian lies of our civilization wither and die, to be replaced by pure exercises of imagination, that have the futility, often the charm, and sometimes the deep hidden truthfulness of works of art" (282). Patusan, it has often been observed, is a "land of the imagination" where, as one reader remarks, Conrad hoped to provide "a true rendering of the large and autonomous forces that reign there."[8] But Marlow's ascription of a "deep hidden truthfulness" requires qualification. The world of imagination Jim inhabits in Patusan is, on the face of it, not a realization of profound personal truth but an escape from it. Patusan is not the mortal world of bodies laid out for death, but a deceptive island refuge, defined in protective opposition to the repugnantly decaying body it would transcend. Jim is a striking example of Becker's edict that man cannot "justify his own heroism." He is one of those who cannot fit himself into his own cosmic plan and make it believable and who must, as women are said to do, create a satisfying alternative world from which the agonizing doubts evoked by contact with reality are banished.[9]

As such Jim is more particularly an elaboration of the plight of modernity. For it is a defining failure of the modern condition that it does not provide convincing dramas of heroic apotheosis, creative play, or cultural illusion. Conrad's response to the failure of modernity, as Erdinast-Vulcan points out, is, like Jim's escape, a regression to the earlier mode of epic, myth, and romance.[10] The vivid and powerful imagination that created the problem offers an at least temporary solution. The same imagination that, conjuring a paralyzing image of mortality, deflates his heroic self-image constructs an alternative, nearly hermetic world far removed from the too real scene of his shame. Like a work of idealized romantic art, Patusan is insulated and beautiful, an organic temptation to the creator/ruler's belief in unqualified control and a brand of immortality. It is a land where, in his desperation, Jim convinces himself and allows himself to be convinced by worshipful others that he will be eternally young, immune from aging, decrepitude, and death. Unfortunately, as the conflictual politics of the island and the tragic end testify and as Conrad knew painfully well, the insulation proves porous, the escape temporary and illusory.

Patusan is a "land without a past," hence an erasure of Jim's past, a place where not reality but "his word was the one truth of every passing day" (272). Like blank pages the natives "had got into the habit of taking his word for anything and everything" (268). In Patusan, in other words, Jim is free to obliterate history and rewrite reality. "Having left his earthly failings behind him and that sort of reputation he had," Jim is offered, in this remote and isolated land, "a totally new set of conditions for his imaginative faculty to work upon" (218). Earlier his imaginative faculty had generated a terrible eidetic vision of death more real and certain than the palpable world itself. The objective and saving privilege of art is its provision of a new set of circumstances in which the imagination is subject not to paralyzing certainty but to the imperfect vagueness of human thought that blurs the real and blunts fear's edge.

The atmosphere of Patusan is bathed in a mysterious moonlight, in the diffuse light of approaching darkness, and in distant starlight. As Jim spoke to him, Marlow remembers, "the moon floated away above the chasm between the hills like an ascending spirit out of a grave; its sheen descended, cold and pale, like the ghost of dead sunlight. There is something haunting in the light of the moon; it has all the dispassionateness of a disembodied soul, and something of its inconceivable mystery" (245–46). The Romantic origins of the image are clear, though the moonlight, serviceably, is not. Its function, like that of the diffused light that supplants the harsh glare of the sun, is to cast upon an unexceptional world "the illusion of a calm and pensive greatness." Like the gradually descending night, it settles "silently on all the visible forms, effacing the outlines, burying the shapes deeper and deeper" (306). The starlight too, which Marlow deems appropriate for the "story" of the romance of Jim and Jewel, throws a light so indistinct and distant that it cannot define the shadowy features of the earth (312). The world of art is a world of moonlit and starlit imagination. But more like the world of *Lord Jim* than Byzantium, its light effaces outlines and prevents the resolution of shadows into definable shapes. Patusan is an extreme form of art, a locus for the "pure exercise of imagination" that deviates from Conrad's aesthetic principally in its escapist indifference to the surface facts of quotidian reality. With its luminous color, meaning, and design, Patusan is "like a picture created by fancy on a canvas, upon which, after long contemplation, you turn your back for the last time" (330). Marlow never completely turns his back on this world, never renounces fully what it represents. But unlike Jim, who becomes the slave of the imagined world he would rule (as Kurtz is swallowed by the jungle he would devour), Marlow has access to another realm. "I had turned away from the picture," Marlow reports, and "was going back to the world where events move, men change, light flickers, like flows in a clear stream, no matter whether over mud or over stones. I wasn't going to dive into it; I would have enough to do to keep my head above the surface" (330).

The return to reality, in other words, entails the risk of a confrontation with the dark interior neutralized by a sustaining connection with the surface. A more fastidious devotion to these surfaces, particularly in times of threat, distinguishes the first half of the narrative from the second, Marlow's creative inclinations from Jim's. But the distinction is often blurred, largely because the attention to surfaces is itself the expression of an escapist impulse and because *Lord Jim,* which is ultimately drawn into the moonlit and starlit atmosphere of Patusan, betrays a comparable affinity for the haze. Narrowly construed, Patusan is the world of high Romantic art, more akin to the latter half of the novel than to *Lord Jim* as a whole. But Marlow's art also erases outlines and obscures distinctions. Disembodied, clouded in inconceivable mystery, such islanded, exotic art saves us from the fixed glare of a glimpsed reality that reduces earth to a wandering speck of dust, man's character to a lurking betrayal of his heroic masculine ideal. It preserves us, most critically perhaps, from the unaestheticized and unanesthetized imagination that, as the father of all terrors, is the looming enemy of that ideal. In this diffuse obscuring light, protected by the illusion that there is nothing else to be seen or known, one can create for oneself the further illusion of a calm and pensive greatness. The deep hidden truthfulness of works of art, then, is a confessed need for a saving uncertainty. When Marlow assures Jim that he will always remain for the natives an insoluble mystery, Jim's response is swift and earnest: "Well, then let me always remain here" (306).

As in the tales of Poe, the sanctuary of art is threatened by the reinvasion of excluded reality. The concealed truth Jim hopes to have left behind is the possession of Gentleman Brown, whose own betrayal leads to Jim's undoing and his death. But like the Red Death in Prince Prospero's abbey, the threat to the safety of Jim's secret, to the safe exclusion of forbidden knowledge, is already inside it: in its topography, its metaphoric identity, its history of betrayal and in the jewel that sits at the center probing for revelation. "There's Patusan," Stein promises, "... And the woman is dead now" (219). But the woman, who is, in Conrad's fiction, a recurrent threat to life, integrity, and self-possession, is never dead. The opportunity Patusan offers is described as an "Eastern bride" waiting to be uncovered by the hand of the master. The "story" of Patusan, moreover, is haunted by the melancholy figure of the woman Stein refers to, by a tale of betrayal that lives in her daughter's suspicious probings for the knowledge Jim conceals. To uncover the Eastern bride, then, is to peel away the veil of mystery and expose the woman, an impossible task. As in a large number of Conrad's novels and shorter tales, woman in *Lord Jim* is entangled in a network of ominous associations that make her unveiling precisely as unlikely as it is perilous. Jewel herself is the Eastern bride, but it is not the master who will unveil her. Rather it is she, the embodiment and probing instrument of truth, who threatens to unveil the master.

The image of the dangerous woman in many of Conrad's narratives is no mere emblem of authorial gynophobia. It stands for the danger of truth or knowledge, typically for the protectively hidden truths of the instinctual, uncontrollable, or savage self whose trampling of self-possession is for Conrad tantamount to death or worse. The driven quest for truth, knowledge, and revelation and the contrary recoil from them in these fictions is both mirror and consequence of the ambivalent attitude toward woman as at once the fascinating, inscrutable, and forbidden object of male desire and the annihilating threat of engulfment, unmanning, and helpless dependency. Conrad's male narrators and protagonists frequently identify woman with the enigmatic, mysterious, and unfathomable—with the sea, the wilderness, with truth itself. As noted earlier, in *The Arrow of Gold*, Rita embodies "that something secret and obscure which is in all women" (146). In "The Return" woman is explicitly identified as the repository of the secret of existence itself. Guttering helplessly at the feet of the wife who has betrayed him, Alvan Hervey has been "penetrated by an irresistible belief in an enigma, by the conviction that within his reach and passing away from him was the very secret of existence—its certitude, immaterial and precious" (176). The narrator of "Falk," gazing at Hermann's bewitchingly sensuous niece, identifies her as "the eternal truth of an unerring principle" (*NN* 236). And in what is perhaps the iconic instance of this pervasive trope, the ironically named Felicia, the elusively menacing seductress of "The Planter of Malata," announces her identity as truth itself on four separate occasions: "I have an instinct for truth"; "I stand for truth here"; "It's I who stand for truth here!"; and "Here I stand for truth itself" (43, 47, 75, 78). The woman protests too much, but she makes a point Conrad's evasive narratives make only slightly less insistently elsewhere, and as beckoning objects of pursuit both are dangerous and far more wisely avoided than attained. The saving difference between the woman-obsessed protagonists of these fictions and the texts that contain them is that, through narrative techniques of evasion, recoil, obfuscation, and contradiction, the latter avoid what the hapless suitors fall prey to.[11]

Jewel, as Marlow nervously remarks, is like an inscrutable Sphinx whose questions threaten to drive him out "of that shelter each of us makes for himself to creep under in moments of danger" (313). She wants the impossible from him: "the exact description of the form of a cloud" (307), as Marlow imaginatively phrases it. Where only a meticulous precision can bring out the true horror behind the face of things, exact description threatens to dispel the protective fog that veils the novel and Jim's crime. For all Marlow's transparently elusive talk of Jewel's ignorance, fear of knowledge, and affinity for uncertainty, she alone seeks the forbidden knowledge Jim and Marlow deliberately conceal.

Fiction, wrote Conrad in *A Personal Record*, "is but truth often dragged out of a well and clothed in the painted robe of imaged phrases" (93). As Elliott Gose observes, "'Truth lies at the bottom of a well' can be taken as a more or less conscious epigraph for Conrad's aim and method as a writer."[12] But since, as Conrad wrote in a letter to Galsworthy, he wished to keep the lid on the potentially poisonous well of his emotions,[13] one should not expect too vigorous a plunge. Although it is not her only role, woman in these narratives is the emblem of hidden, heart-dark truths, the most dangerous of which, because most threatening to masculine self-possession, are the passions and instincts that threaten from within. When not embodied in the alluring woman, they are often projected upon her; she becomes the censored self externalized.

The image of the well is suggestively sexual, the urge to clothe it in the painted robes of language an expression of the artist's need to veil its nakedness in words. And it is linked to Jewel as both the locus of truth and the danger of its exposure. Looking into Jewel's eyes, Marlow perceives "a faint stir, such as you may fancy you can detect when you plunge your gaze to the bottom of an immensely deep well." And all but inevitably he pronounces her "more inscrutable in her childish ignorance than the Sphinx propounding childish riddles to wayfarers" (307).

The woman who would know is pronounced unknowable and prevented from knowing. That Jewel does not know or learn the truth about Jim is no more an accident of language or a mirror of the void than the novel's failure to resolve its own conundrums. Jewel is kept in the dark through the deliberate and anxiously protective collusion of Jim and Marlow, and the tale once again allegorizes the technique that renders it. The absence of truth is the child of the failure not of language but of will. Even Jim's death is a form of abandonment and escape. Though often interpreted as an act of redeeming courage, the restoration of integrity at the price of life, Jim's death, as Miller suggests, may be nothing more than his final act of cowardice, "his last failure to face the dark side of himself."[14] To face Gentleman Brown and almost certain death is a form of heroism, but if so it is heroism in the name of illusion, a perpetuation of Jim's image as a man "as unflinching as a hero in a book" (6). To be true to this illusory image requires that he be "false" to Jewel, to whom he promised unalterable fidelity. At the end like the enigmatic novel written in his name, Jim "passes away under a cloud, inscrutable at heart.... He goes away from a living woman to celebrate his pitiless wedding with a shadowy ideal of conduct" (416). The climactic act of abandonment is also the culminating parallel between technique and tale. The shadowy ideal is the one Jim shares with fiction: the construction of a saving illusion that, obscuring the reality of the void, enables one to live or die with coherence, integrity, and purpose.

THE MOLLUSK AND THE SOFT SPOT

The creation and maintenance of this redeeming obscurity requires the active complicity of the narrator. If Jim's flight to Patusan is a metaphor for the use of art as a refuge from the painful realities of self and world, Marlow's narrative is its overt enactment. The ostensible purpose of Marlow's almost obsessive curiosity about Jim and the facts of his "affair" is to dispel the cloud of uncertainty that surrounds them. Like Marlow in *Heart of Darkness*, he ventures into a dark continent apparently in the name of illumination and self-discovery. But the Marlow of *Lord Jim* is a reluctant knight, a still-more-hesitant hunter of the grail of truth and meaning than he was in *Heart of Darkness*—as though the menacing lesson of Kurtz, elaborated while work on *Lord Jim* was suspended, had a residual effect. The relatively inquisitive Marlow of the opening, his curiosity already modified by a self-interested search for extenuation, gives way to a man conspicuously more attracted to the padded than the naked truth. The last-moment withdrawal from the edge that, at the price of final knowledge, preserves Marlow from Kurtz's fate dogs each hesitant step of his journey through *Lord Jim*. The intimidated concession to delusion that, closing *Heart of Darkness*, spares both the Intended and himself marks every stage of his inquiry in the longer narrative. It is by now a critical commonplace that Marlow is not everywhere a reliable spokesman for Conrad in *Lord Jim*, but Marlow's techniques of obfuscation and evasion dominate a novel that in the end only replicates them. One may share Andrzej Gasiorek's inference that the text's uncertainties, like Marlow's, are designed to show that "there is no escape from incertitude," that nothing finally can be decided.[15] But we take a leap denied us, I believe, by Conrad's repeated expressions of anxiety, ambivalence, and preferred denial in the face of threatening knowledge when we separate the novel from the narrative in this regard. As Jim's and Marlow's failures to reveal or discover truth are unmistakably motivated by the rational desire for self-protection Conrad both understands and commends for our salvation, the novel's own evasions, obscurities, and uncertainties are likewise ascribable to that cause. Indeed it seems odd to argue that a novel whose narrator and main characters habitually, willfully, and self-protectively step back from threatening revelation and self-knowledge demonstrates the inherent impossibility or unattainability of such knowledge.

Like almost every object of ambivalent inquiry in Conrad's fiction, the truth about Jim is both fascinating and intimidating. The dynamic of pursuit in these narratives is the hesitant waltz of attraction and repulsion that draws the leering but mortified voyeur to the lady's dressing room but finally confounds his sight. The process is eminently human and unalarming, its candid depiction a tribute to a kind of wisdom that goes relatively unremarked and unheralded. When readers observe it, as they sometimes do, in Conrad's narrators, they drive a wedge between speaker and writer in order to preserve for the latter the presumably nobler virtue of unflinching curiosity and quest. The occluding haze that denies articulable meaning to these fictions is ascribed not to the forces that motivate willful or defensive obfuscation within them but to inadequacies of language or to Conrad's convictions about the impossibility of knowledge or the mythic status of its object. Such readings derive support from Conrad's frequent proclamations about the meaninglessness of human life, the helplessness of language to render its experience, or the protean ephemerality of glimpsed awareness. But Lawrence's edict is instructive here: trust not the teller but the tale. In *Lord Jim* both the internal teller and the tale attest to the value and attraction of denial, obscurity, and flight. And indeed as his letters and essays testify, Conrad acknowledges no less, and often aggressively affirms it.

The novel's failure to define Jim's moral character or resolve the question of his culpability are at the heart of the hazy ambiguity that has aroused so much discussion and rationalized dismay. Marlow's final judgment of Jim pronounces him an "enigma," "inscrutable at heart." But this is only the climactic expression of his chronic bafflement. Marlow punctuates his narrative with insistent declarations that Jim is an impenetrable or "insoluble mystery" (306), that he is "incomprehensible, wavering, and misty," an "elusive spirit" (180) unclear to others, to Marlow, and to himself. He is perturbed by the "mysterious, inexplicable, impalpable striving" (182) of Jim's spirit, locates him under an opaque and unmoving cloud, hedges the distinction between truth and falsehood, reality and illusion, and in a dozen other formulations obscures Jim's visage along with the springs and symbolic meaning of his act.[16] These are the verbal equivalents of the narrative techniques of multiplied perspectives, unjudged alternatives, and spiraling time shifts; the speaker's protestations of obscurity are complemented by a narration that thickens and assures it.

What the narrative does make clear, however, is Marlow's personal stake in illucidity and doubt. Marlow is endearingly candid, if appropriately uncertain, about his motives. He prefaces his confession with the familiar claim of bafflement: "Why I longed to go grubbing into the deplorable details of an occurrence which, after all, concerned me no more than as a member of an obscure body of men held together by a community of inglorious toil and by fidelity to a certain standard of conduct, I can't explain" (50). But he follows and erodes his disclaimer with convincing speculation—a "distinct notion" he calls it—that situates his motive in its own parenthetical and acknowledges his potentially distorting self-interest. What Marlow seeks, he admits, is not the truth, wherever it takes him, but an answer that will drive away the mortifying doubt evoked by Jim's leap. What motivates him is neither an objective nor an "unhealthy curiosity" but the hope to find "some profound and redeeming cause, some merciful explanation, some convincing shadow of an excuse" (50). What he seeks, finally, is less an impartial truth, wherever it may lead him, than an excuse or explanation that will allay his fears.[17]

Marlow wonders if it was for his own sake that he so hungrily seeks this explanation and excuse, but the question is rhetorical. Virtually all of his pained introspective musings on the case indicate that Jim's betrayal menaces his own cherished beliefs and sense of safety. It is because, as Marlow admits, Jim always appeared to him as a symbol that he maintained this relentless interest in his fate (265). And what he symbolizes is the shakiness of a putatively fixed standard of conduct, distinctly masculine and heroic, and, relatedly, the failure of the defenses, modeled in *The Nigger of the "Narcissus"* and *Heart of Darkness*, that secure it.

Jim's weakness, in Marlow's eyes, is "a thing of mystery and terror," a thing of mystery, finally, because a thing of terror. It reverberated for him as a hint of malignant fate awaiting anyone whose youth had resembled Jim's (51). Jim, as Marlow remarks on at least seven occasions, "was one of us," a man "too much like one of us not to be dangerous" (106). The passage in which Marlow first and most expansively identifies Jim, symbolically and tellingly, as "one of us" is central and revealing. "He stood there for all the parentage of his kind," affirms Marlow,

> for men and women by no means clever or amusing, but whose very existence is based upon honest faith, and upon the instinct of courage. I don't mean military courage, or civil courage, or any special kind of courage. I mean just that inborn ability to look temptations straight in the face—a readiness unintellectual enough, goodness knows, but without pose—a power of resistance, don't you see, ungracious if you like, but priceless—an unthinking and blessed stiffness before the outward and inward terrors, before the might of nature,

and the seductive corruption of men—backed by a faith invulnerable to the strength of facts, to the contagion of example, to the solicitation of ideas. (43)

Like women in *Heart of Darkness*, Jim is out of touch with truth.[18] Also like them he should and must be protected from such contact not so much for his own sake but for ours. Since he is importantly like ourselves, as women, despite denials, ultimately are, the preservation of his illusions is essential for the preservation of ours and the consequent tolerability of our lives. This last is crucial. Jim is one of us; he stands for all those blessed with a steadfast faith that insulates them from facts, from ideas, and from the terrifying realities of human and physical nature. The threat to Jim, then, is the threat to the power of denial, the saving gift that clouds Marlow's inquiry into Jim's "case" and that accounts, as I have been arguing, for much of the enriching obscurity of Conrad's fictions.

The primal dangers, as they always are for Conrad, are within; they are in others or "out there" mainly when, like the heart of Africa's darkness, the world's structures are mirrors of the dweller's spirit. The proliferating mirrorings of self and other, inner and outer, break the textual frame. In the 1917 author's note to *Lord Jim*, Conrad, defending the verisimilitude of his hero by claiming to have personally seen his type, echoes his narrator. What is important about that originating figure is that, like Jim for Marlow, he elicits all the sympathy of which Conrad is capable because he too "was 'one of us'" (ix).

Cognizant of the identification and the vulnerabilities it entails, Marlow is apprehensive lest he be drawn into the failure of Jim's illusion and into a fatal admission about himself. But the blending confusion of selves runs deeper than Marlow realizes. It shapes and colors the nature of his telling. Repeatedly, almost habitually, their voices merge, as those of Marlow and the Intended do in the locking scene of *Heart of Darkness*, though more fluidly and indistinguishably. Marlow offers Jim's perceptions and interpretations as though they are his own. He reports what Jim witnessed as though he himself had been there, presumes to know, as only Jim could know, what Jim believed, anticipates events with the defendant's apprehensions, and scans them with Jim's intelligence. Here is one of many examples in which Marlow's "he" is but an elidible substitute for Jim's "I" and the internal narrator acquires a luminous omniscience.

> You must remember he believed, as any other man would have done in his place, that the ship would go down at any moment; the bulging, rust-eaten plates that kept back the ocean, fatally must give way, all at once like an undermined dam, and let in a sudden and overwhelming flood. He stood still looking at these recumbent bodies, a doomed man aware of his fate, surveying the silent company of the dead. They *were* dead! Nothing could save them!

> There were boats enough for half of them perhaps, but there was no time. No time! No time! It did not seem worth while to open his lips, to stir hand or foot. Before he could shout three words, or make three steps, he would be floundering in a sea whitened awfully by the desperate struggles of human beings, clamorous with the distress of cries for help. There was no help. He imagined what would happen perfectly; he went through it all motionless by the hatchway with the lamp in his hand—he went through it to the very last harrowing detail. (86)

As Marlow merges with the Intended in the closing pages of *Heart of Darkness*, here and elsewhere he folds into the dubious identity of Lord Jim, intensifying the danger of revelation and the need to avoid it. It is because Marlow is so profoundly entwined in Jim's identity and act that the implications of his inadequacy appall him. Since Jim is "one of us," his failure, at least potentially, is all of ours, and "not one of us is safe" (43), least of all Marlow, whose absorption of Jim is almost total. If a man like Jim can go wrong like that, Marlow will fling down his hat and, utterly mortified, dance on it. By violating the code, "the solidarity of the craft" that links not only one seaman to another but the sailor to the artist, Jim has, as Marlow sees it, cheated him. He has deprived him (and the writer in need of his saving deceptions) "of a splendid opportunity to keep up the illusion of my beginnings . . . robbed our common life of the last spark of its glamour" (131).

So resonant is Jim's act, so portentously did it speak to Marlow's spirit, that to him the obscure truth involved in Jim's case seemed shattering enough to alter "mankind's conception of itself" (93). The breadth and power of these implied consequences suggest a further reason for Marlow's investment in Jim's failure and the urgency of its clouding. To Marlow, Jim was, prior to his failure and exposure, not only the guardian of the seaman's code and the efficacy of denial but also the embodiment of the elemental virtue that secures them and makes possible the illusory preservation of the ideal. One of those special few whose very existence is based upon honest faith, Jim stands for "just that inborn ability," absent in Kurtz, "to look temptations straight in the face," an unthinking and blessed capacity to stand up, as all men must if they are to survive, to the inner and outer terrors that besiege them (43). We have moved beyond the code of conduct here to character, deeper still to essential nature. In a single act, Jim has cast doubt not only on the inviolability of one's devotion to the principle of fidelity but also on the unthinking power that enables it, the one ostensibly reliable instrument of salvation. The inborn ability to look temptations in the face and not give in is what separates the cannibals from the pilgrims aboard the ship, Marlow from Kurtz in the heart of darkness; and it is the test that Jim, as unmanned by his cowardly eagerness to survive as others are by an enfeebling lust and longing, fails at sea. The solution offered with brimming confidence in *Heart of Darkness* proves inadequate in *Lord Jim*. Even inborn strength may not suffice, may not protect us from the temptations and terrors of experience and imagination and from the loss of self-possession they engender and expose.

The stakes for both Conrad and Marlow could hardly have been higher, the urge not to gaze too long or discerningly on "the obscure truth" hardly more compelling. Where all the old verities have collapsed, defying reconstruction, one seeks partial salvation in a willful semiblindness. Marlow, as he confesses, was "half afraid to see" Jim squirm (42), and the fear contains its own solution. Half afraid to witness, Marlow and the novel will only half or faintly see. The phrase is like an epigraph, defining the novel's unresolved ambivalence toward the objects of its probing—its fascinated curiosity, its skewed, self-interested inquiry, its glancing contact with the suspected monster in the dark, its avoidant surrender to enigma.

Conrad often furrows his fictions with a multitude of declared or enacted responses to the threat of forbidden or dangerous knowledge. In *Heart of Darkness*, only Kurtz confronts such knowledge directly—and is destroyed; others avert their gaze in a variety of self-protective ways. The accountant wards off chaos and darkness by keeping up appearances and devoting himself to his well-ordered books. A simple old sailor named Towser or Towson does not so much keep his books as—with a distracting singleness of purpose, a focused dedication to the right way of going to work—fill them with voluminous diagrams and tables. Kurtz's harlequin admirer inhibits thought with a mindless discipleship and an uncalculating "spirit of adventure . . . [that] consumed all thought of self" (*HD* 126–27). Women fetally enclose themselves in a "beautiful world of their own," while the cannibals are able to breathe dead hippo meat without contamination by finding refuge in their own inborn strength and capacity for faithfulness. Marlow does likewise; more typically, however, he escapes the stench by attending to surface truths that hide the inner truth—luckily, luckily—and in a splendid metaphor for the evasive technique of narrator and narrative, by "digging unostentatious holes to bury the stuff in" (*HD* 117).

Lord Jim is almost as fertile in its multiplication of spokesmen and exemplars for a rich tactical variety of evasions, self-distractions, and escapes. Marlow's half seeing is an attenuated version of Stein's implicit commendation of the self-idealizing closed eye. Unsatisfied with his little heap of mud or a limiting self-perception, man shuts his eyes in order to see himself as "a very fine fellow—so fine as he can never be . . . in a dream." The real trouble, Stein continues, comes because you cannot always keep your eyes shut. "I tell you, my friend," he offers, "it is not good for you to find you cannot make your dream come true" (213). Unlike Jim, the more imaginative and, therefore, the more consuming dreamer, Marlow cannot give himself entirely to the saving illusion of the dream. His more skeptical turn of mind is better served by a deconstruction of the real that breaks it into partial, vaguely glimpsed, and contradictory fragments. He is spared by the almost equally hopeful illusion that there is nothing coherent to be seen.

Marlow's evasions are in a sense legitimated by Brierly's suicide. One of those "lucky fellows" spared the anguish of indecision and self-mistrust (57) and a man of otherwise indomitable courage, Brierly unabashedly commends cowardice, self-concealment, and escape where revelation, as in Jim's case, threatens the good name of his fellow sailors. His recommendation to Jim is that he crawl deep underground and stay there as, he confesses, in comparable circumstances he would himself. When Marlow argues for the higher ground of facing it out, Brierly's response betrays the power of Jim's threat to his integrity and good name. "Courage be hanged!" he barks back. ". . . I don't care a snap for such courage" (67). Barely a week after the termination of the inquiry, unable to live with the implications of Jim's betrayal, Brierly takes his own life. He is Marlow magnified, a man still more fiercely dedicated to the code of fidelity that underpins Marlow's sense of honor and binds him to those who share his commitment.[19] That a man like Brierly, devastated by the implications and possible consequences of Jim's failure, commends the culprit's self-burial and finally buries himself at sea testifies to the weight of the burden of recognition. Full acknowledgement is impossible—for Jim, for Brierly, and for Marlow. Freedom is reduced to the choice of the mode of evasion or escape. Jim takes refuge in Patusan and on an equally insulated internal island of denial. Marlow chooses in effect to creep underground, to bury his head in bafflement and contradiction—in order, perhaps, not to follow Brierly's example. Like Kurtz, Brierly is drawn into the abyss by a horror whose grip he cannot loosen. Marlow draws his foot back, choosing again the saving lie of indeterminate fiction to the truth that is too dark altogether.

Brierly, Stein, and Jim do not exhaust the escape routes. Chester, a rugged seaman and pirate with "an immense girth of chest," suggests another unheroic alternative. To him Jim's weakness is in his emotional susceptibility, in the strangling cord that links emotion to deed. Chester's answer to the shadow is to stare unflinchingly at reality but never take anything to heart (162). Again some form of evasion is indispensable and assumed. Fascinated by the abominable, one may stare boldly into the heart of internal darkness. But one survives such daring, as Brierly did not, only by deafening oneself to the emotional echo, by not taking the heart to heart.

More sensitive than Chester and less brittle than Brierly, the French lieutenant offers a response to forbidden knowledge not unlike Marlow's. A more complex man than either Brierly or Chester, the lieutenant understands that hidden weakness is both universal and irrepressible. The beast of cowardice that stalks us all inevitably springs. When it does, he says bravely, "you have got to live with that truth" (146). The French lieutenant is smugly certain of his ground and wisdom, but the utterance itself is defensively encased, its implications successively distanced. Marlow notes that the lieutenant had issued his pronouncement "as though he had been the mouthpiece of abstract wisdom," and no sooner is it spoken than he "heightened the effect of detachment by beginning to twirl his thumbs slowly." What Chester explicitly and rather coarsely recommends, the officer more subtly and quietly practices. Acknowledging the inevitability of fear, he speaks of it in a way that modifies its effect and enlists his body in the securing of a saving distance. With the seeming courage of self-application, the lieutenant begins an anecdote in which he apparently will be the living exemplar of the sad truth he speaks of. "Take me, for instance," he begins but as quickly trails off. He drains his glass, returns to his twirling, and makes it clear by these gestures "that he did not mean to proceed with the personal anecdote" (147). Channeling his conveyance back toward Jim, he concludes with another pronouncement and his final exit. One may not live without honor, he avers, and "when the honour is gone—*ah ca! par exemple*—I can offer no opinion . . . because—monsieur—I know nothing of it" (148).

Marlow expresses disappointment with the path of the Frenchman's discourse, but in fact it bears no little resemblance to his own. Like the lieutenant Marlow seems prepared to gaze at truth directly, to acknowledge human cowardice and recognize its presence in himself, and to live with the implications of his understanding. And yet the hidden fear the officer speaks of layers him, as it does the French lieutenant, against full exposure. Although more personally linked than the lieutenant, less the mouthpiece of an abstract wisdom, he too will trail off and turn aside. He too, finally, will offer no opinion. Pronouncing Jim an insoluble enigma, inscrutable at heart, he will know, in the end, nothing of it.

The gap that divides the French lieutenant's performance from his announced convictions does not exist for Marlow, whose behavior is syntonic with belief. Marlow's narrative is laced with unashamed acknowledgements that, like Brierly, he too would hang courage in the interest of comfort and survival. Less principled and more indulgently self-protective, however, he prefers the artful dodge to the desperate plunge. Marlow makes no secret of it: thoughtlessness, willful denial, and a saving vagueness are his evasions of acknowledged choice. In issuing these admissions, he both justifies his own ostensible uncertainties and explains in substantial measure the elusiveness and obscurity of the novel.

Marlow confesses, and with no little pride, the contingent nature of his devotion to painful revelation. Supporting with his silence Jim's denial of guilt, he justifies his silence, explaining that he had no intention, "for the sake of barren truth, to rob him of the smallest particle of any saving grace that would come in his way." Claiming amid proliferating disclaimers that he does not know how much Jim himself believed and suspects Jim himself could not say with certainty, Marlow affirms his belief that "no man ever understands quite his own artful dodges to escape from the grim shadow of self-knowledge" (80). Conrad made a noticeably similar observation, with reference to himself, in a letter to a friend. Men have "but very little self-knowledge," he wrote Charles Chasse, "and authors especially are victims of many illusions about themselves."[20] Even had he confirmed Marlow here, the sweeping charge inevitably embraces the writer, whose novels, as readers routinely testify, are artful dodges from the shadow of both knowledge and knowability. It offers a cogent and credible explanation for the elusiveness of *Lord Jim* and Conrad's other famously deceptive texts. The texts are not merely deceptive but deceiving, artful if not always calculated evasions of intolerable awareness. One may argue that Conrad would have withdrawn himself from the tent of Marlow's gathering indictment. But to do so is at once to deny Conrad the quite irrefutable wisdom of Marlow's observation and to ascribe to him a prideful triumph over an ignorance he often claimed to wish away but never to have successfully effaced. The artist who spoke painfully and often of the half truths and whole illusions of existence claimed familiarity neither with the grim shadow of self-knowledge nor with all the roads that lead away from it.

While Marlow's pronouncement speaks knowingly for Conrad, it somewhat disingenuously (and therefore reflexively) obscures the willfulness of many of his evasions. Through Marlow's own elusive habits of narration, it also speaks for the enclosing fiction that compounds with additional voices and perspectives the obscuring consequences of Marlow's narrative involution and abandoning incertitudes. Marlow's artful dodges—principally a dimming vagueness, a blessed ignorance, and deliberate retreat—are grounded in eloquently acknowledged gratitude for the protective cloak they wrap him in, for the saving distance they provide.

Marlow's never-quite-persuasive lamentations in *Heart of Darkness* about the incapacitating limitations of language and the imprecisions of perception are replaced in *Lord Jim* by a series of paeans to the redeeming glory of the haze. The hypnotic attractions of the sea are rooted in this thankful reverence. There is, as he notes, adjectives ringing his enthusiasm, "such magnificent vagueness in the expectations that had driven each of us to sea . . . a glorious indefiniteness." What they got, he coyly suggests, is considerably less; and as is his habit when reality intrudes upon the vague or certain dream, he declines to speak of it. We know enough about the treacherous wiles of the sea to wink with Marlow at his reticence and to understand the protective uses of a watery imprecision. "In no other kind of life," he announces, "is the illusion more wide of reality—in no other is the beginning *all* illusion—the disenchantment more swift—the subjugation more complete" (129). There is, in Conrad's narratives, one other kind of life where the gap between illusion and reality is at least as wide: namely the passionate romances that begin, for the male protagonist, with the promise of ecstasy, lead quickly to subjugation, and end in humiliation, death, or despair. Erotic romance, then, is a pertinent exception, but the point here—indeed in both forms of subjugating romance—is the magnificence of the vagueness, the gloriousness of the indefiniteness that draws us on and finally, with luck aided by a protective wisdom, preserves us. Vagueness, in other words, is neither a terrifying reflection of the chaos in which reality writhes nor a frustratingly inescapable limitation of human discourse. Rather, screening us from the grim shadow of painful knowledge, it provides the illusory hope that keeps the pistol from our temples, that allows us, in the broadest sense, to go to sea.

Vagueness shields the viewer not only from a sinister reality but, more crucially, from the grimmer dangers of the vivifying imagination. What undoes Jim is the eidetic sharpness of his fatal vision and the unshakable certainty of its reality. As Kurtz has kicked loose of the earth, Jim, below in the body of the ship, is in effect under or inside it. Detached in their separate ways, neither is in contact with the redeeming surfaces, the hard facts of existence that distract us from the depths. Both therefore are free to indulge their imaginations without restraint—Kurtz to incorporate all reality within himself, Jim to conjure his own and inhabit it. Both are subject to a frightening certitude beyond the reach of mitigating doubt. The danger of such damning certainty, Marlow indicates, is abated by a refusal of perception that reduces the threat to "the imperfect vagueness of human thought." Swathed in its mists, "imagination, the enemy of men, the father of all terrors," clouds to a tolerable dullness (11).

Mere thought circles in a salutary haze like the one that surrounds *Lord Jim* and Conrad's other obfuscating fictions. But since thought is susceptible to the incursions of a somber reality and a hostile imagination, Marlow finds special solace in its absence. The surest protection against the outward and inward terrors that stalk us is an instinctive courage, "an unthinking and blessed stiffness . . . before the might of nature, and the seductive corruption of men." One must be, as Marlow puts it, impervious to the force of reality and the seductive beckoning of ideas. Marlow would "hang ideas" as contemptible "tramps, vagabonds, knocking at the back-door of your mind, each taking a little of your substance, each carrying away some crumb of that belief in a few simple notions you must cling to if you want to live decently and would like to die easy!" (43).

Conrad tempts us repeatedly with the comforts of denial and deception but, buffeted by ambivalence, at times inhibits our surrender with ironies that embarrass their appeal. Such ironies are audible in Marlow's contempt for the peaceful obliviousness of the pedestrians walking the sepulchral city in *Heart of Darkness*. And they are present, if muted, in *Lord Jim*, where the first narrator speaks of those seamen in whom he detects "the soft spot, the place of decay, the determination to lounge safely through existence" (13). But the deprecation of ignorance and our desire for its harbor is shallow in *Lord Jim*. Appearing early, it wears steadily away under the pressure of a reality whose bleak visage encourages its occlusion. The cry to hang ideas betrays a broader empathy toward those who would live safely and die easy, and Marlow's still later confession of resentment toward Jim marks a further concession to the appeal of self-deception. He is angry at Jim for having, in effect, "cheated me—me!—of a splendid opportunity to keep up the illusion of my beginnings, as though he had robbed our common life of the last spark of its glamour" (131). The glimmer of self-irony returns in this passage. One can hear, even as he longs for the return of the illusion, the mocking repetition of "me" and the chiding slap of exclamation. But the progression of the sentence mirrors the progression of the novel, where, in the glacial shift to Patusan, the pursuit of truth, tempered from the outset by anxiety, yields to the siren call of glamour.

The weight of Marlow's pronouncements, like the disempowering narrative practice of both Conrad and Marlow, testifies to the greater appeal of the muddle Forster complained of. Lacking the unthinking stiffness that stares temptation down, Marlow yields to the temptations of the lotus. As the novel progresses and insight ominously beckons, the ironies diminish and disappear, replaced by an unashamed affirmation of the wisdom of deliberate suppression. Finding little appeal in enervating self-knowledge, Marlow betrays scant ambivalence in his later claim that "the wisdom of life . . . consists in putting out of sight all the reminders of our folly, of our weakness, of our mortality; all that makes against our efficiency—the memory of our failures, the hints of our undying fears, the bodies of our dead friends" (174); still less in his admonition that one kills fear with "an enchanted and poisoned shaft dipped in a lie too subtle to be found on earth" (316) but found everywhere in the fiction.[21] When he speaks next of the "incalculable majority," whose very dullness makes their lives supportable and welcome, he willingly includes himself among them. He speaks now not of "they" but of "we" who, following one of those "rare moments of awakening when we see, hear, understand ever so much—everything—in a flash . . . fall back again into our agreeable somnolence" (143).

Readers are surprised here by the anomalous, almost arrogant claim to a full understanding that precedes retreat. Like so many other of the novel's expressions, this one is an icon of its technique, an interiorized articulation of the novel's pervasive dynamic of approach and recoil, vision and the lowering of eyes. The repeated claim to bafflement is a confessed deception. Truth is not a myth or absence but an intimidating presence that drives us back.[22] Like this Marlow, Conrad is not a nihilist but a perceiver in flight. Events are not devoid of interpretable meaning; rather, like Jim and Marlow in their dealings with Jewel, the narrative is in active collusion against its exposure. Language is not inadequate but a saving disguise, a shelter, as Marlow puts it, under which we crawl when we have been driven into the open.

Fearful of losing Jim and repeating her mother's fate, Jewel tearfully relates to Marlow the tale of her mother's betrayal. Deeply moved and threatened, Marlow feels himself losing his footing in deep waters and experiences "a sudden dread, the dread of the unknown depths" (312). As she does when Jewel prods Marlow for information about Jim's treacherous history and the likelihood of its repetition in her life, woman assaults man's defenses, threatening to drag forbidden truths into the open. Jewel's is a story of woman as the victim of betrayal. But as the narrative earlier makes clear, it is man who has suffered the primal betrayal. Deserted by someone or something more precious than life, further unnerved by the frightening love of woman, which rattles self-possession, man betrays woman in vengeful retribution. As truth betrays its promise to the adventurers who at least ostensibly pursue it, so woman, often truth in its seductive flesh, habitually betrays the men who desire her and, at the price of self-possession, seek futilely to possess her. And her betrayal is identified as a defining element of her nature. In *Victory* Heyst, among others, is stricken with this enervating insight. It flashes through his mind that women can deceive men "so completely. The faculty was inherent in them; they seemed to be created with a special aptitude" (81). More broadly and strongly suggestive of an elemental maternal origin, Marlow interrupts his narrative in *Lord Jim* with this intrusive reflection on the origins of man's retaliatory urge to betray women: "for where is the man—I mean a real sentient man—who does not remember vaguely having been deserted in the fullness of possession by some one or something more precious than life? . . . our common fate fastens upon the women with a peculiar cruelty. It does not punish like a master, but inflicts lingering torment, as if to gratify a secret, unappeasable spite" (276–77).[23] We will never know, of course, but it seems not too great a stretch to suggest the etiology of Conrad's harsh portrayals of betraying women lies half-unburied here.

Jewel's story stirs Marlow's terror of the depths because it is a screen memory for the primal betrayal, because it bespeaks, in her love for both Jim and her mother, an "extra-terrestrial" element that mortifies man, and because its objective is to disinter the anxiously buried knowledge of Jim's past. The tale, Marlow concedes, "had the power to drive me out of my conception of existence, out of that shelter each of us makes for himself to creep under in moments of danger, as a tortoise withdraws within its shell. For a moment," Marlow reflects,

> I had a view of a world that seemed to wear a vast and dismal aspect of disorder, while, in truth, thanks to our unwearied efforts, it is as sunny an arrangement of small conveniences as the mind of man can conceive. But still—it was only a moment: I went back into my shell directly. One *must*—don't you know?—though I seemed to have lost all my words in the chaos of dark thoughts I had contemplated for a second or two beyond the pale. These came back, too, very soon, for words also belong to the sheltering conception of light and order which is our refuge. I had them ready at my disposal before she whispered softly. (313)

Marlow's first words, as it happens, are a subtle lie disguised as amazement at Jewel's incredulity. He expresses transparently unwarranted astonishment at her inability to believe, her "craving for incertitude" (313), induced, in fact, by his own and Jim's concealing (self-)deceptions. But the meditation has broader implications. It affirms both the indispensability of the protective shelter when the saving illusion is shaken by an impending revelation and the role of language in the restoration of illusion. Truth does threaten to pierce the armor of willful self-deception, and when it does, discretion dictates the preserving retreat.

Perhaps the most potent of all shelters is the shell of words that covers the figure wincing at the probes. Without the ordering power of written words, one confronts the chaos of dark thoughts. That is why, when Jim speaks weakly of his loneliness and his own lack of shelter, Marlow takes to his writing desk. Feeling as though there is something dangerous in the room, a beast of enervating pathos that might pounce on him, Marlow seeks refuge in his writing (172). There he feels protected from the "weird power in a spoken word" (174), more dangerous because nearer to reality, nearer the truth of mortal weakness that assaults one's self-possession. Marlow's confession is a crystallized articulation of the narrative technique of *Lord Jim* and of Conrad's other fictions of obscurity and muddle. There are, in Conrad, two saving illusions. One, the conscious deflection, is the use of words and fictions to create only seemingly intelligible pictures, to generate false images and illusory structures of light and order as a refuge against chaos and the dark. When that defense fails, however, or when it seems, on its own, inadequate to hold, Conrad had recourse to an artful dodge he was perhaps less cognizant of: commitment to insoluble mystery and enigma, the saving illusion that there is nothing to be known. He leans with Marlow toward the imperfect haziness of thought that makes fears grow shadowy, toward the "magnificent vagueness" and "glorious indefiniteness" of our untested illusions of the sea.

The pattern repeats itself kaleidoscopically. As in "The Planter of Malata," where Renouard's destabilizing encounters with the sensual and erotic Felicia repeatedly dissolve toward mist and shadows, vagueness, mystery, and protestations of uncertainty are scattered through the novel as shadows that bear traces of what casts them. It is on the back of his admission that Jim's transgression frightens him that Marlow claims with insistent repetitiveness, "He was not . . . clear to me. He was not clear. And there is a suspicion he was not clear to himself either" (177). It is immediately after he acknowledges his urgent wish to be rid and free of Jim so that he might return home with clean hands that he situates Jim in a metaphoric mist, claims he had never seen him distinctly, and speaks of the "doubt which is the inseparable part of our knowledge" (221). Layering his defenses, Marlow also trivializes the distinction between truth and illusion. "There is so little difference," he asserts, "and the difference means so little" (222). His compelling need at this point is to return home with a sense of cleanliness restored. But he can purify himself only by disposing of Jim—physically to Patusan, verbally and conceptually to the realm of mysterious incomprehensibility where truth and illusion are indistinguishable.[24]

The alternating pattern of alluring fascination and retreating vagueness pulses through the novel. Marlow's discussion of Brierly's suicide and of his own self-interested wish to mitigate Jim's transgression culminates in another fall into mystery, an acknowledgement that he did not understand Jim, followed by the conclusion that he was misleading (76). The closing summary is suggestive: first of the comforts of such tidy encapsulation, more pertinently of Marlow's wish to transfer responsibility for his confusion from the pressure of his own need to Jim's deceptiveness.

The discourse between Jim and Marlow that follows this dismissal crystallizes the technique in miniature. Listening to Jim and offering no dissent to his self-absolving speech, Marlow first acknowledges his preference for the saving illusion over painful truth, then tumbles into expressions of personal bafflement that culminate in a sweeping affirmation of the universality of cunning evasion.

> He discovered at once a desire that I should not confound him with his partners in—in crime, let us call it. He was not one of them; he was altogether of another sort. [Deliberate avoidance:] I gave no sign of dissent. I had no intention, for the sake of barren truth, to rob him of the smallest particle of any saving grace that would come in his way. [Uncertainty:] I didn't know how much of it he believed himself. I didn't know what he was playing up to—if he was playing up to anything at all—and [Universalization of uncertainty:] I suspect he did not know either; for it is my belief no man ever understands quite his own artful dodges to escape from the grim shadow of self-knowledge. (79–80)

The presumed validity of this universalized belief ensures and rationalizes its application to the speaker. What Marlow seems less than steadily aware of are the artful dodges that facilitate his own escape from the grim shadow of self-knowledge.

In the context of this pattern of causal succession, Marlow's pervasive habit of juxtaposing mystery and terror in a single phrase seems a conflation of the same turn of mind. Here is a shortened list of such conflations, with the appropriate phrases italicized:

> [Jim's] appearance alone added a touch of personal concern to the thoughts suggested by the knowledge of his weakness—made it a thing of *mystery and terror*—like a hint of destructive fate ready for us all. (51)

I say mysterious, because it was so in a sense though it contained a naked fact, about as naked and ugly as a fact can well be. (35)

"The opinion that whatever was mysterious in this affair would turn out to be tragic as well, began to prevail. (36)

It was not a vulgar and treacherous massacre; it was a lesson, a retribution —a demonstration of some *obscure and awful* attribute of our nature which, I am afraid, is not so very far under the surface as we like to think. (404)

What these utterances reveal is the intimate connection between the terrible and the mysterious. What is ugly, tragic, and awful is also enigmatic and obscure, not principally because mystery itself is frightening—quite the contrary, it is often cause for gratitude—but because terror is the mother of obscurity. Mystery rarely obscures what might otherwise prove neutral or pleasing. What is mysterious will almost invariably prove tragic or worse—unless of course it remains mysterious. A similar dynamic, I think, is at work in two fusions of the epistemological and the moral. Jewel's condemnation of Jim—"You are false"—speaks at once of his lie and his betrayal, and, as always, the cognitive deception obscures the moral transgression. Marlow's observation, spoken more than once, that Jim is "under a cloud" (342, 414) likewise merges the dubiousness of his moral character with his perceptual obscurity. Here too, he walks in a cloud of mist because he is under a cloud of guilt whose full implications are better left obscured.

"THE PLAGUE SPOT"

I have said that Patusan represents a site of danger. Strewn with images of engulfing forests and gloom, its landscape, for Padmini Mongia, is also a metaphor for the body of the woman: "a space of womb-like enclosure, the maternal darkness which produces so much of the fear and terror of the gothic."[25] Jewel, "drowning in a lonely dark place," is confined and asphyxiated here. Jim, "imprisoned within the very freedom of his power," is more tightly caged by her possessive jealousy and by the forests, her accomplices, that guarded him "with vigilant accord, with an air of seclusion, of mystery, of invincible possession" (283). And Marlow, relieved at the end to put this airlessly constricting landscape behind him, lets his eyes roam through space "like a man released from bonds who stretches his cramped limbs, runs, leaps, responds to the inspiring elation of freedom" (331–32).

Patusan is also linked, relatedly and ominously, to burial and death. Stein is reminded of the island by Marlow's recollection of Brierly's suggestion that Jim "creep twenty feet underground and stay there." It is a place, Stein and Marlow agree, that might "bury him in some sort," and Jim would not be the first to be interred there since, as Marlow surmises, Patusan had once before served "as a grave for some sin, transgression, or misfortune" (219). Woman and death, commonly bonded in Conrad's fiction, come chillingly together at Jewel's mother's grave, where, in imagery suggestive of Kurtz's hut, surrounded by staked skulls, "lumps of white coral shone round the dark mound like a chaplet of bleached skulls" (322).

And yet, paradoxically, it is also a place of refuge and escape. Patusan is the small writ large. All of these instantiations of the movement from the grim shadow of reality to protective obscurity I have cited are microcosmic reflections of the novel's controversial shift from the terrified leap and awful inquiry to the remote sanctuary of Patusan. While a number of the novel's critics gloss over the difficulty or find justification for the shift from realism to romance, more perceive it as an unfortunate flaw in the novel. Ian Watt, for example, complains of "a sense of reduced complexity and rapid confluence of the narrative elements," while John Batchelor is disturbed by the "curious simple moral polarity" of the Patusan section, "a brightly colored flatness.... It is as though the end of *Lord Jim* were drawn from a part of Conrad's mind different from, and shallower than, the consciousness that has created the bulk of the novel."[26]

Both are correct. The Patusan episode does betray a substantially reduced complexity and a sequined flatness, and it is a product of a different and shallower—because perhaps less courageous—part of Conrad's mind. Patusan, as almost every reader notices, is what one describes as "a dream-world where the ideal has its full sway for Jim" or what another calls "a romantic escape world in which the dream is allowed to come true."[27] In literary terms Patusan is a world of myth or high romance, a heroic fantasy where "knight and maiden [meet] to exchange vows amongst haunted ruins" (312) and, more important, where Jim may live out his storied self-ideal as the unflinching hero in a book. Patusan, however, is at the same time described in much broader aesthetic terms. As a motionless painting, a locale for the pure exercise of imagination infused with the hidden truthfulness of art, it is also identified with more substantial forms of art or as a salient feature of such imaginative creation. That the Patusan romance occupies such a prominent place in *Lord Jim* ascribes to it an ineradicable place in Conrad's own writing, one that is not confined to the latter portion of this novel but that, as a refuge from the terrible, suffuses this and other fictions. Patusan is the narrative extension of the novel's identifying habit of protective flight. It is a retreat, if not to the world of art per se, then to that aspect of the artistic performance whose function is to leave intolerable truths and realities behind and set up residence in controlled obscurity.

Escaping decay and death, Jim is a sculpted "figure set up on a pedestal [in Patusan], to represent in his persistent youth the power . . . of races that never grow old" (265). Escaping guilt, Jim can in Patusan leave "his earthly failings behind him" (218) and begin with a clean slate—or so at least he hopes. Reality will pursue the fugitive into the sanctuary, but it does so in the early part of the novel as well. Marlow's repeated efforts to obscure the leaping shadows are only temporarily successful. The flickering light of vision and self-blinding, fascination and evasion, clarity and obscurity permeates the novel. It is consummated, not begun, in Patusan, but the objective is clear: to find refuge in an aesthetic world where language is the only truth, where the word goes unquestioned, and where words can assume their pervasive double function as constructors of substitutive reality and clouding obfuscators of what cannot be replaced. More broadly it is to allow Jim the comforts of the dulling ignorance and half blindness that make life tolerable, even welcome, to the incalculable majority.

The flight to Patusan, as the novel's play of light makes clear, marks a turning away from harsh if flickering vision to a more protective haze. In this secluded realm of art, the sun, the eye of the real, whose fixed glare reveals the earth as a pointless point of dust, gives way to the "diffused light . . . [that] seemed to cast upon a world . . . the illusion of a calm and pensive greatness" (305–6). The sight of earth as a restless mote of dust is equivalent to Jim's vision of the corpses laid out for death. It is a vision of mortality, of the inevitability, the imminence, and the crushing effacement of death that makes of earth's inhabitants equally negligible and restless specks of dust. Appearing as it does immediately after Jim's lament that he has not yet forgotten why he fled to Patusan, that his adoration there is a function of the natives' ignorance of "the real truth," the description of the evening sky is an externalization of Jim's internal landscape. It reifies his need to transform the exposing glare of sunlight into a diffused light in whose subtle haze one finds an illusion of serenity. When Marlow predicts that Jim will always remain for the natives "an insoluble mystery," Jim's response is instantaneous and eager. "'Mystery,' he repeated, before looking up. 'Well, then, let me always remain here'" (307). They are the words Conrad often hinted at or spoke in other terms. And they whisper everywhere in the fiction they made possible.

Anticipating his critics, Conrad referred to the transition to Patusan as the "plague spot" in the novel.[28] But the term is more than a vague epithet of dissatisfaction. Speaking of the sailors Jim encounters in the hospital, men who had faced no danger and always had it easy, the frame narrator detects "in their actions, in their looks, in their persons . . . the soft spot, the place of decay, the determination to lounge safely through existence" (13). The plague spot of the novel is the sailor's soft spot, the turn from realism to romance that betrays the writer's determination to pass, if not quite lounge, safely through existence. It is also the "weak spot" in the maze of accusatory facts through which Jim, circling frantically, hopes to "squeeze [him]self and escape" (31). Only a blessed unthinking stiffness or, in its absence, the will and capacity to avert one's gaze can keep one aboard ship when the sea floods its decks and the living are perceived as the already dead. Only with eyes half-shut can one remain true to his craft.

Dichotomous pairs (knowledge and denial, threatening revelation and escape) are essential to Conrad's art, for they represent the two embattled sides of his ambivalent narratives. Patusan is an aesthetic island, neatly landscaped in reductive language and set by narrative technique and Conrad's darkening layers of illusion at a saving remove from truth. Shrouded in fog, however, it only half conceals the menacing geography of the female—the sexual body, the engulfing womb, the interring earth, paradigmatic sites of dangerous knowledge—and the piercingly questioning woman, whose probings threaten to expose the vulnerable female element at the unheroic core. Patusan, then, to alter my metaphor, is a volcanic island, its language the hardened lava that carries within it the fossilized and still smoldering message of its origins. It rests too, if I may give it one more turn, on the still-active volcanic crater refracted half-visibly beneath the waves.

For Conrad, the mind, to sustain itself when most profoundly threatened, must turn at least partially away. For the writer as for Marlow, and for all their real courage and probing determination, it is the withdrawal of the foot from too much knowledge that saves one from the abyss that Kurtz—monstrously, heroically, tragically—plunges into. Only by averting or confounding one's gaze can one return with a voice. Like Marlow that voice may claim to "have nothing to say," but this purported muddle or vacancy of speech has held us for so long, not least because it glows with the molten core it rises from. The fascination with which we listen to and hear it is a product, at least in part, of the abomination that impels it.

4

A MORE DANGEROUS REVOLUTION

Under Western Eyes

More than a political novel, an examination of Russian character, autocracy, and revolution under half-blinded Western eyes, *Under Western Eyes* is a nervous exploration of Conrad's obsessional concern with the problem of knowledge and the wisdom or value of its exposure. The problem begins, perhaps, with the problem of the author's own exposure in this extraordinarily (even for Conrad) autobiographical novel. As he confessed in his author's note to the novel, he "had never been called before to a greater effort of detachment: detachment from all passions, prejudices, and even from personal memories" (viii).[1]

As more than one reader of the novel has discerned, there are, in effect, two writer-narrators here, or more precisely, setting Conrad precariously aside for the moment, one within the novel and the other of it. For Penn R. Szittya, who offers a rich and astute reading of *Under Western Eyes* as metafiction, this "aesthetic double structure is an image and product of a doubleness in Conrad's own life and mind.... [Together] they express the novelist's (and Conrad's) double relation to his fiction; it both is and is not about himself; it is both a confession and a disguise."[2] They also constitute, I would add, an intimately related exploration, deliberate or unwitting, of the question of the desirability of knowledge, self-knowledge, and revelation. The attitude, predictably, is multiply ambivalent if not contradictory; the results, perhaps equally predictably, layered, involuted, and resistant.

Why, after all, Conrad dropped such an opaque narrative veil across this novel. But we may begin with Razumov, whose "confessional" diary, the radically more involved and revealing text within the text, constitutes the principal source of the narrator's information and report. It is this diary, chiefly, that falls under the reluctant and purportedly occluded scrutiny of the language teacher's Western eyes. Razumov becomes, as Jeffrey Berman remarks, Conrad's "most important artist figure," his diary an expression of the "urges that drive a solitary thinker into the perilous world of confessional art."³ Razumov, then, is the writer driven, for solace, for moral redemption, for survival itself, to a self-revelatory form of authorship. And Conrad seems intensely and committedly identified with his protagonist when, recognizing the danger of attempting to escape "the grip of [his] . . . situation" and despising himself for the inclination, he resolves with a passion seen nowhere else to write. "Must Write!" he exclaims. "He! Write! A sudden light flashed upon him. . . . Is it that I am shrinking? It can't be! It's impossible. To shrink now would be worse than moral suicide; it would be nothing less than moral damnation. . . . I must write—I must, indeed! I shall write—never fear. Certainly. That's why I am here" (288–89).⁴

To write was unquestionably why Conrad was "here," why, he would have said, he was dropped so unhappily into this life. But there is an element of excessive protest in all this exclamation, of somewhat hollow, at least anxious bravado in that ringing "never fear." And from a writer who, with ironic courage, sang the saving virtues of the art of protective recoil, there is more candid self-revelation in that "am I shrinking?" than in its denial. Not to write honestly and unflinchingly might, for Conrad, have been a form of moral suicide or damnation. But to venture onto the battlefield without his armored layers of evasion, contradiction, and obfuscation was more dangerous still—without his distant, detached, and presumably muddled primary narrator, we might say in this instance, though as we will see, he is to a degree internalized, incorporated into the confessional text that is in purported contrast with the avoidant containing narrative. The loss of self-possession all but entailed in unguarded self-revelation constitutes an emotional and psychological threat, no less intimidating—more, I would argue—than the thought of moral damnation. And indeed, one may read Conrad's art as a perpetual struggle—as defiantly frustrating as it is enriching—between the presumed moral compulsion to pursue, discover, and reveal and the understandable human recoil at the prospect or experience of revelation. The ambivalence is compounded by Conrad's conviction that where knowledge is predatory, the drive to pursue it to its corner may be not only risky but immoral.

It is a testimony to both the naive candor of this "confessional" inquiry and its defensive retreat from self-perception that it is fraught with Razumov's self-deceptive rationalizations of his betrayal of Victor Haldin, both as a prospect to be pondered and later as an act performed. Convincing himself that he acts in harmonious accord with justifiable conscience, laudable principle, and sound reason, he persuades himself "with a flow of masterly argument" (35), "argue[s] himself into new beliefs" that are "not alarming" (246), recalls the distinctly Conradian epigram "that speech has been given to us for the purpose of concealing our thoughts" (261), and, looking into the mirror "with anguish, with anger or despair . . . as a threatened man may look fearfully at his own face in the glass, formulat[es] to himself reassuring excuses for his appearance" (214).⁵ When they do not suffice, or to supplement these calming rationalizations, Razumov takes refuge in "the trivialities of daily existence [that] were an armour for the soul" (53). And if we are tempted, as we surely, perhaps calculatingly are, to discover dismissive authorial contempt for such deflections, our confidence is weakened by the recognition that Razumov's trivialities of daily existence are, in motive and effect, the surface facts Marlow escapes to, quite undeniably with his creator's indulgent sanction, as he sails nearer the heart of African darkness. When he "messes about" with the strips of woolen blanket to bandage the leaky steam pipes, watches the steering, watches out for sunken stones, or keeps a lookout for signs of dead wood to cut up for the next day's steaming, Marlow attends, as he puts it, "to the mere incidents of the surface" that hide, luckily and savingly, the menacing "inner truth" (*HD* 93) that Razumov no more contemptibly obscures.

The reader is brought into the forgiving enterprise, made more sympathetic to Razumov's evasions and denials, by the anguished nature of his thoughts. The narrator sees in his weighty gaze "the stare of a man who lies unwinking in the dark, angrily passive in the toils of disastrous thoughts" (183). To Natalie Haldin "he seems to be a man who has suffered more from his thoughts than from evil fortune" (168). From such thinking some forgiveness, surely, some permissible escape; and the latitude is confirmed and strengthened by its adoption—undeniably with authorial as well as narrative support—in other contexts. Everyone who has contact with the older Mrs. Haldin, who knows the truth about her son's death and has the opportunity to reveal it, agrees without hesitation or compunction that it should be mercifully withheld, if necessary by deliberate deception.⁶ As the compassionate *dame de compagnie* puts it, speaking more inclusively and echoing Conrad in a dozen direct as well as fictional expressions, "To give one's life for the cause is nothing. But to have one's illusions destroyed—that is really almost more than one can bear" (148). Late in the novel, volunteering to work with Razumov as his humble companion, she commends herself to him—and by this time almost as appealingly to the reader—with the assurance that "I would not want to know anything.... I would know how to keep dumb" (233–34, 236–37).

Ironically, then, Razumov is the internal author of a work of presumably confessional art rife with rationalizations, self-deceptions, and evasions, a work concerned principally with the anguished effort to avoid detection and the need, finally, to confess. In this the young man's diary is a revealing image of Conrad's revealingly covert fictions: their ostensible search for truth, knowledge, or self-awareness, their deeper urge to conceal or obscure whatever dark, self-betraying truths glimmer or peek through, and their tacit acknowledgement by exposure of that profounder need. In the end, of course, Razumov does confess, and in some measure it is his journal that brings him to this unburdening and seemingly soul-saving revelation. Tracking what seem to be quite blatant and transparent textual cues, most readers have come to regard Razumov's confession as a moral and spiritual triumph endorsed by the novel and its creator. Tony Tanner speaks for many when he credits Razumov with the acquisition of "great station, not only because of what he suffers, but because in the depths of that suffering he discovers that no matter what is in the balance he cannot live a lie."[7] There are grounds for such an affirmation, and I do not reject it. After all once he has decided to "confess, go out—and perish," he discovers "there is air to breathe at last—air!" (361). And he expresses gratitude to Natalie Haldin, whose "light of truth" shone the way from evil and made him "betray myself back into truth and peace" (358).

But the addendum "go out—and perish" to the determination to confess is symptomatic, for virtually every expression of relief that attaches to Razumov's confession is similarly qualified by a chilling recognition of the terrible cost. "I am independent," announces the repentant sinner, "—and therefore perdition is my lot" (362). It is a curious salvation that ends in perdition, but the confessor will not have to wait for the afterlife to experience his damnation. In what have been accurately identified as perhaps the most violent and vicious passages in all of Conrad, Razumov is cruelly beaten, deafened, run over, and crippled by a passing tramcar he does not hear and condemned to live—if such it can be called—as the helplessly pathetic charge of the disillusioned *dame de compagnie*. For Berman, who vividly describes this punishment and recognizes some of its important implications, the violence is so aberrantly brutal and protracted that one questions the author's pent-up violence no less than that of the revolutionaries.[8] But the extremity is less mystifying, I think, if recognized as the author's visceral revenge upon a character who has dared what he would not. The narrator's lurid description of the confession as a tortured self-stabbing supports this reading: "It was as though he had stabbed himself outside," shivers the speaker, "and had come in there to show it . . . as though he were turning the knife in the wound and watching the effect" (350–51). What Conrad seems to betray here is, at the least, a revulsion indicative of profound ambivalence toward the confessional act. Figuring it, as he does, as a grotesque act of moral and physical masochism, he mitigates its earlier characterization as a moral victory and release. As he does in the severity of the punishment he inflicts on his confessed sinner, he betrays in this grim conceit his revulsion at what in a more hopeful compartment of his spirit he commends.

It is for more and more symbolic reasons than affection or disguise that, closing his diary with the self-canceling introspection that he is independent yet doomed to perdition, Razumov stops writing, closes the book, and wraps it in the black veil he has taken from Natalie Haldin. Whatever else it represents, the veil, a poignantly chosen prop, is also the visual icon of the obscuring hiddenness within, the fabric of ambivalence and contradiction that comes between

Razumov's (and Conrad's) confessional art and lucid self-exposure or a univocal attitude toward it.

It is also a textile representation of the more opaquely layered textual veil in which Conrad wraps Razumov's conflicted diary. I am speaking, of course, of the English teacher, the novel's perplexed and perplexing narrator, whose insertion into the story and whose transforming effect upon it have been the controversial subjects of critical discussion since the novel's first appearance. A 1908 letter to Galsworthy reveals that *Under Western Eyes* was first conceived as a short story, tentatively titled "Razumov." Two years later, with the addition of two new sections, it had grown into a full-sized novel. Although the ending was altered, the plot stood basically unchanged. The radically transforming difference was the addition of a narrator under whose distant and myopic eye Razumov's story would be half-comprehendingly perceived (*CL* 4:8–9).[9]

The question of why Conrad, at considerable apparent cost to immediacy, intensity, and credibility, chose to interpose this strangely baffled and more than mildly bewildering narrator has generated a small cottage industry of explanations. However, an understanding of the full scope of the consequences of Conrad's decision requires a somewhat more detailed and critical examination of the narrator's reliability—or lack of it—than I have seen, one that raises more serious questions about the novel's coherence and interpretability and makes it, I believe, a more aporic fiction than is generally acknowledged.

Anthony Winner, one of the relatively few readers to bring the novel's ultimate coherence into question, observes persuasively that expectations are "frustrated by the spate of mutually canceling ironies that pervades the novel," interpretation sabotaged by "an outbreak of anarchy or entropy that calls all prescriptions and definitions into question."[10] Since the narrator is sometimes transparently obtuse, at other times an equally transparent purveyor of familiar Conradian convictions, one of the novel's principal sources of misrule is the difficulty of sorting out the teacher's reliable from his dismissible interpretations and beliefs. How, except in the most obvious instances at either end, do we distinguish the novel's dramatic irony from the internal author's insight? But long before we feel the effect of this problem or the other sources of hermeneutic anarchy, we are confronted with a narrator whose smugly confessed ignorance of his subject and unabashed disclaimers about the reliability of his medium—language itself—are compounded by what appears to be disingenuousness at best, or perhaps quite blatant dishonesty.

The English teacher opens his narrative with the wish "to disclaim the possession of those high gifts of imagination and expression" but proves through much of what follows to be an imaginative reporter often quite as eloquent as the Russian diarist or the great English novelist. He compounds our apprehensions with the surprising acknowledgement—he is in many ways a more effusive confessor than Razumov—that as a teacher of languages he has come to perceive words as "the great foes of reality" (3), the study of which long ago smothered whatever gifts of imagination or expression he may have once possessed. All this is intended, paradoxically, to render him, because unimaginative and inexpressive, a more reliably restrained and objective reporter of Razumov's story. He is, he implies, a faceless conduit for that inner narrative, which he will offer virtually unsupplemented, uninterpreted, and unalloyed. So scrupulous is he, he insists somewhat further on, that "I would not try (were I able) to invent anything.... I would not even invent a transition" (100). Clearly Conrad, if not the teacher himself, is bent on irony here. One of them (more likely both) surely knows very well that no narrative is conceivable under such constraints, certainly not this one. And indeed the narrator, who on more than one occasion somehow knows what he could not know and sees what he could not have seen, invents routinely a great deal more than a transition.[11]

The Western teacher strengthens his claim to the objectivity of a detached observer by insisting he has nothing in common with his mystifying Russian subjects. But they are alike, as more than one reader has remarked, in several poignant ways. The narrator shares with Razumov the struggle for a strictly rational bias and self-control that contrasts starkly with Russia's clouding mysticism and irrationality. Like Razumov—and Conrad, it should be noted—he seeks a "form or ... formula for peace" (*UWE* 5). And of course, no less than Razumov, if less able finally to acknowledge it, he is in love with Natalie Haldin.[12] More to the point, however, since in some of these ways Razumov is more Western than Russian, the teacher's narrative, as Bernard Meyer discerns, bears the imprint of a number of minor as well as major Russian literary masters and "reflects an unmistakable identification ... with the Slavic temperament and people of the story." Meyer also notes the empathic implications and, I would add, the markedly Slavic coloration of his only partially muted cry: "Who knows what true loneliness is—not the conventional word, but the naked terror?"[13]

Most significantly, perhaps, the English teacher's repeated profession of a stunning incomprehension of his subject is belied by analyses of the Russian character quite unmistakably reflective of Conrad's own. "I have no comprehension of the Russian character," he announces at the outset (4), and he punctuates the ensuing narrative with similar disclaimers: "I suppose one must be a Russian to understand Russian simplicity" (104); "her sayings always seemed to me to have enigmatical prolongations vanishing somewhere beyond my reach" (118); "once more I had the sense of being out of it" (170); "it is a vain enterprise for sophisticated Europe to try and understand these doings" (126); and there are more. Earlier on he claimed that to a teacher of languages "the world is but a place of many words and man appears a mere talking animal not much more wonderful than a parrot" (3). Since parrots, presumably, are mere motiveless mouthers of human speech, one wonders why one group of such birds—Russians, for example—would prove more opaque to another's understanding than any other. But we may set that aside, for the narrator quite frequently betrays not only an irrepressible willingness to interpret the allegedly inscrutable behavior and mutterings of these colorful creatures, but also an understanding revealed in the very utterance of his disclaimer. "I have no comprehension of the Russian character," he declares, only to erode the absolutism of his claim with a markedly comprehending account of what ostensibly eludes him: "The illogicality of their attitude, the arbitrariness of their conclusions, the frequency of the exceptional . . . [and their] extraordinary love of words" (4).

To a teacher of languages, whose universe consists of "a wilderness of words," a people so in love with words that they gather them up, cherish them, then "pour them out . . . with an enthusiasm, a sweeping abundance" (4), should be quite accessible to his understanding. And so, as he reveals in this self-unraveling observation and intermittently throughout, they are. Examples of his astute readings of Russian character are as common as his claims of incomprehension and the obtuse observations that seem to confirm them. "It is the peculiarity of Russian natures," he remarks, speaking of Inspector Mikunin, "that, however strongly engaged in the drama of action, they are still turning their ear to the murmur of abstract ideas" (294). Here it is the peculiarity of Russian natures that the narrator quite shrewdly understands. But it is not always. Razumov, for example, "took the attitude of an inscrutable listener, a listener of the kind that hears you out intelligently and then—just changes the subject" (5). "This sort of trick," he elaborates, "which may arise either from intellectual insufficiency or from an imperfect trust in one's own convictions, procured for Mr. Razumov a reputation of profundity" (5–6). This observation, revealing in itself of a capacity for insight the language teacher renounces, points further. By categorizing his subject as a particular kind of listener, he acknowledges that the Russian's nature is by no means entirely alien, peculiar, or unfamiliar. He repeats the contradictory performance when, speaking of the solace he assumes Razumov must have found in the writing and ultimate exposure of his journal, he offers what he labels an "inscrutable" motive he immediately parses. The ostensibly impenetrable motive, which he elucidates, more than situating Razumov's behavior in a familiar class, universalizes it. The Russian, it seems, was after "what all men are really after . . . some form or perhaps only some formula of peace" (5). Pursuing what all men do, Russians, it seems, are neither incomprehensible nor exceptional—poor instantiations, in short, of impenetrability.[14] No sooner does he offer this explanation than he retreats into his shell of professed ignorance: "What sort of peace Kirylo Sidorovitch Razumov expected to find in the writing up of his record," he shrugs, "it passeth my understanding to guess" (5). He knows very well, of course—the antiquated language suggests a tongue half in cheek—and will later unflinchingly reveal it.

A writer given to universal generalizations about human nature, which he applies routinely to members of a national cohort, can hardly lay persuasive claim to "no comprehension" of these luminously inscrutable people. But the knots multiply and pull tighter, resisting, I believe, even the Polish sailor's capacity to untie them, if indeed he wished to. For one thing the narrator's claim that "words ... are the great foes of reality" (3) teeters—if *reality* is a synonym for *truth* here— on the brink of antinomy. Unless this statement marks a rare exception to the rule it adduces, since it uses words, inevitably, to argue their uselessness, it is true only if, by being true, it proves itself false. But if this is too clever (or obtuse), there are other, perhaps less avoidable turns in this labyrinth of retractive affirmation. Early on the narrator self- and truth-effacingly acknowledges that his profession as a teacher of languages is "fatal to whatever share of imagination, observation, and insight an ordinary person may be heir to" (3). For to such a man the world is but a sea of words, man a mere talking animal like a parrot. It is not long after, however, that, exchanging the impossibility for the more manageable "difficulty" of his task, he proclaims the writer's struggle and obligation—his own in this instance—is to seek the "key-word" that, "if not truth itself, may perchance hold truth enough to help the moral discovery which should be the object of every tale" (67). The blind and helpless teacher of languages, it seems, only recently an ornithologist at large in a chattering jungle, has been resurrected as a probing, half-tormented Marlow grappling with a resistant truth he is determined to approach, if never to discover. And as with Marlow, his enterprise is eroded as severely by the language it is couched in as by the dangers of menacing exposure. The keyword in this tale, he informs us proudly, the one that holds truth enough to constitute a moral revelation, is *cynicism,* a word that, by definition, minimally implies if it does not entail the disbelief in either reliable truth or dependable moral conviction.

Where are Conrad and his novel in all this, inviting us to witness events through a lens as prismatic, shifting, and opaque as this one? How much clarity or understanding can we expect or derive from a fiction seen through the eyes—*Western* scarcely begins to describe them—of a narrator who, ostensibly devoid of imagination and expression and dead by profession to observation and insight, admits to utter incomprehension of a subject he will render, unavoidably, in a medium hostile to reality. A narrator, moreover, who, renouncing the will or capacity to invent even a transition, editorializes, condenses, and elaborately supplements the journal he is ostensibly bound to; and who, proclaiming utter bewilderment in the face of his subject, addles the reader with a flurry of alternately foolish and enviably trenchant insights.

Conrad offers, through this dubious instrument, glimmers of illumination that fade to a more viscous darkness. On one of the not infrequent occasions when the allegedly giftless teacher acquires his creator's tongue, eye, and oft-repeated convictions, this sprinkler of intermittent falsehoods asks for the reader's understanding that falsehood is never really false. Rooted in the necessities of existence, in our secret fears, self-mistrust, and half-formed ambitions, our love of hope and dread of all that is uncertain (33–34), it is an expression more of mortal frailty than willful dishonesty. Toward the other end of his narrative, he returns to this familiar Conradian conviction with a crucial twist. He pleads now for a comparable tolerance grounded in a recognition not only of these ambitions, hopes, and fears but also of our "many passions and our miserable ingenuity in error" (305). With this, falsehood is rationalized not only as the forgivable consequence of uncontrollable emotions, but also as a product of artfully self-serving misdirection. In Russia, the teacher remarks, with his familiarly comprehending incomprehension, "many brave minds have turned away" from the futility of endless conflict to the land and "to autocracy for the peace of their patriotic conscience ... [and the] blessing of spiritual rest" (34). Since this observation is appended as illustration to his reflection on the origins of falsehood in the necessities of existence, it may be read, I think, as a politicized expression of his own protective habit of avoidance: his own somewhat less heroic turning away from threatening unreason and desire, his own turning, for the peace of his conscience and the blessing of spiritual rest, to the safety of professed ignorance and the ordering autocratic aloofness of Western reason as he adapts it.

Everything is done here to win latitude for Razumov's train of falsehoods and mortal errors. But in their comprehensive reach, they apply, inevitably and reflexively, to the supplicant. As a lonely, repressed, and timid man subject to many fears and apprehensions, intensified in the threatening environment of Russian irrationality, the anxious alien has a vested interest in rationalization, self-deception, and denial. The inclination is most conspicuous in his unexamined commitment to Western reason and detachment and the tenderly protective denial of his transparent desire for Natalie Haldin. But where else might this "miserable ingenuity for error" exhibit itself? In his expressed attitudes not only toward Victor and Natalie Haldin but also toward Razumov, Russian aristocracy, and the revolution that would destroy it and, he claims, inevitably reassume its clothing? In the demonstrably unsupportable denials of the gifts of imagination and expression? In his dubious claim to categorical incomprehension? In his similarly deceptive renunciation of an editorializing inclination and the analytic capability he frequently exercises? Most radically and inclusively in his ostensibly unaltered rendering of the text of Razumov's diary—"I would not try (were I able) to invent anything.... I would not even invent a transition" (100)—in which case, as in Poe's tale of a different tell-tale heart, everything is thrown into chaotic question?

To narrow the inquiry, is the narrator's unpersuasive denial of any understanding of or affinity with Russian character an expression of artfully defensive ignorance and dissociation, or is it the unavoidable product of a habit of self-deception he is neither aware of nor able to control? And in which of these, if either, does he parrot his creator? Where, in other words, does Conrad stand in relation to this narrator, his narration, and the text of this novel? Is he ironically judgmental of the teacher's fitfully real and pretended ignorance, or, afflicted by the same "miserable ingenuity in error" he shares with all mere mortal men and the same need to deny the Russian sediment in his own nature, does he share it? In a 1924 letter previously cited, after denying any knowledge of the Russian language, literature, or the culture's formative influence on his own distinctly Western development and character, Conrad surprisingly acknowledges the possibility of self-deception in this refusal. "This is the truth as far as I know," he confesses. "Men have but very little self knowledge, and authors especially are victims of many illusions about themselves. I put before you my claim to Westernism for no other reason but because I feel myself profoundly in accord with it."[15]

However these questions are answered, if indeed they are answerable, it seems undeniable that the interposition of the language teacher between the writer and his tale immeasurably complicates comprehension of the novel and any effort to interpret it. As Albert Guerard understates it, the narrator "creates unnecessary obstacles by raising the question of authority."[16] That the story is also layered, deepened, and enriched by his insertion, bringing Guerard's "unnecessary" into question, does not simplify the task. *Under Western Eyes* is by no means utterly meaningless. A plethora of insights, attitudes, and observations—political, moral, and psychological—squeeze or flicker through the chain-mail curtain drawn across the novel by this inhospitable host. They emerge, however, largely with the aid of our indulgence, our saving refusal to consider the ultimate consequences of the narrator's potentially limitless unreliability—or, if we do consider these implications, the reluctance to allow them to muddle our understanding altogether. I will not press this point, only the softer, more palatable, and less assailable claim that Conrad's decision to add this narrator to his original story of Razumov performs, in a far more sweeping and inclusive manner, the function of Marlow's obscuring mystifications, evasions, and retreats in *Heart of Darkness* and *Lord Jim*. The strobe-light quality of flashing recognition and retraction of those novels is replaced here by a pervasive dimming, if not the utter darkening, of the hall.

The insistent question—and it is one critics continue to debate—is why Conrad chose to place this particular story of Russian autocracy and revolution, passion, crime, and guilt under just these vastly more than merely Western eyes. In his author's note to the novel, written nine years after its first publication in 1911, Conrad offered his own partial and somewhat artfully dodgy explanation. The English teacher, he wrote, was a useful agent of actuality and credibility. Eyewitness to the events in Geneva and a sympathetic friend to Natalie Haldin, he would validate her experience (ix). Although he does not connect it directly to his employment of the narrator, Conrad implies a far more persuasive explanation in this note when he speaks of his effort to achieve a necessary "detachment from all passions, prejudices, and even from personal memories" (viii). What Conrad coolly justifies as a quest for detachment many readers have perceived, in Penn Szittya's terms, as a form of "authorial retreat: from direct involvement with the hero [Razumov] and his suffering; from revealing too much of himself in his story; from taking a clear position in judgment or in sympathy toward his hero."[17] Jeffrey Berman is more explicit about what he thinks the writer behind the mask of this narrator is retreating from: the "agonies of self-conflict" Conrad painfully acknowledges in *A Personal Record*, the lifelong guilt he suffered over what he regarded as his abandonment of his Polish homeland, his "unforgivable betrayal of family, country, and religion."[18] Presumably sane, stable, and protectively detached, the English teacher reduced the looming threat of overidentification with the tortured, self-destructive, and too mirroringly familiar author of the betrayer's diary. A still personal, if more politically inflected, explanation is inferable from recent discussions of what has come to be known as the "Russian issue" in Conrad studies: Conrad's declared loathing for Russia and everything associated with it, his repeated, language-teacherish denials of any connection with or formative knowledge of that detested nation and its people, and the affinity, familiarity, and passion that belied those too vigorous denials.[19]

Conrad's notoriously tormented struggle with a number of his novels were less often the product of relentless Flaubertian quests for *le mot juste*, the right form or the appropriate voice or style, than anguished engagements with the rats and roaches swarming in his personal and historical basement. Conrad was candid about what he regarded as the inevitably autobiographical nature of his profession. "I know that a novelist lives in his work," he wrote in *A Personal Record*. "He stands there, the only reality in an invented world, among imaginary things, happenings, and people. Writing about them, he is only writing about himself." Betraying his characteristic urge toward retraction and concealment, he adds that the disclosure is never complete. The writer of this dangerously revealing fiction "remains to a certain extent, a figure behind the veil; a suspected rather than a seen presence—a movement and a voice behind the draperies of fiction" (xiii). Given his lacerated psyche and tortured relationship with his past, Conrad's writing was most difficult—often to the point of breakdown or beyond—when the draperies of fiction were too thin or frayed, the movement behind them too conspicuous, the voice too resonant and familiar. The problem he faced in this encounter was that in its earlier form as the short story "Razumov" there was virtually no veil or drapery at all. And while even with the interposition of the narrator, *Under Western Eyes* remained, as many have called it, the most autobiographical of all his fictions, he required this screen if the protracted effort were to be possible at all.

What aspect of his autobiography required the most protective shielding is suggested in his author's note to the novel. The need, he wrote, for "impartiality" and "absolute fairness"—his euphemism for the distance and detachment he later acknowledged—was imposed on him "historically and hereditarily, by the peculiar experience of race and family," by the need to separate himself from "personal memories" (viii). The most unnerving dangers, this suggests, reside in memories linked to race, family, heredity, and personal history. They are, therefore, historical in the broadest sense—not confined to the personal guilt of abandonment and betrayal summoned by Razumov's betrayal of Victor Haldin and his tortured effort to conceal the crime, but vivid and menacing in the pervasive confrontation with the Russia and Russianness he despised, denied all connection with, but could not escape or successfully disown: in short with the entire subject of the novel.

In a number of letters written over the years and to a variety of correspondents, Conrad claimed, like the English teacher, to know "practically nothing of Russia or its people." He denied repeatedly that he knew the Russian language, even its alphabet, or, having read only a few novels in translation, that he knew Russian literature or was in any way influenced by it, particularly by Fyodor Dostoyevsky, whose writing he analogized to "fierce mouthings from prehistoric ages" and claimed not at all to understand.[20] As Lewitter, speaking for many, remarks, these denials are "an obvious affectation of ignorance in the teeth of abundant evidence to the contrary, internal and external."[21] A reading of Conrad's essay "Autocracy and War," together with the flagrantly Dostoyevskian plot of *Under Western Eyes*, is enough to dispel most of these disclaimers. But they are important as testimony. They reveal, narrowly, the compelling power of his need to distance himself from the intimidating subject of his novel, to avoid at almost any cost a bonding identification with his Russian subject and all it embodied. More broadly these denials are personal manifestations of the literary practice of defensive avoidance or escape I have been arguing throughout: the drive in his fictions, at times unwitting or subconscious, at times willful and contrived, to evade or obscure whatever crouching knowledge or self-awareness threatened his fragile sense of self-possession and of self.

One prominent source of revulsion and recoil was political. Conrad harbored, first, a lasting detestation for Russia's political tradition—the ferocity, imbecility, and moral anarchism of its autocratic rule, on the one hand, and the equally imbecilic and atrocious response it provokes in the form of violent and destructive revolution on the other. "The oppressors and oppressed are all Russians together," he concluded in his author's note (x), a prima facie condemnation of the harshest kind, since Russians, as he wrote elsewhere, "are born rotten."[22] Geographically Russia was the cruel predator that had carved, swallowed, and devoured Poland like a slaughtered lamb. And still closer to home, as close as one can come, in fact, he held it culpably responsible for the persecution of his dissident parents, the jailing of his father, their joint exile under debilitating conditions, and the early death of both when Josef was still a child. As Edward Crankshaw dramatically described it, "Russia had killed first his mother, then his father—to say nothing of other relatives and family friends. How can one imagine that the sense of Russia as a source of evil was not burnt into him?"[23]

But to Conrad there was something more menacing about Russia, Russians, and the Russian subject of his novel than their politics, even their murderous abuse of his nation and family. I am speaking of its embodiment in his mind of all the primitive, passionate, nightmare elements of his own tormented nature that he sought to keep at bay. It rings out in the "fierce mouthings from prehistoric ages" he claimed to hear in the writer he so unpersuasively disowned. And psychological critics and literary historians, as one of their own remarks, "increasingly have become aware of Conrad's intense unconscious identification with the hated Russian novelist, and his use of denial as a defense against the repressed Dostoyevskian elements of his own self."[24] They are unquestionably right about the origins of Conrad's need to distance himself from Dostoyevsky, but there is another point to be made here: namely that the same internal conflict dictated the inclusion of a detached and distant narrator with whom the writer is both identified and critically or ironically at odds. What Conrad, with predictably partial success, sought to tame, distance, and in large measure deny through the adoption of his rational, repressed, and dubiously uncomprehending Western narrator are the alien and familiar, alluring and endangering dark forces of destabilizing passion, internal and external that threaten the self-possession upon which personal honor, integrity, and moral behavior depend. "I never knew Russian," Conrad wrote to George Keating in 1922. "Their mentality and their emotionalism have been always repugnant to me, hereditarily and individually."[25] In "Autocracy and War" Conrad describes Russia as an "ill-omened creation ... a fantasy of a madman's brain ... a figure out of a nightmare ... held by an evil spell, suffering from an awful visitation" (*NLL* 91, 98). The projective implications of this passage seem to me strident. Whose bad omen? Whose fantasy nightmare and awful visitation? And in that same essay, Conrad fleshlessly fleshes out the horrid fantasy in terms he frequently applied to the gaping menace of intemperate passion, whether as wilderness or woman, urban chaos or the treacherous sea. "She is not an empty void," he writes, gendering his subject and sounding for all the world like the Marlow of *Chance*; "she is a yawning chasm open between East and West; a bottomless abyss that has swallowed up every hope of mercy, every aspiration towards personal dignity ... every redeeming whisper of conscience" (100). He draws her still closer to these ungovernable human and natural forces when he speaks of Russia as "a nation so difficult to understand," a creature whose "arbitrary will" gives rise to "her impenetrability to whatever is true in Western thought. . . . Hence the contradictions, the riddles of her national life, which are looked upon with such curiosity by the rest of the world" (98). It is the novel's preoccupation with this image and conception of Russia that demanded the insertion of the protectively naive and detached narrator and drove him and the narrative into incomprehension, contradiction, and retreat. As the language teacher is timidly cerebral, ruminative, and self-restrained in his vulnerable commitment to reason, order, egoistic detachment, and control, revolutionary Russia is irrational, volatile, and capricious. Antithetical to his values and threatening to his composure, it is therefore, in the economy of Conrad's fictions, inscrutable. "I have no comprehension of the Russian character," concedes the teacher. "The illogicality of their attitude, the arbitrariness of their conclusions, the frequency of the exceptional" elude his understanding (4).

Like the archetypal female in many of Conrad's fictions, the revolution and its activists are typically naive, impractical, and utopian, unable, like women as Marlow defines them in *Heart of Darkness*, to stare directly into the blank or sinister face of a reality that would decompose their fantasies. They share with Natalie Haldin the "lofty ignorance of the baser instincts of mankind" (*UWE* 142) that enables its blind journey. Like woman to her captivated suitor and like the sea and wilderness to the questing but overwhelmed adventurer in Conrad's romantic narratives, the revolution offers "indefinite promises" it crushingly disappoints or betrays. To the autocracy of male governance and rule—psychological and political—it represents the danger of passion, "intoxication," and "hysteria," of disruption, a "horrible discord," and the violent betrayal of indefinite promises. It is in these terms that Councillor Mikunin and the early Razumov describe it (*UWE* 294, 21). Clearly speaking for Conrad and echoing the cry of a dozen betrayed protagonists in his narratives, the narrator, with uncharacteristic vigor, argues that the victims of the revolution are "the victims of disgust, of disenchantment—often of remorse. Hopes grotesquely betrayed, ideals caricatured—that is the definition of revolutionary success." As in the destructive upheaval of personal romance, "there have been in every revolution hearts broken by such successes" (134–35).[26]

As the ruling autocracy is a cruel and minatory form of the rage for order of threatened male self-possession, the revolution that threatens to disrupt it is identifiably sensual, passionate, and indulgent. Indeed as one may read *Heart of Darkness* as an interior and psychological voyage as well as a geographical journey to and within the Congo, one may read this aspect of *Under Western Eyes* as an internal struggle between forces of defensive (the narrator) and tyrannical (the autocracy) control, on the one hand, and those of rebellious and libidinal disruption (the revolutionaries) on the other. And this in turn has ramifications for the struggle between the impulsive drive toward revelation and the constraining need for concealment.[27]

Conrad's anxious engagement with the subject of *Under Western Eyes* and his consequent need for an intervening narrator of the teacher's remote and uncomprehending stripe arise, then, from the poisonous mixture in this tureen, the especially potent merger of these toxically compatible ingredients. Conrad recoils from a complex of reified threats—the abyss, the yawning chasm, the devouring maw, the enveloping darkness, the passionate, the irrational or chaotic, the sensual and intoxicating—all that repels as it draws one on, all that envelops and devours. And he locates them in several menacing sources: the savage wilderness or jungle, the void or darkness, the beckoning and betraying sea, Russia, and the seductive woman. And all, to add a further complication, are both cause and embodiment, externalized manifestations of a turbulent inner nature they call to and threaten to exhume. Which, if any, is primary in any given venture is less important than the recognition that in the face of these threats Conrad's narratives step back—sometimes gingerly, sometimes hastily or in near panic. And if they do not actively dodge, obfuscate, or turn away, their road to these inviting terrors is clouded over or obstructed by a variety of defenses of varying thickness and efficacy. The result, typically, is a derationalizing of the text, a conversion of the narrative into a hermeneutic replication of the very void, darkness, or abyss it recoils from.

Russia, thought Conrad, leaves all opposition "impotent." And the word or its synonym, as one reader observes, appears frequently in Conrad's writings, "usually in the context of Russian partitioning or severing of the Polish body politic."[28] It appears no less frequently, I would add, as a description of the pathetic male protagonist in his surrender to the lure of the dangerous woman or the helpless adventurer in the grip of forces beyond his meager capacity for control. As rendered these forces are external and palpable. But they are reification as well as causes, hypostatized projections of the debilitating susceptibility to passion that threatens self-possession.

The narrator's scramble for refuge to an ostensible opacity, complexity, or enigma in his personal contacts with Natalie Haldin,[29] is the large writ small. The separate techniques of evasion summoned fitfully to ward off a dangerous attraction perform in their localized application the same function as, more thickly and pervasively, the imposed presence of the narrator performs for the writer. They are defensive interventions between the self and a threat that, like Conrad's denied but undeniable Russianness, was also a vulnerable and rejected aspect of the self. The Russian squeezed into a dark corner of the insistently Western and assiduously Westernized Pole is the ethnogeographic equivalent of the libidinal self that, thinly buried, resonates to the siren call of its human and natural cognates beyond its porously armored skin.

What Conrad fears and recoils from in Russia and the Russian character is what Marlow fears in the "wild and passionate uproar" in which he recognizes his kinship and, more broadly, what a number of male protagonists in these fictions fear in the alluring sensuous female: their resonant emotionalism and their passion, their too-familiar arbitrariness and irrationality, the threat of engulfment and possession (the undoing of self-possession) they embody.

Put another way, the dread of unraveled self-possession Conrad's male protagonists share with their creator is a psychological manifestation of his nationalistic fear of geographical and political dominance and possession. The danger to both is the defeat or overthrow of a "local regime": of a Westernized Poland identified with reason, stability, and restraint, in one of its manifestations, of the internal order and principled control of masculine self-possession in the other. What tumultuous Russia was to Poland, Conrad's insistent Polishness and his adopted Englishness, the seductive wilderness, woman, and the traitorous sea are to heroic self- composure. The threat is particularly menacing, the defensive need extreme because the caged figure resonates with a reluctant but unmistakable sympathy to the danger from without.

On the narrow road away from a shattering confrontation with the passionate internal demon, there are two dividing paths that ultimately converge. One, as in *Heart of Darkness* and *Lord Jim*, is the imposition of a haze, a fog, or darkness spread and thickened by a scattering of calculated or disingenuous evasions, denials, and professions of blindness by a narrator ostensibly in relentless pursuit of knowledge. The result is the famously indeterminate text, the epistemological void, chasm, or abyss that is the narrative replication of the engulfing female body. The other route, adopted in *Under Western Eyes*, is the sluice-gate interposition of a narrator who, in his hostile detachment from his subject, does not wish to see and who, in his general if not categorical obtuseness, presumably could not if he wished to. The result in this novel is a style Conrad argumentatively praised for its unmistakable "virility," but which, in its defensive male detachment and remove, brushes nervously against a protective refusal of awareness reminiscent of the scorned, unthinking masses of the sepulchral city. Conrad, as many have remarked, often seems to take a mockingly ironic distance from his own distanced and distancing narrator in this novel. Since it is often extremely difficult to tell precisely when he does so and to what degree, the problems of interpretation only deepen. That he does so at all, however, as surely he does, marks the trace of another wave in the sea of authorial ambivalence. Conrad intermittently mocks his own indispensable defenses—more profoundly, I believe, the very need for safety, avoidance, and illusion he readily acknowledges but no less demonstrably disdains.

Overwhelmed by the protracted immersion, Conrad suffered his severest emotional breakdown upon the completion of *Under Western Eyes*. In her biography of her husband, Jessie Conrad described what Conrad later referred to as a "horrible nightmare" and what was clearly a long psychotic episode. After threatening to burn his only copy of the manuscript, he fell into a delirium and "lay with his eyes closed and his arms folded, repeating snatches of orders in an Eastern language." With the manuscript on a table at the foot of his bed, she wrote in a desperate letter to a friend, "he lives mixed up in the scenes and holds converse with the characters."[30] In both Razumov and the insufficiently protective teacher of languages, in his buried Russian history and his denied Russian shadow, Conrad had poured too much of himself into *Under Western Eyes*. In the last of the novel's leakages, its scenes and characters were taking their revenge.

5

DROWNING IN THE ROMANCE OF THE SHALLOWS

The Rescue

Before Conrad learned the squid's art of obscuring his escape by darkening the waters of his inventions, on one protracted occasion at least he all but fled the waters altogether—and that for twenty years. In his author's note to the 1920 edition of *The Rescue*, he wrote, with a sigh of understandable relief, that "of the three long novels of mine which suffered an interruption, 'The Rescue' was the one that had to wait the longest for the good pleasure of the Fates" (vii). Actually it was not the good pleasure of the Fates completion had to wait for but the subsidence of a protracted and paralyzing inability to see it through. Exactly when Conrad set the book aside, how much he had written to that point, and when he once again hefted the burden on his back are questions that hover in something of the haze that shimmers through many of the writer's tales. Conrad claimed to have put it aside in the summer of 1898 and picked it up again twenty years later, in 1918. Frederick Karl and Daniel Schwarz believe he abandoned what was then "The Rescuer" in 1899; Karl thought that at the time he was somewhere near the beginning of part 4, Schwarz nearer the middle. And while Owen Knowles and Gene M. Moore argue for cessation in 1898, they place the stopping point somewhere around the third and fourth chapters of part 4.[1]

Because of the difficulty dating the final sections of "The Rescuer" manuscript, it is unclear exactly where in his writing and at what time Conrad abandoned it. But the crucial question and the one that has busied professional readers almost since the novel's long-delayed completion in 1920 is why this, of all Conrad's novels, endured the most tormented history—why, more particularly, he stopped writing the novel when and where he did (if these can be fixed, even approximately), why he agonized so painfully and despairingly over his inability to go on with it; and why, despite repeatedly declared intentions and several brief failed efforts, he proved unable to reassume the burden for nearly twenty years. Conrad himself blamed what he called his failure to find "the proper formula of expression, the only formula that would suit" (R viii). The real problem, he claimed, insisting on explanations in terms of style and language, "was, in reality, the doubt of my prose, the doubt of its adequacy, of its power to master both the colours and the shades" (ix). Of all Conrad's compulsive obfuscations, this is surely among the most disingenuous and least convincing. Conrad's own expressions of profound dread and loathing testify that something much deeper and more powerful was driving him away. In February 1898 he complained to his friend Edward Garnett of "the slough of despond that damned and muddy romance" had tossed him in. A month later, in a letter to the same correspondent, he declared, "I hate the thing with such great hatred that I don't want to look at it again" (CL 2:32, 47). And a few months after that: "I am paralyzed by doubt and have just sense enough to feel the agony but am powerless to invent a way out of it.... I had bad moments with The Outcast, but never anything so ghastly or hopeless. I feel I have forgotten how to think—worse, how to write"[2]

Clearly more than a failure of the proper formula of expression or a prose adequate to master the colors and shades of this none too vividly colored or subtly shaded novel is at issue here, and few students of the novel's tormented history have believed him. Alternative explanations are numerous and varied. Thomas Moser and Bernard Meyer ascribe Conrad's anguished paralysis to problems with love and sex—Moser to the writer's characterological difficulty with this "uncongenial" subject, and Meyer to a more localized symptom: his anxiety at the expanded sexual demands of his recent marriage.[3] Peter J. Glassman attributes Conrad's failure more broadly to a severe and consuming depression, an inability to write grounded in a wider defeat in his struggle with life itself.[4] Responding somewhat credulously to Conrad's claims that he could not touch or get hold of his story's fluid and evading shape and could not see its images, Katherine Baxter and Robert Caserio adopt a symptom for its cause when they attribute Conrad's writing off of his novel to his difficulty "seeing his own narrative," a failure, in Caserio's terms, "of veracious representation."[5]

The problem with speculations that ascribe Conrad's struggle with *The Rescue* to the recalcitrance of a given subject or to his mood or situation at the time of writing is that between 1899, when he apparently abandoned the novel, and 1918, when he probably picked it up again and at last completed it, Conrad was able to write virtually everything else he was to write: *The Nigger of the "Narcissus"* almost immediately after giving up on *The Rescue*, *Heart of Darkness* and *Lord Jim* within the next two years, and virtually all of his prodigious and impressive corpus after that. More disturbing still to some of these interpretations, as John Gordan's documented history of the novel's tortured progress testifies, is that Conrad's anguished wrestling with it persisted to the last day of its writing. He complained to Curle in 1918 of his failed and feeble efforts to complete it. He worked arduously on the serial version before publishing it in book form, understatedly confessed to Garnett in 1919 "the vague uneasiness I always felt from the first while writing the Rescue," admitted as late as January 1920 that he could not "even tackle the text of the Resc. My mental state is awful," and, beset with its difficulties, abandoned the labor for several more weeks. "Slaving at it," as he wrote, "all the morning and often in the afternoon" to meet the promised deadline, he kept his promise but was overcome by the strain and finished the revision in bed.[6]

What all this seems quite undeniably to suggest is that Conrad's problems with *The Rescue* were owed not to style, prose, marriage problems, veracious perception, or an acute depression but to something—perhaps, as I argue, many things—in the novel itself, quite specific elements or resonances of subject and content. On at least one occasion, Conrad, in a more than usually candid moment, acknowledged as much. "It is strange," he wrote of his failed effort to complete the manuscript. "The unreality of it seems to enter one's real life, penetrate into the bones, make the very heart beats pulsate illusions through the arteries" (*CL* 2:205). Since Conrad's declared unrealities are often the monstrous realities he protectively turned from or obscured, when he speaks, as he does, of the fluid and evading shape of the novel that prevents his "get[ting] hold of it," one may wonder if it is not something writhing and repulsive he would rather not take hold of. And aware of his penchant for dimming perception of what is too dark or terrible to behold, one may read his claim that "in the matter of R. [*The Rescue*] I ... can't see *images*" (*CL* 2:66) as we read many of Marlow's protests of a blinding obscurity of vision: as a saving preference not to see. For Conrad the inability to see or touch is typically a manifestation of the preference for a protective haze or distance, the inability to express—"I had lost the proper formula for expression"—a defense against the anxiety of engraving description or definition. A failure of veracity, in short, is the paw print of something voracious underneath, the ineffable a screen for the abominable.

There is, then, in and about *The Rescue*, something that intimidates its author, induces in him, to put it in terms nearer his own laments, a state of morbid anxiety that drives him from it. Soon after, particularly in *Heart of Darkness* and *Lord Jim*, Conrad developed a strategy for dealing with material of this kind—the incorporation of techniques of evasion, obscurity, and obfuscation into the fictions that darken, bewilder, and, by withholding, incomparably enrich them. Whether Conrad would have agreed or not, this, I believe, is "the proper formula, the only formula that would suit," the one that eluded him and that might have rescued *The Rescue*. Perhaps because he had not yet discovered the formula, more likely because even when he had developed and all but perfected it, aspects of the novel remained too menacingly aggressive to subdue, Conrad's only recourse was to abandon the project as Lingard abandons his brig. And therein, as I hope to show, lies the tale that labored so long to become one.

That whatever dogged every approach to *The Rescue* and plagued every contact with it lay within the novel and the writer's deeply problematic relation to it has not gone unnoticed. And those who have remarked on it have quite uniformly located the problem in Conrad's immobilizing overidentification with King Tom Lingard, the novel's protagonist and compulsive rescuer manqué. For Erdinast-Vulcan, Conrad, like Lingard, was engaged in a doomed struggle to sustain the mythical mode of perception. Like Lingard, with whom, as artist, he is fatefully entangled, he struggled ineffectually to resist the downward slide into romance and, cognizant of his inability to resist it, abandoned the struggle.[7] For Daniel Schwarz, Conrad, similarly overidentified with a protagonist projectively identified as an artist and as an incarnation of his own earlier, less perplexed, and more autonomous existence, replicated Lingard's debilitating slide into listless inaction.[8] And in a particularly insightful study of Conrad's vexed relationship with *The Rescue*, Royal Roussel, linking the author with Lingard's absorption of Edith Travers's annihilating vision of the infinite and eternal darkness, locates Conrad's abandonment in that damaging association. "*The Rescue* was such a threat to Conrad," Roussel concludes, "precisely because it required him to identify himself with Lingard and, therefore, undergo Lingard's experience of the darkness."[9] More intimidating, I would say, because the identification with Lingard entails a paralyzing incorporation of Edith Travers, forms part of the complex that makes of her, in fact, his feminine doppelgänger.

Conrad's variegated identification with Captain Lingard offers promising answers to the question of the writer's singularly perplexed involvement with *The Rescue*. But the nearly suicidal despair that accompanied his failure and the unconscionable length of time required for the novel's resurrection suggest an especially profound and dangerous bonding, a kind of Siamese joining at the heart. "It's all faded," Conrad wrote to Garnett about his struggle as early as 1896, "my very being seems faded and thin like the ghost of a blonde and sentimental woman, haunting romantic ruins pervaded by rats" (*CL* 1:289). The rats in this crumbling house, I believe, gnaw more deeply and more damagingly than we have seen. And they are aided in their erosive work by the woman who haunts so many of Conrad's fictions and accounts for the obfuscating haze or darkness that invades them—in this instance for the writer's mortified flight from its walls.

Like Marlow, Kurtz, and Jim, Lingard is indeed an artist. Like Kurtz he is first introduced as "a voice," and like Lord Jim he masters his limited and primitive environment through the commanding power of his language. In short, as Schwarz remarks, he is, for a time, "a kind of Prospero figure, a magician-artist who can control the world in which he lives."[10] But it is in the confessional tale of his commitment to restore Rajah Hassim and his sister to their kingdom, told to the invitingly trustful Mrs. Travers, that his distinctly Conradian artistry is most evident, most vulnerable, and most damagingly betrayed. Everything about this tale, its telling, and its reception suggest it is, in a sense, Conrad's ur-tale, the story he dreamed of telling, was in a sense compelled to tell—at least to attempt—in nearly every tale he wrote; also that he is telling it to a listener who is in one sense his ideal audience, precursor to the riveted narrator-listener to Marlow's yarn in *Heart of Darkness* and yet, because a beautiful, trusted, and unwarily desired woman, so much more dangerous a confidante. And finally, because it "concealed nothing" from her but laid bare the workings of its teller's soul, it was the tale he most feared telling, would learn never quite to tell, and could not author here.

The story is an autobiographical narrative of the life of "King Tom" Lingard among the barbarous souls who regard him as a near deific model of heroic integrity, honesty, and reliability. More specifically it is the story of Lingard's promise, his commitment to restore to his country a banished prince who had saved his life and to whom he owed this commanding debt. As such it is of course the narrative embodiment of Conrad's highest value: the principle of uncompromising fidelity to a cause, a "fixed standard of conduct," ultimately to one's most exalted conception of oneself. Hearing him relate it, Mrs. Travers recognizes that, like the grandest (and wickedest) of Conrad's heroes, "that simple soul was possessed by the greatness of the idea" that alone redeems an enterprise. She intuits too that "there was nothing sordid in its flaming impulses," in other words that this story, "truth or fiction, presented in picturesque speech" (163) was purified of the "menace of fanaticism[,] . . . intolerance," and "arid despair" that alone of all human impulses Conrad deemed inadmissible to the house of fiction (*PR* xx, 93). As the narrative's ideal listener, Edith "looked into it through the guileless enthusiasm of the narrator" and, transportingly enthralled, "forgot where she was. . . . Suddenly, in a flash of acute discernment, she saw herself involved helplessly in that story, as one is involved in a natural cataclysm" (*R* 162–63). As she loses track of time, nakedly exposed to "the effect of his words," the story enters her life—as Conrad complained *The Rescue* had far more cataclysmically entered his—and became "a fact of her own existence." Its characters came alive for her, "belonged now to her life . . . imposed themselves upon her senses" (163), as they would to Conrad in his breakdown. Achieving Conrad's writerly ambition, set out in the preface to *The Nigger of the "Narcissus,"* which he wrote almost immediately after giving up on *The Rescue*, Lingard has made her *see*. He has made her, as surely Conrad wished to make us all, feel "intensely alive . . . in a flush of strength, with an impression of novelty as though life had been the gift of this very moment" (*R* 165). That Lingard's rescue story enters Edith's life as Conrad's comparable narrative entered, invaded, and nearly destroyed his own, points to what I take to be the seminal cause of Conrad's extraordinarily anguished struggle with this novel: the marking of Edith, the dangerous woman/truth in this novel, as Conrad's internal double, his anima, if you will, the feminine aspect, whose invitation to a debilitating passion and to the dark, nihilistic vision he labored a lifetime to rise above overwhelmed his defenses and his tale.

Like Conrad's tales and novels, Lingard's story is told under a kind of internal compulsion. He tells it "because I—because I had to." The risk in this enterprise, the mortal danger lurking in the telling, is that he has told Edith what "I have told nobody." He tells her because he instinctively trusted her, told no one else because, breaching the walls of Conrad's always endangered sanctuary of self-possession, he laid bare the workings of his soul; he "concealed nothing." "This man," the woman muses, "had presented his innermost self unclothed by any subterfuge. There were in plain sight his desires, his perplexities, affections, doubts, his violence, his folly" (162–66). He presents all this, though in his naive trust and "guileless enthusiasm" he does not consider it, to the woman soon to become the object of his helpless and debilitating passion, the purveyor of the darkness he will unresistingly absorb. The woman, too, seeing his story through his own eyes and knowing him completely, will possess him at the inevitable price of his own self-possession.[11] What this extraordinary knowledge, empathy, and inhabitance suggest—together with her sensuality and her surprising affinity for the obliterating darkness that mortified the author—is that Edith is not merely another of the many dangerously alluring women that destabilize Conrad's protagonists and the tales that contain them. As Roussel observed, there are striking parallels between the darkness that envelops and ultimately immobilizes first Mrs. Travers, then Lingard within the narrative and Conrad's pained descriptions of his own insurmountably black-walled confrontation with *The Rescue* before he first abandoned it in 1898 or 1899.[12] Edith, then, is the fictionalized projection of the instinctual, seductive, yet effete, depressive element—female in Conrad's lexicon—that attention to work and surface fact and the unswerving commitment to a saving illusion or idea that are the staples of masculine self-possession kept him from. Until they could not. What I am suggesting, in short, is that like *Heart of Darkness, The Secret Sharer, Lord Jim* in a measure, and other of Conrad's fictions, *The Rescue* is a doppelgänger tale, an interior narrative whose progress was impeded by its more ominous personal implications. Conrad was able to get on with those other tellings because neither the criminal sharer, the deserting seaman, nor the demonic Kurtz, with whom Conrad perhaps too vigorously denied affiliation, registered as loudly or unnervingly with him. More susceptible than the feminine to the control of his technique, including that of protective evasion, they did not so aggressively invade his life and overwhelm his writing, the protective job of work that kept him intact.

Lingard, then, is not simply the first in Conrad's long chain of narrator- or protagonist-artists. He is the bearer and riskily endangered barer of Conrad's essential tale of loyalty and fidelity, the ideal artist who captivates his audience with the greatness of an idea, the picturesque power of his words, and the purity of his motives. He is also the impassioned speaker who conjures his tale to vivid life and drives it directly and transformingly into the altered life of a listener who is also an extension or projection of his weaker self. In effect the heroic male and masculine self has exposed its vulnerability to the woman, out there and in here, most likely to exploit it, as inevitably she will. By concealing nothing from her, mirroring the containing narrative that reflexively reveals too much, the teller of the internal tale threatens the stability of the art that carries it, art that in later works would survive and flourish by withholding. The principal failure of concealment in *The Rescue*, it should be said, lies not in Lingard's confession, decorously filtered through the eyes of its auditor, but in the author's destabilizing overidentification with the two principal figures and too much else in a story that, as he admitted, oozed threateningly into his life.

For Conrad the artistic objective is mastery through language and idea, the danger a crushing of the spirit and the power of expression through unguarded exposure. Possessed by the listener, who, knowing completely the mind of the teller, knows too much, the carrier of the tale—Lingard within it, Conrad struggling to drive it forward—falls into a paralyzing state of lassitude. The alternatives are prophetically captured and condensed in two passages Conrad cut from "The Rescuer" when he composed his final revision around 1918. In one Lingard expects his brig to respond "without hesitation to every perverse demand of his desire." In the other the narrator describes Lingard's quite different mood as he brings his brig to anchor: "A sudden listlessness seemed to come over him. It was one of his peculiarities that whenever he had to call upon his unerring knowledge of his craft, upon his skill and readiness in matters of his calling that big body of his lost its alertness, seemed to sink as if some inward prop had been suddenly withdrawn."[13]

The complex identity of the brig as at once woman and the artist's craft is, I think, quite evident here, as it is in a number of other revealingly metaphoric descriptions of the captain's intensely bonded relation to his brig in the finished novel. References in Conrad's fiction to the seaman's "knowledge of his craft" or his skill in "matters of his calling" are frequent and unmistakable allusions to the writer's own craft and calling. And what the excised narration reveals here, as in a number of the novel's surviving descriptions, is the replacement of a sense of mastery by an enervation ascribable both to the speaker's hopeless passion for the elusive Mrs. Travers and his gradual absorption of her own sapping vision of the darkness. On the one hand, Lingard expects both woman and verbal craft to respond swiftly and obediently to the demands of his desire—as both gratifyingly do when he relates his powerful narrative to his seductively receptive auditor. In time, however, passion undermines and replaces commitment, and self-possession yields to a lapdog subservience by one who, knowing him too well, controls him. Translated into the terms in which I read this novel and believe it lends itself to be read, the stoically and committedly self-possessed male loses control of the shadow self, at once passionate and helpless, desperate and despairing, whose presence within him Conrad was always aware of, always feared, always strove precariously to hold in check. With that failure of control, the inward prop of purposive self-possession is withdrawn, mastery gives way to impotence and languor, and the brig that is this narrative cannot properly be brought to anchor.

The dual identification of Lingard's brig with both artistic craft and the indispensable woman is manifest in virtually every protracted description of the captain's sense of its nature and importance. Lingard, the reader learns early, was aware that "his little vessel" gave him something no other thing or person in the world could give him, "something specially his own." "She—the craft—had all the qualities of a living thing: speed, obedience, trustworthiness, endurance, beauty, capacity to do and to suffer—all but life. He—the man—was the inspirer of that thing. . . . His will was its will, his thought was its impulse, his breath was the breath of its existence. . . . To him she was unique and dear . . . a kingdom!" (11). Again his brig was "perfect because a wandering home; his independence, his love—and his anxiety. . . . He had often heard men say that Tom Lingard cared for nothing on earth but for his brig. . . . To him she was as full of life as the great world. . . . To him she was always precious—like old love; always desirable—like a strange woman; always tender—like a mother" (10).

Quite transparently, I believe, these heated portrayals of the brig simultaneously describe the artist's pride in his skill, his consuming devotion to his craft, and the comparable centrality and importance of the desired woman. In both of these passages, subtle condensations of the troubled progress of the narrative and its writing, the account begins with a clearer and more emphatic application to the artist's craft—his breath was the breath of its existence; she was as full of life as the great world—and shifts, gradually or suddenly, toward the woman, as Lingard will in his abandonment of the brig to his uncontrollable passion for Mrs. Travers and as Conrad, comparably susceptible to her influence, will by abandoning his enterprise.

When, about midway through part 4, Lingard acknowledges the full measure and irreversibility of his defeat, understands that his attempt to rescue Mrs. Travers and the stranded crew of her yacht has doomed his primary commitment to repay his debt to the Malay prince and princess, he juxtaposes his horror at the prospect of permanently abandoning his brig with a lament at having told his too-revealing tale to the woman whose hold has undone him. Drawn away from his brig to do battle on Mrs. Travers's behalf for the release of her husband and a friend, Lingard utters a bravura declaration that seems to signal Conrad's recognition of his own loosening hold on the story and the "craft" that enables it. "They fear the brig," he announces, "because when I am on board her, the brig and I are one. An armed man—don't you see? Without the brig I am disarmed" (226–27). This sense of disarmed, almost suicidal helplessness is precisely what Conrad reported to Garnett and others in letters written at this time; the letters cry out with "the horror of that powerlessness I must face through a day of vain efforts," the "lack of strenght [sic], of power—of an uplifting belief in oneself" (*CL* 2:49, 204). Here too the brig is an internalized objectification of Conrad's narrative vessel and the craft required to keep it afloat. Speaking for the author's lack of an uplifting belief in himself, Lingard expresses his horror that for the first time in his experience—it is also Conrad's first crippling confrontation with the loss of faith in the persuasive power of his gift—"Nobody believes me. . . . By all the stars they doubt me!" (227). And Lingard is aware of the source of both the failure of belief and the abandonment of the commitment that parallels Conrad's own commitment to the immediate task and grander project of his art. "It is as though you had brought a curse on me in your yacht," he cries out to Mrs. Travers. "Ought I to have kept it all in—told no one—no one—not even you? Are they waiting for what will never come now?" (227).

All these surprising parallels may be mere coincidence, though it seems unlikely. In this pained reflection at the beginning of the fourth chapter of part 4, we are very near the point where, I would argue for this reason, Conrad abandoned the novel. Linking the feared abandonment of his brig with the too-revealing telling of his tale, Lingard seems to recognize their connection. And now, speaking no less of the novel's imagined readership than of those within the fiction to whom he had made what he believed to be an inviolable commitment, he wonders if they are "waiting for what will never come now." Earlier on the narrator affirms what Lingard, in his blinded passion, will require more time, experience, and personal courage to confront. In a passage that reflects at once Conrad's recognition of the magnitude of his artistic gift and the disaster that would befall it, the narrator remarks: "[The sea] had made him owner and commander of the finest brig afloat; it had lulled him into a belief in himself, in his strength, in his luck—and suddenly, by its complicity in a fatal accident"—the grounding of the boat that brings the resonant Mrs. Travers into the narrative and Lingard's life—"it had brought him face to face with a difficulty that looked like the beginning of disaster" (127). There can be little question as to the cause of both disasters. It is, predictably, the dangerous woman, in this instance the woman as both the eliciter of a distracting and paralyzing passion and the hypnotic purveyor of an annihilating vision of the darkness that strips all human action of its meaning, writing no less than the fulfillment of a more conventionally heroic promise. The siren has such power, of course, because she sings to her counterpart within the listener: the chaotically instinctual, passionate, potentially hopeless, and despairing element that always threatens the self-possession it necessitates. It is this same element, emotionally indulgent, nihilistic, and despairing, that Conrad insistently warned the writer committed to the moral obligations of his craft must not surrender to (*LE* 132).

The early Lingard, the one we hear of before his catastrophic encounter with Mrs. Travers and the relation of the history that holds nothing back, is a paradigmatic Conradian hero: forceful, devoted, loyally and single-mindedly committed, and in full and purposeful possession of himself. He is a man who, as Jörgenson thinks of him, "knew nothing of the black skepticism of the grave" (*R* 117). Lingard compellingly insists that he "will let no man's play interfere with my work." "I belong where I am," he announces with deific simplicity and certitude. "I am just Tom Lingard, no more, no less, wherever I happen to be" (*R* 121). And he is a man committed—irreversibly, he believes, by debt, by promise, and by the core integrity of his personality—to the restoration of the royal couple who had rescued him. Like virtually all the male protagonists in Conrad's tales of emasculating romance, Lingard will lose all this, systematically and utterly, under the influence of his passion for the captivating woman. No sooner does he notice the telltale "abundance of pale fair hair, fine as silk, undulating like the sea . . . a throat white, smooth, palpitating with life, a round neck modelled with strength and delicacy, support[ing] gloriously that radiant face and that pale mass of hair unkissed by sunshine," than this man of unimpedible action is overcome by the stupefied paralysis his too-enmeshed author will inherit. He gazes at and listens to her with "the stupor of a new sensation" (139, 141). His speech rambles on disconnectedly, and as he stares into her violet eyes and feels his mind "overpowered and troubled," the man who previously was just Tom Lingard, no more, no less, is now, in a revealing phrase, "beside himself" (144). The process is too familiar to bear elaboration. Before long, losing the knowledge and certainty of his own mind, Lingard feels light, "powerless as a feather in a hurricane" (179), like a swimmer swept out to sea by the undertow (219). And near the end, having abandoned his commitment and sacrificed his reputation, his integrity, and his place in the world and in his own esteem, he is reduced, sitting at her feet, to the pathetic declaration that he cares for nothing in the world but her and the weary plea that she grant him the rest that is in her (418).

The decline is familiar. It is repeated in a variety of forms in a number of Conrad's later novels and tales, none of which gave him anything like the difficulty he encountered in his anguished struggle to complete *The Rescue*. What is especially poignant about Lingard's confession of exclusive dedication to Mrs. Travers is that it is a telling replication of his earlier regard for the brig, so closely identified with his art.[14] Where once he had cared "for nothing on earth but his brig," now he cares "for nothing in the world but" this woman (418). The fatally paralyzing woman, in other words, the woman engulfed in Conrad's nihilistic darkness, has assumed the place previously occupied by his (artist's) craft. And the exchange is crystallized and emphasized by repetition. Where once it had been the brig that was "always precious—like old love; always desirable," now it is she. Where previously the brig, the craft, had seemed the most perfect of its kind, that exalted place and power are now hers. And where the narrator notes a bit earlier—where, I would argue, Conrad abandoned the novel—that, saying goodbye to his beloved, Lingard felt as though he were "saying good-bye to all the world, . . . taking a last leave of his own self" (234), he assigns to the woman the identity, meaning, and importance once reserved for the brig-as-art. "The brig and I are one," Lingard had declared in more promising and productive times. His breath was the breath of its existence.

In all of these passages and many more, Conrad offered the reader an internalized account of his failing "romance" with the novel, his plaguing recognition of its imminent abandonment. Echoing language and complaints he expressed in letters to Garnett and others about his punishing battle with *The Rescue,* Conrad seems, consciously or otherwise, to have been writing of his losing struggle with his manuscript when he writes that Lingard had a sense of confusion within him and mystery without, that this affair did not seem comprehensible ("It had somehow a subtlety that affected him" [183]), and that Shaw sees "a mysterious iniquity in a dangerous relation to himself and begins to lose his head" in the affair. As Conrad desperately tried to, "he washed his hands of everything" (191). When the narrator remarks that the impenetrable darkness Lingard had to combat was "too impalpable to be cleft by a blow—too dense to be pierced by the eye" and that "the mysterious obscurity . . . descended upon his fortunes so that his eyes could no longer see the work of his hands" (*R* 202), he is describing the state of paralyzing blindness Conrad described in a number of his anguished letters about his inability to see or carry on with *The Rescue.*

As Mrs. Travers feels herself helplessly involved in Lingard's story, Conrad felt himself as helplessly if far more damagingly gathered up in Lingard's, Mrs. Travers's, and his own; and thus drawn in, he is infected by the enervation that disables him. When Lingard shouts angrily to the woman who was privy to his confessional narrative, "You heard it. And now it's gone. . . . There's nothing left to tell any more" (233), he is speaking also of the narrative that contained it and that Conrad for so many years could not tell.[15]

It is because of Mrs. Travers, as all who know him realize, that the captain has abandoned his brig; and the damaging effect the story Conrad is struggling to tell has on his ability to complete it is intensified by an identification with Mrs. Travers no less invasive and debilitating than the one entwining him with Lingard. It is more devastating, finally, because identification with the woman entails, in fact if not by definition, an identity- and gender-threatening incorporation—the woman as "enemy within"—against which he has no adequate defense.

Edith Travers's protean role as an alter ego to the artist, his muse, and an artist herself is but another of the many ways in which her nature entwines and merges with that of both Lingard and the author. As Conrad's perfect listener, who views, through the guileless enthusiasm of the author, a story that draws her so richly and utterly inside it that its characters belong to her life and impose themselves upon her senses, Travers re-authors and relives in her stirred imagination the experience of its creator. Later in the novel, in a section written after Conrad resumed its writing, D'Alcacer, the author's reflective raisonneur, identifies her as "a representative woman," one of those rare creatures for whom "artists of all sorts invoke their inspiration" (411). And for Conrad this perfect recipient of the inspiration's production must, like the sensitive and eloquent reconstructor of Marlow's tale in *Heart of Darkness,* be herself an artist. As Erdinast-Vulcan has noticed, Mrs. Travers, has, like Lingard, the capacity of "magic words" and a mastery of language to which Lingard's will eventually surrender, hanging on her words "as if it were only for the sake of the sound" (255).[16] Like Rita in *The Arrow of Gold,* as Ruth Nadelhaft remarks, Mrs. Travers represents the artist at work, for whom, as for Conrad, the line between invention and reality mysteriously blurs: The occurrences of the afternoon were strange in themselves, "but what struck her artistic sense was the vigour of their presentation. They outlined themselves before her memory. . . . They were mysterious, but she felt certain they were absolutely true" (152–53). In all her representations, as Nadelhaft rightly observes, Conrad is multiply identified with this representative woman. In all her incarnations—as artist, as marginalized figure, as artifact, and as recalcitrant and articulate lover—she is a feminized embodiment of Conrad's personal situation and history.[17] And like her creator, she "longed to know"—I would say, rather, managed to convince herself she longed to know—"the naked truth of life and passion buried under the growth of centuries" (153), where Conrad, like the ultimately reluctant and recoiling Mr. Travers, wished them to remain.

But it is principally in her experience of the eternal void and darkness, her sense that reality is "less palpable than a cloud" (247), her engulfment in "the everlasting night that fills the universe . . . like a suspicion of an evil truth" (151) that she is nearest—in a sense an internal mouthpiece for—the panicked author, who, in letters written as he struggled with this novel, spoke of his feeling that he too had lost the sense of reality. All is darkness and illusion, everything impalpable to the touch. And "in the matter of R. [*The Rescue*] . . . I can't see *images*" (*CL* 2:66). Edith Travers is not only "representative woman." She is also, and in large measure, the cause and projected embodiment of the anxious male protagonist's susceptibility to a consuming and distracting passion and, consequently, to the mindless, sentimental lethargy that unmans the purposive man of action and drains his dedication to his task. As such she acquires a double identity and role. She is, in other words, the principal threat to Conrad's cherished self-possession, the dreaded woman or female element within. Moreover, aimlessly adrift herself and stripping man of purpose and the capacity to pursue it, she becomes as well the emblem and emissary of darkness, the hollowness at the core of self and creation that drains all effort, including all creative and heroic effort as well as purpose and worth.

The dangerously alluring woman in Conrad's fictions is almost invariably such a projection. She acquires her power over the previously self-contained, determined, and forthrightly masculine hero of the tale from her all-but-demonic capacity to address and elicit the latent anima, the "womanish" sentimentality, passion, and weakness quivering under the stiffened surface. Conrad's own vulnerable duality is captured concisely in Nadelhaft's observation that while over time Conrad's female characters came to represent many of his own deeply harbored attitudes, convictions, and desires, at the conscious level he asserted his maleness, vigorously associated his artistry with his masculinity, and indignantly resented any suggestion of a feminine element in either himself or his work.[18] The mortal blow to the common enterprise of Lingard and his creator is the abandonment of the brig tightly identified with the seaman's ideal self and Conrad's artistry or craft. The maintenance of this resonant vessel and the owner's or author's devoted captaincy and steerage are essential to the fulfillment of the task and promise on which their worth and integrity depend: Lingard's fidelity to the young rajah and his sister, Conrad's to his writing. And it is because of a "representative woman" who at once stands for and threatens the precariously contained woman or female element within that the brig in both constructions is abandoned.

Conrad seems to have recognized his own identification with this woman, externalized here in the form of Edith Travers. Writing to Garnett of his anguished inability to shape a coherent narrative from the chaos of his sensations, he complained that his story had faded. His very being, he repined, seemed to him as gossamer as the ghost of a sentimental blonde woman haunting romantic, rat-infested ruins (CL, 1:289). While most of Conrad's alluring women are dark-haired—all have sensuously long and abundant tresses—Mrs. Travers is notably fair. As the fascinated response of this bourgeois dabbler to the simple and violent workings of a roving seaman, king of jungle, forest, and primitive peoples attests, she is also a sentimental woman haunting romantic ruins—most notably when she gazes delusionally into the eyes of the Malay princess and imagines she is looking into her own heart (140), more theatrically when she parades barefoot in a native costume. As a young girl, Edith was often "reproved for her romantic ideas ... she had dreams where the sincerity of a great passion appeared like the ideal fulfilment and the only truth of life" (151). That these are romantic ruins is indicated in personal terms by her more mature realization that the dreams are unattainable, politically by the novel's urged implication that the incursion of the imperious whites into the island realm has already begun to corrode and will eventually destroy its purity. These whites, of course, most saliently Mr. Travers, are the rats gnawing at these impending ruins. In a pale but chilling presage of Kurtz's mortifying document, Travers proclaims the sacred "duty to civilize" these brutes. If they perish in the process, he adds coldly, it is a step toward the perfection of society and a mark of progress (148).

The story, Conrad said, had eerily invaded his life, significantly in the reciprocal overlap and influence of the dark vision he shared with Mrs. Travers, as balefully in his paralyzing identification with the "womanish" weakness that surrenders to her. It is no surprise that, as Conrad announces in his author's note to the novel, he abandoned it not to surrender to idleness and regret but to begin *The Nigger of the "Narcissus,"* a novel "purged" entirely of female presence. Although Conrad's retroactive explanations of his motives are partial truths at best, he is on the mark, I believe, if unaware of the deeper cause, when he reports his recognition that throwing himself into the writing of the second novel was the refuge he required from this undoubted "crisis." "There only," he clearly and emphatically understood, "was the road to salvation, the clear way out for an uneasy conscience"(*R* ix). There only could he rediscover the "mastery which could accomplish something" lost in his unnerving identification with the blonde and sentimental woman. And it was there, of course, in the now famous preface to the womanless *Nigger of the "Narcissus,"* that he felt secure enough to place at the center of his aesthetic manifesto the overriding determination to "make [us] see" (*NN* x).

Lingard is more forcefully assertive and only a word or name shy of explicit recognition of the origin and location of his failure. Although he comes late to the discovery, in a scene constructed after Conrad resumed the writing of *The Rescue*, it had always been apparent. The real cause of the disaster, he reflects in a rare moment of blazing insight, lay not outside, in others, but "in himself . . . somewhere in the unexplored depths of his nature, something fatal and unavoidable." The powers he faced were "within, as though he had been betrayed by somebody, by some secret enemy," a "traitor" he shatteringly recognizes as "myself." That he "could not defend himself" (329) against this revelation locates the unintrospective Lingard, together with virtually everyone else in the novel, in the teeming company of Conrad's characters for whom knowledge, particularly self-knowledge, is a Greek gift wisely left beyond the gate. That the enemy or traitor within the defeated adventurer is the unmanned male or internal female is evident everywhere in the novel, glaring in the events and dialogue that surround and generate Lingard's pained epiphany. Having broken his word to the natives and doomed both the success of his mission and the integrity of his soul, the man of action cannot act. Acknowledging to his inamorata, moments prior to his discovery of the traitor within, that he is "nothing now. Just nothing," Lingard is drawn to what has made him so. Losing himself in the contemplation of her face, he can do nothing but stare at it "in a world which had lost its consistency, its shape and its promises in a moment" (328). There is unmistakable causal implication in this proximity. The enemy within him is the capacity for obsessive passion that has reduced his world to this countenance, his potency to the fleeting capacity to hold it in view. More alert because less needily defended against the recognition, Jörgenson identifies the problem much earlier. Seeing that Lingard has brought this woman to the scene of impending battle, he is stunned. "I thought I knew you," he blurts out. "How could you, King Tom[,] . . . leave your weapons twenty miles behind you, your men, your guns, your brig that is your strength, and come along here . . . bare-handed and with a woman in tow. . . . Hasn't King Tom a mind of his own? What has come over him? . . . Has he put himself in the hands of a strange woman?" (249, 255–56). The woman in tow is not only Mrs. Travers; it is also the unthinking, disarmed, dethroned Tom Lingard, whom Jörgenson scarcely recognizes as the man he once knew. What has come over him is what has emerged from inside him and, as for Conrad, likewise identified with the sentimental blonde woman, driven him from his strength. His mind belongs to a strange woman because, responding to her, the still stranger creature trembling with helpless desire within him has taken control. And the seeds of this transfer of power, this seepage of the dangerous woman into the core of the always-vulnerable "king," were sown early: in the telling of the tale that, concealing nothing, gave her controlling access to his mind. *The Rescue*, in this sense, plays out the consequences of an interior dramatic monologue: the heroic ideal's ill-advised confession of vulnerability to the suppressed but powerful libidinal impulses and depressive inclinations that are its most virulent enemy.

Here, then, I believe, are the complex internal equations that both describe and explain Conrad's anguished abandonment of the novel: Captain Lingard, with whom he is overidentified as at once his ideal and most vulnerably exposed artistic self, abandons the brig metaphorically identified as the artist's "craft" and the work (*The Rescue*) he is struggling to "bring to anchor." He does this under the sway of Edith Travers, the feminine aspect and double with whom the writer is similarly identified, both as ideally creative auditor and as one who shares with her creator a paralyzing vision of the infinite and eternal darkness that empties life and action of all meaning. Seeing "through" him in both senses and privy to his every thought, feeling, and desire, this penetrating reader-author, for whom the artist invokes his inspiration, controls him, undermining his capacity to fulfill his promise and commitment. Similarly as the obsessive object of those thoughts and of his uncontrollable yet futile desire, she infects him with her nihilistic vision and the attendant world-weariness that compounds his incapacity for effective action. It is with this woman "in tow," that is, with this debilitating interior enemy, that the craft's once powerful and committed but now disarmed commander/writer goes to a battle within and with this narrative, dooming both the rescue and *The Rescue* to two decades of failure.

In a passage written just before Conrad abandoned his commitment in despair, Lingard, saying goodbye to his beloved, feels as though he is taking leave "of his own self," as indeed he is. Mrs. Travers, however, will not let him leave, and to assure her continued possession of his soul, she speaks the words that name its source. "I do know him," she says. Then, "speaking slowly and with emphasis: 'There is not, I verily believe, a single thought or act of his life that I don't know'— 'It's true—it's true,' muttered Lingard to himself" (236). Like many others in Conrad's short and longer narratives, Mrs. Travers is woman-as-knower, more dangerous for knowing so much more. As Conrad's subsequently cultivated habit of protective concealment tacitly testifies, one forfeits masculine self-possession essential to effective action to possession by the fascinating, abominable, and mirroring other by revealing too much, by holding nothing back. Where everything in naive enthusiasm is revealed, everything—one's integrity, one's fidelity to his craft, one's own self—will follow. In the beginning is the word. And then the flood that drowned the early writing of *The Rescue*.

A PSYCHOANALYTIC SUPPLEMENT

While I share, to some degree, the contemporary hesitation before relatively uninflected Freudian readings of literary texts, I offer one here, as a supplement[19] to my attempt to account for the extraordinarily long and anguished journey Conrad traveled with this novel. It was extraordinary even for Conrad, whose writing was often punished and occasionally interrupted by bouts of anxiety, depression, or difficulties specific to the task. A psychoanalytic inquiry is justified, I believe, first, because exceptional circumstances are often ascribable to, if they do not demand, exceptional explanations; second, because the interiority of the narrative I have just argued for suggests a powerful psychological connection between author and text; and third because the explanatory phenomenon I am about to introduce—the "rescue fantasy" as a driving force within *The Rescue*—offers a remarkably close fit. It is, in fact, one of those rare instances when the literary text seems to validate the psychoanalytic theory at least as persuasively as the theory "understands" the text.[20]

Freud introduced his theory of the rescue fantasy in a 1910 essay cumbersomely titled "Contributions to the Psychology of Love: A Special Type of Choice of Object Made by Men." There is, I believe, compelling evidence for the presence of just such a rescue fantasy in *The Rescue*—two in fact, both doomed to failure, in part because they are in conflict with one another, their success mutually exclusive. What I am suggesting is that the novel's direct and pointed address to painful and problematic aspects of Conrad's personal history and its arousal, below the level of awareness, of powerfully charged fantasy material made the writing of this book the nearly impossible adventure it turned out to be. The difficulty may have been compounded by the novel's dramatization of the soul-crushing conflict between two such fantasies: one in the service of the masculine ideal of unflinching dedication to a heroic purpose, the other promising satisfaction to the equally potent demands of emotional and sexual desire.

The strong initial hint of the fantasy's presence, clearly, is the novel's title, changed, apparently in 1897, from "The Rescuer" to *The Rescue*. Why Conrad changed its name is not clear, though one possibility is that the early title imposed a burden of success on the novel's protagonist—perhaps its author as well—a challenge Conrad had already begun to suspect he could not meet. Explaining unconvincingly why, even after he had recovered his confidence with the writing of *The Nigger of the "Narcissus,"* he did not return to *The Rescue*, he spoke of the subsequent "irresistible claim[s]" of "Youth" and *Heart of Darkness*. "Every stroke," he wrote, "was taking me further away from the abandoned 'Rescue'"(*R* x). My contention, of course, is that Conrad was rowing for his life. But while the syntactic absorption of the title here may be nothing more than play, it may also point to another covert abandoned rescue behind the pair the plot poses in fatal opposition to one another. The rescue fantasy, as Freud and Karl Abraham described it, is the compulsive attraction of certain men to women of a given description whom they become obsessed with and desire urgently to rescue from a real or imagined state of degradation. The phenomenon is identified by several defining features. First the woman must be attached to another man—a husband, fiancé, or the like, who has primary right of possession. Second she should be sexually discredited, her fidelity or loyalty sufficiently in doubt to arouse the jealous pangs and longings the would-be rescuer requires. Third the man invests this love object with the highest value, such that his relations with her absorb his entire mental energy "to the exclusion of all other interests." And crucially, he experiences an irrepressible desire to rescue her.[21]

It should be immediately apparent from this brief summary that the relationship between Lingard and Edith Travers curls up comfortably with at least three of these criteria. Mrs. Travers is solidly if discontentedly married to a coldly contemptuous and unresponsive spouse. She is indeed a treasure of immeasurable value in the glazed eyes of her pursuer, whose exclusive obsession with her proves fatal to his earlier commitment and destroys him utterly. And he is driven, by motives inexplicable to Mrs. Travers's companions and only vaguely and flickeringly understood by Lingard himself, to rescue her and her rock-stranded yacht at any cost. All that is missing to complete the fit is the sexual discreditation of the woman, though her fidelity and loyalty to her husband, while finally reaffirmed to Lingard's agonized dismay, are called early and repeatedly into question by her fascinated and more-than-flirtatious attachment to her impassioned suitor.

Freud, in one of his own protective disclaimers, maintained that not all of these criteria need be met, that one or two may be sufficient to identify the type.

But *The Rescue* is in no need of permissive dispensation. As the title suggests it may, the novel unfolds as a powerfully confirming dramatization of the fantasy as Freud described it. For Freud the fantasy, unsurprisingly, is Oedipal. All of its features are derived from a fixation of the lover's infantile feelings of tenderness for the mother, and it is most often associated with the early loss of that parent. Conrad's beloved mother died when Joseph was only seven, and the loss may have been intensified by what Jocelyn Baines describes as his father's cultish absorption with his dead wife.[22] That Lingard rescues Mrs. Travers, her husband, and her companions from a yacht that has foundered on the rocks gives added poignancy to Freud's claim that saving dramas in dreams and fantasies "are especially clearly recognizable where they occur in some connection with water"; when a man dreams or imagines rescuing a woman from water, it means he makes her a mother, his mother.[23] As noted, Freud's analysis of the fantasy is distinctly Oedipal, and there is enough in *The Rescue*, particularly in the second of the two rescue attempts, for a comparable account of its presence in the novel. But later discussions of the phenomenon have widened its base. The explanatory focus, as Emanuel Berman observes, has shifted from the Oedipal triangle "to the earliest ties to the mother, to experiences of loss and restitution, to a reparation of damage caused by aggression, to the need to save a depressed or helpless parent, to the rescue of oneself as projected onto the other."[24] And it is on this wider foundation, I suggest, that the rescue fantasies of *The Rescue* are constructed.

One of the factors inhibiting a satisfactory resolution of the rescue fantasies in the novel is the deeply complicating if not inherently irresolvable contradiction between two types and origins of the fantasy. The first, demonstrably restorative—Conrad's father died but five years after his mother, leaving Conrad orphaned by the age of twelve—requires the restoration of the youthfully innocent (parental) couple to their rightful seat of power. The second, manifestly sexual, plots an illicit romantic relationship with the female (maternal) surrogate that marginalizes and demonizes the male. While the shallows are rife with dangerous formations, the novel, like Lingard's dual enterprise, founders, among others, on these rocks.

That Conrad construes his novel as a marvelous fantasy of some kind is established immediately by the quotation from Chaucer's Franklin's Tale Conrad selected to serve as an epigraph: "'*Alas!' quod she, / 'that ever this sholde happe! / For wende I never, by possibilitee, / that swich a monstre or / Merveille might be!*" That it will be, in addition, a rescue fantasy is suggested by the same selection, for the Franklin's Tale, like Conrad's novel, is the heroic tale of a young knight's illicit love for a married woman. The wife refuses Arveragus's love at first out of devotion to her husband but agrees to become his lover on the provision that he make the rocks of the sea—on which she fears her husband's ship will shatter—

disappear. As for Lingard, in other words, the possession of the beloved but previously attached object is conceivable, paradoxically, only if the husband/rival is rescued. Chaucer's tale ends more nobly and satisfactorily for all concerned than Conrad's tragic narrative. But the identity of the novel as a marvelous tale of illicit romance and rescue whose dream of possession will contain its own undoing is forecast in this prefatory inscription.

Conrad seeds his acknowledged fantasy with a proliferation of references to the story as "strange," "mysterious" and "incomprehensible." The story is identified as a "dream," a "fantastic" tale whose "significance [is] impossible to perceive." And it is peopled by real or ostensible kings and rajahs, "chivalric" knights, and witches who speak "magic" words and experience, in the midst of a "romantic" if ultimately tragic "adventure," divine and ecstatic visions of an illusory "Paradise."[25] That this is, more particularly, a rescue fantasy is manifest not only in the title and the entangled double plot but also in the revealing dramatis personae plucked handily from the dream of a model patient in a psychoanalytic session. One of the thwarting complications of Conrad's plot is the hero's need and commitment to rescue the rival husband as proof and testament of his devotion to the beloved woman. The Franklin's Tale provides a literary context for the motif, psychoanalytic theory a subtler cause. For Freud it is when the child learns that he owes his life to his parents that he forms a desire to repay them for this gift. He then creates a fantasy in which, risking danger, he saves his father's life, thereby erasing this debt and presumably clearing the way to the guiltless possession of the mother. This fantasy, writes Freud, is typically displaced onto a king, emperor, or any other great man, at which point it may be accepted into consciousness and exploited by poets. Or novelists. As in Conrad's fiction, the hostile attitude toward the rescued father in these fantasies is contrasted with the tenderness directed toward the mother,[26] rescued by the childlike knight from her unhappy and unfulfilling connection with the father.

The reader familiar with this novel needs little help matching figures here. "King Tom" Lingard is perfectly cast as the determined, devoted, one might say compulsive rescuer, "defenceless as a child before the shadowy impulses of his own heart." This child was "uplifted at times," the narrator relates, "by the awakened lyrism of his heart into regions" as "charming . . . and dangerous" as his guilty longing (11). And later, as the garroting complexities and implications of his adventure tighten around him, he feels within him "crime, sacrifice, tenderness, devotion, and the madness of a fixed idea" (215).

Tom is also "guilty" of every inclination and excess of the driven rescuer. Writing specifically of the dangers of its incursion into the therapeutic process but with obvious relevance to the fantasy in general, Berman names three characterizing temptations threatening the would-be rescuer. The first is a belief in his own omnipotence, the delusional conviction that one can single-handedly transform another's life from misery to happiness. Another, clearly related to the first, is self-idealization and romanticization, the rescuer's glorifying tendency to portray himself as a benevolent, pure-hearted knight, thereby occluding awareness of both his limitations and his more egoistic motives. The third is the tendency to demonize a guilty party—the woman's husband or parents, perhaps—a simplistic splitting of good and evil that may blind the would-be savior to the complexity of his undertaking and its unforeseen consequences, principally the danger of being drawn unconsciously into the psychic patterns and disturbances of the person to be saved.[27]

It requires no strain to demonstrate that these childlike and romantic habits of mind characterize the novel's protagonist in his doomed determination to meet the conflicting obligations of his commitments. Lingard's unqualified belief in his omnipotence, his unique, almost preternatural power to save, conquer, and restore, is notable for both the strength of its rooted conviction and the hubristic bravado with which it is proclaimed. Urged on by "the proud conviction that of all the men in the world, in his world, he alone had the means and the pluck 'to lift up the big end' of such an adventure," Lingard assures the reenergized Hassim and Immada of the inevitable fulfillment of his promise to bring them home (106). And no man convinced of his possession of such resurrective power is likely to balk at the seemingly simpler challenge of rescuing the crew of a yacht stranded in hostile territory. "I am a white man inside and out," he announces thumpingly to the yacht's captain; "I won't let inoffensive people—and a woman, too—come to harm if I can help it. And if I can't help, nobody can. You understand—nobody!" (39).

Where such pride prances, self-idealization and romanticization cannot be far behind, and Lingard is a quixotic knight from an only slightly less palatial neighborhood of La Mancha. The narrator speaks admiringly of the "romantic side" of his nature, his "chivalrous character," and the stirring "heart of [this] . . . true adventurer" (74, 80). And Lingard unfailingly confirms his assessment. Throwing himself body and soul into the great enterprise of restoring the young rajah and his sister, Lingard revels in the "long intoxication" of preparing its success, allows no thought of failure to cross his mind, and regards no price too high to pay "for such a magnificent achievement . . . nothing less than bringing Hassim triumphantly back to that country seen once at night under the low clouds and in the incessant tumult of thunder" (106).[28]

Demonization, especially in the Oedipal version of the fantasy, is the third identifying scar on the enterprising dreamer. And while we have already mentioned the contemptuously aloof, heartless, and rejecting Travers, it is worth noting again the unmistakably Kurtzian snarl of this man "whose life and thought, ignorant of human passion, were devoted to extracting the greatest possible amount of personal advantage from human institutions" (123). Unlike Kurtz, who begins with a dream of civilizing the savages and only later, transformed by exposure, temptation, and a hollowness at the core, recommends their extermination, the comparably demonic if less potently menacing Travers recognizes early and with satisfaction that civilizing them might well be tantamount to their evolutionarily desirable eradication.

The danger latent in the rescuer's prideful idealization of himself, his romantic idealization of the object of his illicit passion, and the simplistic division of good and evil is a menacing failure to recognize his own unavoidable human limitations and egoistic motives. Self-blinded, the would-be rescuer is also unlikely to anticipate dangers inherent in his project, chief among them the corrupting incorporation of the idealized object's unrecognized disturbances and defects. Self-inflatingly assured of his capacity to effect the rescue of Mrs. Travers and her entourage without cost to his prior commitment to Hassim and Immada and driven to attempt it by a helplessly impassioned desire he recognizes too late, Lingard, though superficially successful in the preservation of all their lives, pays with his reputation as a man of honor and his sense of his own integrity and worth—in short, and as he experiences it, his soul. Like Conrad, unable to complete his own artistic and psychological attempt at restitution, restoration, and romantic conquest, Lingard fatally ingests his beloved's blackening and debilitating awareness of the encompassing and obliterating dark.

Lingard, the fixated child-hero in this fantastic adventure, is torn between two parental couples: Hassim and Immada in the noble drama of restoration and Mr. and Mrs. Travers in the more sordid tragedy of Oedipal hunger and replacement. The flawlessly innocent (presexual) pair are the deposed Rajah Hassim and his sister, Immada. It is to their rescue, their restoration to their usurped place at the head of their nation, that Lingard first pledges himself in insistent payment of his unforgettable "debt" to Hassim. They are the first set of symbolic parents in this conflictual drama: Hassim as the rajah and "a person of authority" who has "perfect knowledge" of Lingard's mind; Immada by her royal heritage, perhaps also by the audial implications of her name, resonant with the Hebrew *ima*, the Arabic *yamma*, and with the informal *ma* or *mama* in English and innumerable other tongues. But when Lingard happens on the fateful yacht stranded on the rocks, a second rescue effort supersedes the first and dictates its abandonment. Confused by his own motives—partly the romantically compulsive need to rescue whoever is in need, partly his as-yet-unacknowledged attraction to Mrs. Travers—Lingard swerves from his initial obligation and devotes himself totally, obsessively, and with a fatal forgetfulness to the eager rescue of the at once sexual and angelic Mrs. Travers, her husband, and their companions on the foundered yacht. A second pair of parental objects, likewise savable only by a dangerous rescue effort, replaces the first, and here the substitutive identities are more transparently insistent and distinct.

That Edith Travers is an idealized mother in this tainted struggle to rescue a woman in both marital and watery distress is evident in her "perfection," which "seemed [to Lingard] to have come into the world complete, mature, and without any hesitation or weakness" (304). Also in his experience of her as both a "vision" of "unconscious ecstasy" (214) and a "priceless and disputed possession" (235) the exclusive possession of whom, despite her oft-affirmed attachment to her husband, consumes him (335). Her maternal role in this fantasy is complicated but deepened by the Madonna-whore portrait that paints her at once as a radiant and haloed saint or angel and a seductively sensuous woman, "undulating" and "palpitating" with vivid, sexual life (139). And it is confirmed—characteristically in this fantasy—by her entrapment in the cold, loveless, and unsatisfying relationship from which the aspirant would save her at any cost, substituting his own virile passion for his rival's effete and bloodless remove.

The counterpart to the longed-for mother in the Oedipal version of the rescue fantasy is the stern, hostile, and negatively perceived, sometimes demonized father. Travers, as already noted, is a candidate measured neatly to the role. His eyes, a chill and naive blue, bespeak a rigid, self-preoccupied, and icily controlled nature devoid of human decency and feeling (337). As he impressed his wife's imagination by his "impenetrability" (152), he faces Lingard with an air of congenital invulnerability (127). And like the threatened Oedipal father sensing danger from below, he identifies Lingard as the kind of man "I would be least disposed to trust" and denounces him, without apparent cause, as a "violent scoundrel" (138, 145). Small wonder he is such an unsatisfactory partner for the ripely frustrated Mrs. Travers, whose life with him is devoid of "sincerity[,] . . . true passion[, or] . . . a single true emotion" (152).

Lingard's rescue efforts are multiply perplexed and, like the novel, impossible to bring to anchor. Since, like Dorigen in Chaucer's tale, Mrs. Travers demands that Lingard rescue her husband from captivity and seems, despite her glaring discontent and craving, determined to remain with him, Lingard's hopes of possessing his rescued beauty are doomed almost from the outset. But there is more, and worse. For viewed as rescue fantasies, Lingard's two primary commitments are in direct conflict with one another—in the obvious sense that, falling helplessly in love with Edith Travers, he finds himself forgetting and ultimately abandoning his prior commitment to Hassim and Immada; but also, and more covertly, because the two fantasies posit contradictory psychological dramas. In the first his effort, pure and noble in intent and apparently unsullied by more selfish motives, is to restore a royal pair to their rightful place of leadership. The second rescue, on the other hand, itself internally and fatefully inconsistent, is a more conspicuously Oedipal drama, whose purpose is the eroticized possession of the idealized mother to the exclusion of the rejecting and detested father. The unconscious, of course, can sustain contradictory fantasies. But here, it seems, Conrad's commitments as a novelist came into irresolvable conflict with his half-hidden regressive wishes. His craft-based recognition of the need to choose, I would suggest, was among the principal causes of the novel's stalled, tormented history. The choice is especially freighted because, as I have argued, it is between the two elemental warring elements of Conrad's character: the heroic ideal marked by masculine self-possession and devotion to a cause and the passionate, libidinal, feminine principle of uncontrollable desire. And it is all but irresolvable because Conrad seems to know early on what he is able to accept and put in writing when, a considerably older man, he resumes the novel: namely that with a tragic inevitability born of his fatal weakness, the vulnerably yearning and dependent "woman" within him, Lingard will sacrifice the nobler for the needy, sordid, and ultimately more hopeless enterprise. There are many such conflicts and posed choices in Conrad's narratives between the heroic commitment and the seductive woman. What distinguishes *The Rescue* from other dramatizations of the struggle is what emerges overtly and repeatedly in the closing pages of the novel. Lingard has not merely surrendered to the dangerous woman, emblem and eliciter of uncontrolled emotion; he has become her.

The thwarting complexities do not end here. For even were the sacrifice made on behalf of an achievable cause, the successful possession of the incomparable Mrs. Travers, the achievement would unravel with the skein of the quite unmistakable association of Lingard's brig with yet another idealized mother, to whom he is bonded, from whom he derives his strength, and to whose preservation he is hardly less passionately committed. As I have indicated, almost all the earlier cited descriptions of Lingard's precious brig point toward this covert maternal spirit of the craft. The brig was his "wandering home . . . his love—and his anxiety. . . . To him she was always precious—like old love" (10). "Unique and dear . . . —a kingdom!" she had, moreover, "all the qualities of a living thing: . . . trustworthiness, endurance, beauty, capacity to do and to suffer"—all, like Conrad's dear, long-suffering, and long-deceased mother, "all but life" (11). And again: "Lingard's love for his brig was a man's love, and was so great that it could never be appeased unless he called on her to put forth all her qualities and her power, to repay his exacting affection by a faithfulness tried to the very utmost limit of endurance" (54). Clearly this is the sort of limitless emotional exchange one organizes primally with a mother, the kind and degree of faithfulness one expects or demands only from the woman who bears and nurtures us.

We are accustomed, in Conrad, to hyperbolic paeans to the sea and the ships that sail it, but little or nothing quite like this. Both in the romantic intensity of their heated rhetoric and in the pointed particulars of their language, they suggest that more is afloat here than a mere water-going vessel. Part of this rapturous intensity and import is ascribable to the ship's metaphoric association with the art and artistry to which the writer was so consumingly and sacrificially devoted—as much, I believe, to its suggested linkage to the beloved lost mother he would, through that writing, somehow rescue and restore, over and over in romanticized tales of attempted, if almost invariably thwarted, rescue. When Lingard abandons his brig to rescue Travers in the name of his desperate love for the miscreant's wife, echoing his author, he is not only abandoning his art for the haunting sentimental blonde woman within him and without. In the attempt to rescue one incarnation of the idealized mother, he is unavoidably turning away from another: the lost and priceless mother whose spirit haunted the mast and hull and every polished plank of that magnificent but always storm-tossed craft.

My point in all this is dual: First, the vivid and intricately elaborated presence of a scarcely hidden rescue fantasy—laden with unnerving resonances, memories, and significances Conrad could hardly have been sufficiently aware of to control—accounts in no small measure for the exceptionally long and tortured history of his enterprise. Second, the difficulty was compounded by the incompatibility of two rival but almost equally powerful rescue fantasies: one serving the heroic ideal of loyalty, commitment, and sacrifice, the other rewarding the equally potent but contrary drive toward sensual, romantic, and emotional satisfaction. Twenty years had to pass for Conrad to complete this journey successfully. Only when these memories of the lost mother had dimmed; when he had achieved sufficient detachment from Lingard as a vulnerably confessional artist, insistent lover, and absorptive victim of the woman's paralyzing vision of the darkness; and when he had gained a safer distance from the dreaded enemy within, the sentimental woman haunting the romantic ruins of his childhood and early experience—only then could he rescue a novel that even at the end reached up from the watery depths of his unstable psyche and threatened to pull him down. How poignantly ironic his subtitling this novel "A Romance of the Shallows."

EPILOGUE

The movement through the last four chapters of this study has been in a sense (and to a degree chronologically) progressive. The Marlow tales, *Heart of Darkness* and *Lord Jim*, are governed by a narrator ostensibly committed to the pursuit of knowledge and understanding but palpably intimidated by the anticipated consequences of their acquisition and at least as strongly committed to their avoidance. The phrase "the fascination of the abomination" captures well the conflicted psychological impulse that directs his hesitant and fitful quests—more ostensible than determined—and it is clear from both the persistence of the occlusions at crucial moments and Marlow's acknowledged preference for an escape from thought and threatening knowledge that the fascination will at almost every turn give way. It yields repeatedly to a defensive preference for illusion and the preservation of the well-being that accompanies a willingly adopted ignorance.

In both novels Marlow steps back from an edge beyond which some destabilizing truth of self or other lies, and he is not alone. Both landscapes teem with figures engaged in similar, if less ambivalent, projects of avoidance, some willfully and admittedly, some by the example of their practiced incuriosity or bunkering devices of distraction. Jim, Stein, Brierly, Chester, and the French lieutenant in *Lord Jim* fall principally into the former category; the accountant, the manager, the brick maker, the Intended, "women" as a collective or species, and the citizens of the "sepulchral city" in *Heart of Darkness* into the latter. Although he began *Lord Jim* before *Heart of Darkness*, he set the novel aside and returned to it only after he had finished the novella. The emphasis, in other words, shifts with the progression: from ingrained but unarticulated and undefended habits of avoidance in the earlier narrative, often overtly or implicitly condemned as cowardly or hollow, to explicit commendations of denial or flight in the later one, often acknowledged as wisely and essentially self-protective. Both tales, then, are rife with evidence, often the persuasive counseling, of avoidance. But in both, the narrator's pursuit of understanding is, if considerably more avoidant than determined, to a degree ambivalent, and there is nothing in the structure of either narrative that inherently precludes discovery.

In *Under Western Eyes*, published twelve years after *Heart of Darkness* and eleven years after *Lord Jim*, there is, and it was imposed on the novel years after it was first conceived, almost certainly as a consciously adopted instrument of occlusion. I am speaking, of course, of the narrator of *Under Western Eyes*, the language teacher who denies the communicative efficacy of language, proudly acknowledges that he understands little or nothing of the detested Russian character and culture that constitute the subject of his self-defeating inquiry, and contradicts himself so conspicuously and often as to cast irresolvable doubt on the elemental reliability of his narrative. Flights from painful (self-)revelation and recommendations of evasion, denial, and concealment riddle this novel, as they do *Heart of Darkness* and *Lord Jim*, but they pale as instruments of obfuscation and avoidance beside the looming darkness of the language teacher's baffled, contradictory, and finally incoherent narration.

The Rescue, begun before any of the three other novels studied here at length but given up midway and finished long after the last of them, marks a further intensification of this cross-textual drama of evasion, denial, and retreat. Or rather, under the pressure of a radically intensified urgency, it signals a progression from narrative evasion and denial to physical abandonment and escape. Conrad, who suffered often from doubts about his projects and abilities, experienced considerable difficulty with several of his novels but nothing comparable to the twenty-year history of repeatedly failed and confessedly tortured efforts to cope with, return to, or complete *The Rescue*. The reasons for Conrad's extraordinary and anguished difficulty with *The Rescue* are no doubt overdetermined, but if anything is nearly certain, it is that Conrad's own explanations—his failure to find "the proper formula of expression, the only formula that would suit," or the failure of his prose "to master both the colours and the shades" of this adventure—are woefully unpersuasive. In partial agreement with others, I believe the principal cause is to be found in the writer's many-faceted and threatening overidentification with both of the novel's principal figures: the storytelling male "hero" and the seductively attentive woman who, summoning the helplessly desirous female element within him and infecting him with her nihilistic vision of despair, destroys at once the heroic mission he has undertaken, the reliability of the word on which his worth and reputation depend, and his heroic sense of self.

Here as elsewhere, the source of avoidance lies in one or more of the many manifestations of the female—literal and figurative, biological and psychological, out there and within. But the source, which varies from work to work, is less important than the identification of the need for avoidance as the source of flight. In this regard the anguished twenty-year history of Conrad's struggle with

Epilogue

The Rescue is the small writ broad and carved deep. It is the enactment across a twenty-year expanse of the dynamic repeatedly manifest within the given tales and novels: the ambivalent approach to and anxiously protective retreat from something that can neither be successfully turned away from nor stared down.

What we witness in elusive tale after tale is not, principally, the frustrating retreat of clarity or knowledge relentlessly sought after and pursued but the nervous, often conviction-backed refusal to risk that last—at times even the first—endangering step toward full discovery. We see not truth or knowledge slipping elusively away or seductively beckoning as it disappears behind a curtain but the drawing down of that curtain by the very hand that seems to lift it. And this should not surprise us. For while Conrad vacillated confusingly on the question of the existence of something we might properly identify as truth or, if it does exist, the possibility of its acquisition or conveyance, he was uncharacteristically consistent about at least two things: the virtual equivalence of evil and (when he did declare it) truth; and, as consequence, a driving preference for the avoidance of threatening (self-)knowledge. This avoidance may be variously come by. If one is lucky, he may be the beneficiary of an inherent and distinctly blessed ignorance. More often, however, it must be worked for, either in the dedication to work or action that distracts and refocuses one's attention or, when even that fails, in the willful preference for mystery, uncertainty, or a saving illusion. All are protective alternatives to the sustained reflection that brings some fearful revelation roaring from its cave or, more dangerously still to one's sustaining self-possession, steaming upward from within.

APPENDIX

Woman and Truth,
the History of an Association

The association of woman with truth so prevalent in Conrad's fictions is ancient, multiply grounded, and deeply rooted.[1] It owes much to the primitive association between woman and earth or matter, or between woman and nature, which, in the post-Renaissance world, was the penetrable repository of knowledge and truth. As Carolyn Merchant, speaking for many, observes, women and nature "have an age-old association—an affiliation that has persisted throughout culture, language, and history."[2] In both Western and non-Western cultures, in ancient and early modern times, Nature, contrasted with art and the artificially created, was personified as a female being. Variously perceived as a prudent lady, an empress, and Dame Nature, as virgin, bride, witch, whore, and mother, her identity was essentially dual. She was the beneficent, cornucopic, and nurturing mother whose bounty provided generously for nature's inhabitants. But as expressed in earthquakes, flood, storms, and droughts, she was also the menacing embodiment of violence and chaos. In either form, however, nature was insistently woman,[3] the assumptive truths and realities of one entangled with those of the other.

The Greek notion of truth as *aletheia* makes of truth that which is hidden, buried, out of reach, drawn up, often by force or struggle from the forgotten (*Lethe*).[4] In Greek and other pagan mythologies, the journey toward truth, knowledge, or self-discovery is typically inward and downward. Returning from his journey through the underworld, Odysseus says: "I will recount all the a-letheia, all the truth."[5] Hades itself (*Aides*), du Bois speculates, may be an alpha-privative form from the verb of seeing and knowing, *idein*. Odysseus's journey, like that of other mythological heroes, is, as Campbell observes, "fundamentally . . . inward—into depths where obscure resistances are overcome, and long lost, forgotten powers are revivified, to be made available for the transfiguration of the world."[6] And that descent into the earth's interior marks the return of the hero to the mother's body. The earth, after all, is traditionally a goddess, nature the maternal guardian of the living and the dead. And it was through the body of the priestess of Pythian Apollo at Delphi that divine truth was transmitted. Odysseus's journey—across the "stream of the Ocean," through "a thickly wooded shore, and the groves of Persephone," into "the moldering home of Hades"—is fraught with imagery of the return to the woman's body, as, by resonant association, many such journeys are.

Traditionally the invisible world of earth that lies beneath the surface, in the space of burial, was associated with the mother, with the woman's body. As a vessel, a container, a body filled with an interiority itself full of potential for holding, for entreasuring or warming, the woman's body was seen as analogous to the earth, with its caves, crevasses, openings into an invisible world from which the living emerged, into which the dead departed.[7]

Descent into this interior female world was fraught with danger and prohibition. Where nature is identified with the body of the mother, its violation, most vividly and ravishingly effected in the practice of mining, is haunted by fear, inhibition, and restriction. As Merchant remarks, normative constraints against the mining of Mother Earth were commonplace among aboriginal populations and in the ancient and early modern world.[8] The Columbian Indian Smohall wrote: "You ask me to plow the ground! Shall I take a knife and tear my mother's breast? ... You ask me to dig for a stone. Shall I dig under her skin for her bones?"[9] Pliny's response was less poetic and more directly concerned with consequences than with the moral affront that provoked them. He warned against mining the depths of Mother Earth and suggested that earthquakes were an expression of her rage at this violation. "It is what is concealed from our view," he wrote in his *Natural History*, "what is sunk far beneath her surface, objects, in fact, of no rapid formation, that urge us to our ruin, that send us to the very depths of hell."[10] Spenser's treatment of this "great Grandmother" in *The Faerie Queen* equates digging into the "quiet wombe" of earth for hidden metals with man's lustful invasion of the female flesh for pleasure. And latent in all these penetrations of nature's female body for secret treasures is the analogy with the quest for truth that surfaces with Francis Bacon. While Bacon would of course legitimate this penetration, his insistence on a chaste relationship between the scientific mind and the female body of nature whose veil it draws back shows him mindful of the fears and inhibitions that threaten the enterprise. As the tale of Pandora makes painfully evident, the release of the secrets of the female body is a seductive invitation to disaster. The retreat from truth is driven by forces more primitive than the detachment of language from the world, and its footprints lead down many roads.

Recoil from a woman-centered truth seems to have played a substantial role in the substitution of masculine reason for oracular mystery as the ultimate repository of truth in the ancient world. The dark oracular truths of earth and nature associated with the cults of the earth goddesses and the body of woman were gradually deposed by the forces of reason embodied in the triumphant male gods. With the marginalization of these cults, divine and mysterious truth was pejoratively redefined as mere illusion or deception. In his *Iphigenia in Tauris* (ca. 413 B.C.E.), Euripides dramatized this victory of reason over the earlier mysteries of the chthonic interior. When the infant Apollo kills the python that guards the oracle, he shatters the power of the earth goddess in the name of lucidity and reason. The goddess seeks to avenge her defeat by clouding the minds of her male adversaries with a "dark dream truth," but her dream oracles are dispelled by Zeus, who replaces her rule at Delphi with the masculine forces of reason.

Greek philosophical thought marks the partly defensive institutionalization of this new order. In the history of Greek philosophy from Pythagoras through Aristotle and beyond, reason and the feminine are antithetical and exclusive. In the Pythagorean table of opposites, as Genevieve Lloyd points out, "femaleness was explicitly linked with the unbounded—the vague and indeterminate," maleness with the precise and clearly determined, with the reason that had become synonymous with the truth it now monopolized.[11] The undefined and formless once associated with the dark dream truths of the earth goddess retained their connection with the feminine but were forcefully disengaged from the claim to truth. Maleness was identified with definable form, the female with indeterminate matter, and since form was now the exclusive domain of truth and reason, all that was knowable to the mind was quite literally of man, and the feminine was relegated to a cognitive location beyond the pale of truth.

Such relegation, however, was no mere neutral repositioning. To be outside the boundaries of reason, order, and determinacy is to be linked with the dark and turbulent forces of the irrational that threatened man's control over the external world and, more important, over his own instinctual forces, likewise identified as feminine. Friedrich Nietzsche's vaunted woman-as-absence or untruth, later elaborated by Jacques Derrida and the French feminists,[12] is entwined with the image of woman as monstrous truth of the interior, projected outward in the innumerable mythic images of the female siren, witch, or monster. Woman as the absence of truth, then, as indeterminate and unknowable, is portentously tied through the chaos and turbulence of the irrational with woman's other identity as the rampant, often monstrous truth of instinct and the unconscious; tied as tightly, through her identity with perishable matter, to suffering, decay, and death. When, in a movement that begins with Aristotle and culminates in Bacon, woman-as-matter is readmitted as an object of knowledge, new (or old) defenses are required to neutralize or disarm her. In Baconian science the distance between subject and object widens, the relationship is defined as analytic and objective, the goal a form of dominance and conquest.[13] In art, where such distance and conquering detachment are unavailable or damaging to the enterprise, other more indigenous and appropriate defenses are invoked. When reality or suspected truth threatens to assume this disfigured, feminized form in Conrad's fictions, her classical association with mystery, obscurity, and indeterminacy, exhumed by Nietzsche, is protectively summoned (or trails after), and glimpsed truth enshrouds itself in delphic mist.

The reinstatement of woman as a locus of truth begins with Aristotle, who de-etherealizes the forms and binds them and their incumbent knowability to the material world of things. Matter that had once to be transcended in the search for truth was, in Aristotle, a principal constituent, and genderization of the relation, which again culminates in Bacon, became inevitable. "From ancient to modern times," as Londa Schiebinger points out, "nature—the object of scientific study—has been conceived as female."[14] Because philosophy and science are all but exclusively male pursuits, nature and the matter they explore identified with woman, the pursuit of knowledge becomes an expression of male courtship, pursuit, and attempted conquest of the female. The tradition becomes graphically entrenched in seventeenth- and eighteenth-century frontispiece engravings of science as a woman, more pertinently in the all-but-ubiquitous depiction of the probing scientist as male, the object of his inquiries, truth and nature, as a female figure[15]—often veiled. The male, a near synonym for the intellect, studied the female "body" of knowledge that nature contained and science organized.

The transition toward matter as the proper object of inquiry and knowledge culminates in the work of Bacon, where, as Lloyd observes, "the gap between form and matter is completely closed. The split between knowable forms and unknowable matter is repudiated; and with it the model of knowledge as contemplation of forms."[16] Bacon's descriptions of the scientific enterprise are rife with sexual metaphors. Attuned to the dangers of nature/woman's carnality and sex, Bacon insists on a chastely sanctified marriage between mind and nature. In an early work called "The Masculine Birth of Time," the narrator announces himself as one who has "come in very truth, leading to you Nature with all her children to bind her to your service and make her your slave."[17] One may make various uses of such slaves, but Bacon is unequivocal, if somewhat coy. "My dear, dear boy," he writes as if chiding, "what I propose is to unite you with *things themselves* in a chaste, holy and legal wedlock"[18]

The metaphorizing habit was by no means exclusive to Bacon, and other writers were more candid about the erotic nature of the pursuit of truth and knowledge. René Descartes, who dedicated his *Principles of Philosophy* to Princess Elizabeth of Bohemia, identified her as the representation of knowledge itself, the living incarnation of wisdom who, as the object of the philosopher's analysis and study, was also the object of his desire.[19] Thomas Vaughan spoke suggestively of the scientist's need to penetrate "the innermost core of Nature."[20] Abraham Cowley wrote in his ode in praise of the Royal Society of the male philosopher's probing into the "privatest recess" of a conspicuously feminized nature.[21] And John Locke, speaking of "Truth" in his *Essay Concerning Human Understanding*, praised Pembroke's "intimate Acquaintance with her, in her more retired recesses."[22]

Metaphorized associations of woman as nature's truth awaiting the male scientist's "penetration" and discovery are commonplace in the prose and poetry of the period, and Brian Easlea, arguing for the continuity between alchemy and science, remarks that both shared the same phallic dream: "to expose, pierce, penetrate—and thereby to dominate Nature."[23] Walker likewise notes that Locke's use of the sexualized terms "Acquaintance" for sexual acquaintance and "recess" for womb "suggests that it is an erotic engagement which is invoked by Locke to define the intellectual advancement of Pembroke and the aim of philosophy in general."[24] The sexualized female identity of nature as an object of scientific exploration is reified in a nineteenth-century statue in the Paris medical faculty. Typical of many, it is named *Nature Unveiling before Science* and shows nature as a beautiful woman with exposed breasts. Unveiling, as Ludmilla Jordanova remarks, "has specially female connotations, not just because of the eroticism of the female body, but because of the female personification of both Nature and Truth."[25] What is perhaps most significant about the iconography of this and similar statues is that "it is only the head and upper part of the body that are to be revealed, not the lower part, the unveiling of which can be deemed profoundly threatening."[26] In this persistently erotic character of woman/nature as the object of man's search for knowledge lies one of the principal dangers of his pursuit. Where truth and nature are the erotic and often forbidden objects of male probing, where knowledge is carnal knowledge of the woman's body and the product of phallic penetration, the sexual threat is imminent and knowledge acquires the features of a menace that, like Medusa, must not be gazed upon directly.

The relationship between the cognitive and a fatal form of carnal knowledge is an essential feature of man's Fall. We are often baffled by the pernicious consequences of knowledge in the Genesis narrative, but it may be at least partially explained by the hypothesis that the sycamore fig, probably the Tree of Knowledge, was an important symbol at the shrines of the goddess Astorath. These trees, argues Merlin Stone, represented the knowledge of life and the creative power of the goddess. According to Egyptian texts, to eat ceremonially of the fruit of this tree was to eat of the flesh and fluid of the goddess of sexual pleasure and reproduction.[27] Contravening the common ascription of phallic import to the serpent, Stone, following the archeologist Stephen Langdon, argues that the serpent was originally the emblem of a female divinity associated with wisdom and prophetic counsel—another link between woman and truth.[28] In Christianity the reptilian symbol of woman's truth inevitably lost its identity as wisdom and became associated with seduction, carnality, and evil in its most heinous aspect.[29]

But the threat of woman as the truth of nature's body is by no means sexual alone. Simone de Beauvoir vividly and articulately binds aging, decay, and death to the body of woman. The link is present in the identification of woman with the dark recesses of the earth's interior, for while it is there that seeds take root and grow, it is also there that the dead are buried and begin the grotesque process of decay. As it is the mother who cradles the dead or dying infant so recently taken from her womb, it is the earth that reaccepts the dead. As the serpent of evil is latent in the serpent of wisdom, death squats patiently in the transient specter of life. And this, writes Beauvoir, is woman's first lie, her first treason. Life itself, "though clothed in the most attractive forms, is always infested by the ferments of age and death.... It takes only the passage of time to alter her charm—infirm, homely, old, woman is horrifying." While old men are comparably repulsive, "normally, man does not experience older men as flesh; he has only an abstract unity with these separate and strange bodies. It is upon woman's body—this body which is destined for him—that man really encounters deterioration of the flesh."[30]

In the dichotomy the Judeo-Christian tradition shares with the Greek, woman is assigned the realm of flesh and body, man the loftier realm of spirit. The cave of Plato's allegory, which is also the darkened cave of woman's body, is the seat of a false and inferior material knowledge mind and spirit must transcend. Locus of the transitory and impermanent, the realm of matter/woman is the home of all that is deceptive and all that vilely degenerates and dies. Eve, constructed of a part of Adam's body, brings death as well as lust into the world. And the offspring of John Milton's hound-hipped Sin is Death. Knowledge of woman, in other words, is knowledge of the material, hence mortal, world. It is in the very nature of matter to decay, and since, as Wolfgang Lederer points out, mother is mater, which in turn is matter and materiel, unlike the eternal (masculine) spirit, she is perishable.[31] One may trace the dread of woman's body, as many do, to the primitive fear of menstrual blood and menstruation as a form of defilement[32] or, as others do, to fear of the vagina.[33] But the source matters less than the tradition it has begotten: the identification of woman's body not only with a terrifying sexuality but also with mortality, decay, and death. As in Conrad, to "know" woman-as-truth is to know her carnally and to risk the dangers of castration and defilement. But it is also to know the perhaps still more paralyzing truth of the mortal coil that reduces the pursuit of all other knowledge to an absurd indulgence.

The opposite of woman-as-death is, of course, woman as maternal source of life. But it is in the nature of woman, as a male-dominated tradition has defined her, to watch her ostensible virtues metamorphose into objects of dread. That death is inherent in all life is one expression of this duality. But the image of mother as life-giving woman and primary nurturer likewise contains the seeds of its own rejection. It is as difficult as inadvisable to seek a single cause for the traditional association between woman and truth, though the mother's role as the child's first and principal object of knowledge and experience is a viable candidate. The mother, who begins as an undifferentiated extension of the child's unified —Freud called it "oceanic"—sense of self and world, is gradually distinguished.

She becomes, in effect, the first and, typically for years, the primary object of the child's awareness. As the source of food and warmth, and as what Winnicott calls the "mirror" of the child's moods and feelings, whose obligation it is to reflect the child's gaze and accompanying emotions back to itself, she is the principal object of attention; it is knowledge of the mother, as the first introjected object, that in largest measure determines the child's sense of self and self-regard.[34] She is also that from which the infant, later the child, must separate in order to achieve first a sense of the self's own boundaries, then, in approximately the second year, what Erik Erikson called autonomy and Margaret Mahler identified as separation and individuation. At both these stages, often for a lifetime, the relationship is plagued by ambivalence. The lure of fusion and amniotic sleep is balanced by the terror of the loss of self, the drowning of personal identity in regressive reunion.

"The earliest roots of antagonism to women," Dorothy Dinnerstein argues, "lie in the period before the infant has any clear idea where the self ends and the outside world begins."[35] The mother is the threatening embodiment of the smothering engulfment against which the child must define itself. The very achievement of self-definition, Winnicott argues, is dependent on the mother's disappointing of the child and on the child's aggression against the source of that enraging frustration.[36] The mother provides warmth, love, food, nurture, comfort, body contact—everything the child cherishes and depends upon. But in this capacity the mother, hence later femaleness in general, is defined into a position that inevitably invites fear, hostility, or both. Unavoidably the mother disappoints the child, fails at times to provide the instantaneous satisfaction the demanding child requires. Such frustration is essential to the development of the child's recognition of the "not me" who fails to provide, hence to the definition of the "me" who remains, in its newfound isolation, unsatisfied. But what is essential for development is hardly salutary for the introjection of the maternal object in the child's mind. For the inevitable by-product of maternal disappointment is infantile rage and the gathering perception of the primary internalized female object as the mother of privation. Where the dominant perception of the mother remains that of the inexhaustible supplier and the undifferentiated extension of the pre-fallen self, the incompletely differentiated child, later the adult, vacillates anxiously between powerful attraction toward the engulfing womb or body and dread of obliteration within it. What little sense of self or autonomous ego has been developed remains precariously fearful of reabsorption within the corpus of the earliest object of all knowledge.[37]

It is this fear of obliteration in the woman's body that colors numerous descriptions of the dangers of excessive learning and knowledge. John Chrysostom, for example, warned against the dangers of engulfment in a seductive sea of spiritual knowledge, indicating that divine-learning-as-Sophia is beset by the repressed terror of maternal absorption. Folklore is replete with lurid tales of men driven mad by excessive study or an overabundance of knowledge. And the seduction of this goddess, writes Lederer in *The Fear of Women,* "can lead to insanity, to loss of self and dissolution, as in a deep water, as in a dark and bottomless lake."[38]

In nearly all of woman's traditional identities, her association with truth is a virtual prescription for its avoidance. It is her identity as the object of the child's desire for merger and of his dread of its obliterating consequence that leads Evelyn Fox Keller to her psychological reading of the scientific insistence on distanced objectivity and its quest for mastery. "It has seemed to me," writes Fox Keller, "that central aspects of this problem belong to the psychological domain, and further, that this is the domain least accounted for in most discussions of scientific thought."[39] "Science," she suggests, "has been influenced by its unconscious mythology,"[40] in this instance by the scientist's fear of the return to primary narcissistic identity with the mother who, like dangerous knowledge, both lures and terrifies. For Fox Keller the uniform insistence on the objectivist perspective is not an inevitable entailment of the scientific enterprise. At least in part, she argues, the obsessive securing of distance and the demand for absolute mastery reflect the prober's fear of the obliterating lure of the woman-as-nature he is obliged to pierce and penetrate, to marry and embrace.

Whether or not one accepts this provocative hypothesis, certain aspects of the problem of man's relationship with truth are illuminated by this perspective; writers as well as scientists are influenced by unconscious mythologies. Where truth is a woman in any of her guises, when, in fact, truth, in whatever form, inspires fear or apprehension, it is likely to invoke defense. For Fox Keller the danger is the inviting mother of regressive fusion, the fear a loss of identity, the response a retreat to objectivity and the quest for dominance. For Conrad the fear and danger are awesomely compounded, the response a saving mystification and confusion that, in its obliteration of boundaries, effects a simultaneous return to the object it obscures.

NOTES

Prologue

1. Mencken, *Book of Prefaces*, 11, 16.

2. Forster, "Joseph Conrad," 134–35. Thinking mainly of *Heart of Darkness*, F. R. Leavis agreed. He found the novel hazy and evasive, particularly where it strives for profundity or horror. Conrad, he claimed, used words such as *inexpressible, inconceivable, unspeakable,* and *incomprehensible* to magnify a "thrilled sense of the unspeakable potentialities of the human soul." But the actual effect, concluded Leavis, "is not to magnify but rather to muffle." In the end he seems "intent on making a virtue out of not knowing what he means" (*Great Tradition*, 179–80). Part of this prologue and parts of the "Saving Illusion" section of chapter 1 originally appeared in my essay "Conrad and the Anxiety of Knowledge," *Conradian* 35 (2010): 1–12.

3. Said, "Conrad," 32. This reading of Conrad is very widely shared and appears in a variety of permutations. Cedric Watts finds Conrad's novels characteristically "deceptive" and "Janiform," that is, crucially paradoxical or contradictory (*Deceptive Text*). Fredric Jameson describes Conrad's style as the "impressionistic strategy of modernism whose function is to derealize the content and make it available for consumption on some purely aesthetic level" (*Political Unconscious*, 214). Kenneth Graham likewise ascribes Conrad's elusiveness to modernist inclinations, finding in his work the skepticism, enigmatic contingency, and provisionality typical of Modernist writings ("Conrad and Modernism," 206). Sandra Dodson has argued that "the image of the abyss in Conrad repeatedly conveys a sense of the world experienced as absence, aporia, signification without significance" ("Conrad and the Politics of the Sublime," 20).

Paul B. Armstrong reads Conrad's novels as, among other things, "a prolonged meditation on the meaning and significance of contingency," revealing that "the 'real' is not simply there for judgment to uncover but is, rather, a collection of constructs" (*Challenge of Bewilderment*, 110, 3). One of Armstrong's hypotheses about the value of this pervasive contingency in Conrad and others recalls one of the justifications of reader entrapment in Jonathan Swift frequently proposed by his critics. It may bring us, Armstrong suggests, to "an increased self-consciousness about how we interpret and signify, including a new awareness of the limits and vulnerability of everyday semiotic processes" (262). Alongside the relatively intelligible aspects of *Under Western Eyes*, Frank Kermode finds "another plot, misty, full of phantoms" (*Art of Telling*,

145). Conrad's writing is "an outbreak of anarchy or entropy," in Anthony Winner's words, "that calls all prescriptions and definitions into question" (*Culture and Irony*, 100).

Robert Hampson reads *Victory* as a "polysemous, indeterminate fiction" whose inconclusiveness accurately reflects the novel's skepticism about truth, facts, and reason (*Joseph Conrad*, 250). Harold Bloom accuses *Heart of Darkness* of a "fall into obscurantism" and wonders if *Lord Jim* is "simply an instance of such obscurantism on a larger scale" (introduction, 5). For J. Hillis Miller, *Lord Jim* passes over the bounds of general intelligibility. The ambiguity of metaphor and symbol, Miller writes, the shifting points of view, and the multiplication of incompatible yet equally plausible explanations conspire to make of *Lord Jim* a woven "fabric of words which is incapable of being interpreted unambiguously, as a fixed pattern of meaning" (*Fiction and Repetition*, 31). Douglas Hewitt has an unsettling explanation for this confusion. "The effect of muddlement which is so commonly found in *Lord Jim* comes," he suggests, ". . . from this—that Marlow is himself muddled" and that this muddle is the surface manifestation of a deeper "confusion [that] seems to extend to Conrad's conception of the story" (*Conrad*, 37, 38). And Sooyoung Chon argues that "the solid and distinctively articulated, but opaque texture of the narrative in *Nostromo* resists a search for truth beyond. The creation of a depthless and opaque surface in postmodern art is based on the idea that there is no ultimate truth behind appearance, and this also seems to be the attitude behind the narrative strategy in *Nostromo*" ("*Nostromo*," 59).

Although efforts to ascribe definable meanings to individual works persist, they are typically presented in the context of confessed obscurity. For some the pervasive mistiness of Conrad's work is at least occasionally a defect. For others, more numerous, it is the ingenious point and purpose of his work. Disagreement on this issue, in other words, has narrowed principally to a choice between the reflective significance and the faulty obscurantism of the haze.

4. Roberts, *Conrad and Masculinity*, 118.
5. Daleski, *Joseph Conrad*, 20.

Chapter 1. Forbidden Knowledge and the Saving Illusion

1. For a useful survey of the history of forbidden and threatening knowledge, see Shattuck, *Forbidden Knowledge*.
2. Rank, *Will Therapy*, 251.
3. Becker, *Denial of Death*, 269.
4. Freud, *Ego and the Mechanisms of Defense*, 70–71.
5. Hartmann, *Essays in Ego Psychology*, 12–13, 22. For a fuller discussion of the relationship between literature and denial, see my chapter "On Literature and Denial" in *Porous Sanctuary*, 1–19.
6. Although it is structured into the language and obvious to all who speak it, for an illuminating and detailed discussion of the relationship between seeing and knowing, see (or know) Jay, *Downcast Eyes*, particularly the first two chapters: "The Noblest of the Senses: Vision from Plato to Descartes" and "Dialectic of EnLIGHTenment," 21–48.

7. Quoted in Shattuck, *Forbidden Knowledge*, 28.

8. See Ricouer, "'Original Sin.'"

9. Also, of course, in Rafael's and Michael's angelic admonitions to Adam that certain events are "perhaps / Not lawful to reveal," to be content to be "lowly wise" and to "let thine own inventions hope / Things not revealed." The narrator himself wishes that Adam and Eve may "Sleep on / Blest pair" and declares that they will be "O yet happiest if ye seek / No happier state and know to know no more" (*Paradise Lost*, 4:774–76). As the doctrine of the Fortunate Fall, which dominates the later books of *Paradise Lost*, indicates, however, Milton, like Conrad, is demonstrably ambivalent, hence inconsistent on the question of the desirability of forbidden or dangerous knowledge. Like the later writer, he is simultaneously or alternately attracted by and admonishingly wary of such knowledge.

10. Rousseau, "Dissertation on the Effects," 20–21.

11. Foucault, *History of Sexuality*, 53. Because the fit is so precise and because Foucault's observations about the discourse of sex between the late seventeenth and early twentieth centuries constitute not mere analogical background but, in large measure, a causal explanation of the avoidant nature of the fictions we will examine here, I allow myself a relatively elaborate and heavily quoted summary of his remarks.

12. Elisabeth Bronfen observes that there is a "cultural convention that the mother's gift of birth is also the gift of death, and that the embrace of the beloved also signifies a dissolution of the self. Woman functions as privileged trope for the uncanniness of unity and loss, of independent identity and self-dissolution, of the pleasure of the body and its decay.... Given that woman is culturally constructed as the object of a plethora of contradictory drives, the death drive and the drive for femininity are readily aligned" ("death-drive [Freud]," 56). For Simone de Beauvoir, the "gift" of life is woman's first lie, her first treason. For life itself, however appealingly dressed, "is always infested by the ferments of age and death.... [And it] is upon woman's body—this body which is destined for him—that man really encounters deterioration of the flesh" (*Second Sex*, 160). For additional discussions of woman as the symbolic incarnation of body and, therefore, of sex, defilement, decay, and death, see Lederer, *Fear of Women*, 20ff; and Noddings, *Women and Evil*, 10, 34–43.

13. Cave, "Joseph Conrad," 62.

14. For an essay-length study of the historic, mythic, philosophical, and psychological identification of woman with truth, see my "Conrad's 'Woman as Truth' Topos."

15. Sex, Foucault argued, was a matter not only of sensation, pleasure, and taboo but also of truth and falsehood. The truth of sex was perceived as something "fundamental, useful, or dangerous, precious or formidable." It was constituted, in fact, "as a problem of truth" and as such was "driven out, denied, and reduced to silence" (*History*, 56, 4).

16. Ibid., 4, 55.

17. Qtd. in ibid., 24.

18. Ibid., 56.

19. Ibid., 72.

20. See Becker, *Denial of Death*, for an excellent survey and study of man's historic denial of mortality.

21. Letter to *New York Times*, August 29, 1901, qtd. in Graver, *Conrad's Short Fiction*, 43–44.

22. Curle, *Last Twelve Years*, 12–13. It is noteworthy that the hesitancy, vacillation, and instability that define Conrad's relationship with threatening knowledge were identified by his uncle and guardian, Taseusz Bobrowski (who knew his sister's son as well as anyone), as being among the defining marks—he saw them as weaknesses—of Conrad's character. And this with Conrad's candid confirmation. Responding to Conrad's request that he "indicate those shortcomings of your character that I have observed during the thirty-four years of your life, with the help of my 'cold reason,'" Bobrowski weighed in: "I consider," he wrote back, "that you have always lacked endurance and perseverance in decisions, which is the result of your instability in your aims and desires. *You lack endurance, panie Bracie, in the face of facts*—and, I suppose, in the face of people too?" (letter from T. Bobrowski to Korzeniowski [Conrad's birth name], July 30, 1891; qtd. in Najder, *Joseph Conrad*, 147–48; emphasis added). And Conrad, as this same biographer remarks, "was quite ready to agree." "One admires what one lacks," he wrote soon after to another correspondent. "That is why I admire perseverance and fidelity and constancy" (letter from Korzeniowski to M. Poradowska, August 26, 1891; qtd. in Najder, *Joseph Conrad*, 149). Although he is unsympathetic toward Bobrowska on a number of counts and wary of his influence on Conrad, Najder readily acknowledges his "sober judgment" (166).

23. Guetti, "'Heart of Darkness.'"

24. Cox, *Joseph Conrad*, 176.

25. Senn, *Conrad's Narrative Voice*, 9.

26. Daleski, *Joseph Conrad*, 27. See also Jeremy Hawthorn's comparable observation that while writing, stripped of the forms of nonverbal expression that accompany and enhance speech, can readily lie, "what the eye has seen is truth" (*Language and Fictional Self-Consciousness*, 103). And relying heavily on Conrad's celebratory declaration that when the writer does succeed, "behold!—all the truth of life is there: a moment of vision, a sigh, a smile—and the return to an eternal rest," Neville H. Newhouse endorses his encouraging if transitory conviction that the writer's word picture can indeed "reveal the substance of the moment's truth" (*Joseph Conrad*, 45–46).

27. Billy, *Wilderness of Words*, 1. See also pages 3, 6, and 8.

28. Said, "Conrad and Nietzsche," 69. See also Hawthorn, *Language and Fictional Self-Consciousness*, 107, 108; and Raval, *Art of Failure*, 2–3. As Raval remarks, speaking for many, Conrad's narrators "often struggle with the inadequacy of language, striving for a sense of clarity which at times turns out, by their own admission, to be unattainable or illusory." Conrad, he maintains, labored under the burden of a "relentlessly skeptical attitude toward both language and fiction" (3).

29. Miller, *Poets of Reality*, 18–34.

30. Roussel, *Metaphysics of Darkness*, 4, 14. Speaking exclusively, if projectably, of *Heart of Darkness*, Jerry Wasserman suggests that "the abundance of abstract,

imprecise adjectives reflects the verbally inexpressible nature of the darkness as well as the tentative nature of language itself" ("Narrative Presence," 112).

31. Watt, "Impressionism and Symbolism," esp. 38–43, 51.

32. Johnson, "Conrad's Impressionism." Conrad, writes C. B. Cox, "does not believe that the human mind can uncover absolute truth; instead we can only substitute an ability to describe objectively the veil of appearance. We cannot describe the universe in isolation from an observer; things are seen relative to some particular individual, rather than absolutely" (173). For Conrad, as Anthony Winner reads him, "the fact of truth as fiction, of the idea as illusion, sets the stage for irony upon irony" (*Culture and Irony*, 5).

33. Warren, introduction, xx.

34. Wollaeger, *Joseph Conrad*, 11, 10.

35. Peters, *Conrad and Impressionism*, 124.

36. Conrad evokes the full absurdity of modern life, which was expressed more radically by his contemporary Alfred Jarry and later disseminated in its most influential forms by Albert Camus's "The Myth of Sisyphus." All the writers "rediscover Hume's insight that uncurtailed skepticism leads to conclusions that are as irrefutable as they are absurd, and all spin fictions that provide shelter from a skepticism that threatens to become more extreme" (Wollaeger, *Joseph Conrad*, 3).

37. Peters, *Conrad and Impressionism*, 125. For J. M. Kertzer, who draws a distinction between an agnostic skepticism and an atheistic cynicism, it is the latter that is to be shunned ("Bitterness of Our Wisdom"). Others, like Watt, draw the red line at nihilism and deny that "Conrad's social and moral purport [can] be regarded as ultimately nihilist" (*Conrad in the Nineteenth Century*, 252). Similarly Raval maintains that Conrad's "refusal to believe that there is anything like abstract meaning or value in reality apart from man's social-political life does not make him a nihilist, except in the view of those who believe in absolutist transcendental ideals of objectivity, truth, and meaning" (*Art of Failure*, 167). In his review essay of Watt's book, Kertzer holds that for Watt, "in revealing meaning . . . Conrad does not assert truths to which we accede; he follows 'a process of prolonged moral and psychological probing,' a questioning that entices us to find answers. Everything is a clue to the 'revelation of moral essences'" ("Watt on Conrad," 91). My quite different claim is that when reading Conrad we are at times enticed not to find answers and, when they cannot be borne, encouraged to evade or obscure them. I claim further that not everything in his narratives is a clue to moral or any other essences, though there are many clues to the advisability of heeding Jocasta's desperate counsel not to probe further.

38. Since, as Eve Kosofsky Sedgwick suggests, ignorance is "not a single Manichean, aboriginal maw of darkness . . . perhaps there exists instead a plethora of *ignorances*, and we may begin to ask questions about the labor, erotics, and economics of their human production and distribution" (*Epistemology of the Closet*, 8). Such a belief in the overdetermination of the evasiveness and elusiveness of these productions is the motivating force behind this study. The questions I wish to ask about the blurring obscurities and professions of ignorance in and of so much of Conrad's writing are

principally psychological and ideological. Rooted as these ostensible ignorances often are in a defensive avoidance of the feminine or sexual, they are pertinently related to the erotics of their production.

39. There is wide agreement that, as Zdzisław Najder remarks, "the basis of Conrad's 'impressionism' is his striving after suggestiveness; to evoke in the reader specific moods or visions—not by means of mirror-like descriptions or reports communicated to the intellect, but by direct appeal to feelings and imagination" (*Joseph Conrad*, 212).

40. David Thorburn, for example, suggests that Conrad was led to his frustrated conviction about the inadequacy of language not only by professional experience but by Romantic poetry and theory. "Conrad, like the English Romantic poets, holds to a meager but partly sustaining faith in the power of language to make sense of the world . . . however imperfectly." His Wordsworthian "preoccupation with the limits of language," then, is at least partly responsible for the "failures" of language Leavis remarked and criticized. Marlow's "vocabulary of uncertainty . . . reinforces his stated conviction that his telling must fall short of perfect truth" (*Conrad's Romanticism*, 127, 118). Edward Said speaks of the writer's "general loss of faith in the mimetic powers of language" ("Conrad," 38). And Sandra Dodson makes a similar point more recently: "Conrad's descriptions of a shadowy, illegible, non-signifying Nature in works like *The Nigger of the 'Narcissus'*, *Heart of Darkness* and *Lord Jim* invariably coincide with an obsessive preoccupation with the failure of language to signify truths or, in the famous words of the 1897 Preface to *The Nigger of the 'Narcissus,'* 'to make you see'" (Dodson, "Conrad," 20).

41. There are, of course, minority views, some well worthy of attention. Daphna Erdinast-Vulcan, in her illuminating *Joseph Conrad and the Modern Temper*, finds in Conrad a lifelong struggle against a Nietzschean nihilism that drew him toward despair and argues that he succumbed to the darker side of his spirit only in the later novels, which suffer for their surrender. For Erdinast-Vulcan, Conrad was a didactic writer concerned chiefly with the problem of "how to be." "The view of reality as a text" that characterizes his late phase "could not be a joyful celebration of an endless play of indeterminate meanings. It was an admission of ethical and aesthetic bankruptcy" (155). Suresh Raval, while acknowledging Conrad's relentlessly skeptical attitude toward both language and fiction, locates the principal source of the fiction's indeterminacy elsewhere. He situates it not in Conrad's nihilism, not in postmodernist reflexivity or its abandonment of literary authority, but in the writer's fascination with the contradictions he perceived in human affairs and his effort to dramatize "their implications for social and personal life." The contradictions that pervade and perplex Conrad's stories, then, are "not simply matters of logical or epistemological impasse; they point to dilemmas which lie at the heart of our social-political life" (*Art of Failure*, 4).

42. Billy, *Wilderness of Words*, 8.

43. In its more nearly complete form, Conrad's messages was that "words, groups of words, words standing alone, are symbols of life, have the power in their sound or their aspect to present the very thing you wish to hold up before the mental vision

of our readers. The things 'as they are' exist in words; therefore words should be handled with care lest the picture, the image of truth abiding in facts, should become distorted—or blurred" (letter to Sir Hugh Clifford, October 5, 1899, *CL* 2:200).

44. Miller, *Poets of Reality*, 33.

45. *The Secret Agent*, as Bernard Meyer argues, is "an avowal of the elemental savagery which lurks in the human breast, a renewed affirmation and a renewed confession that 'man is an evil animal'" (*Joseph Conrad*, 97). Savage and cannibalistic impulses reside not only in the heart of Africa but also in the heart of "civilized" London as well. Throughout his fiction, remarks H. M. Daleski, Conrad "asserts the liability that to be despicably less than human is part of the human condition" (*Joseph Conrad*, 84–85).

46. Cave, "Joseph Conrad," 65.

47. Conrad expressed contempt for "The Return." "The work is vile," he wrote to Garnett, "—or else good. I don't know. I can't know.... I have a physical horror of that story. I simply won't look at it any more. It has embittered five months of my life. I hate it" (Conrad to Garnett, September 27, 1897, in Garnett, *Letters from Conrad*, 92). Tormented throughout his career by self-doubt and protracted bouts of creative impotence, Conrad expressed loathing for a number of his productions, often compounded by a rage at the suffering they had caused him. But as I hope my readings of "The Planter of Malata" and *The Rescue* demonstrate and as Daphna Erdinast-Vulcan shows persuasively, Conrad's minor and least successful works may tell us the most about the covert forces that drive his major novels: "There are ... a number of short stories which are indeed strange; which do not seem to lend themselves to readerly consumption; which generate the same sense of aesthetic discomfort induced by Conrad's undisputedly great novels" (*Strange Short Fiction*, 1–2).

48. The narrator provides brief background to this experience a little earlier in the novel. "There are in our lives short periods," he reflects, when "we are absorbed in the contemplation of that something, within our bodies, which rejoices or suffers while the body goes on breathing, instinctively runs away or, not less instinctively, fights—perhaps dies. But death in such a moment is the privilege of the fortunate, it is a high and rare favour, a supreme grace" (72). It is infinitely preferable, apparently, to such contemplation.

49. Although a number of Conrad's critics have commented on his escapist commendation of ignorance and avoidance and his praise for the value of illusion, very few have connected this powerful and acknowledged inclination to the evasiveness and obscurantism of his narratives. Edward Said does so briefly when he notes that "often obscurity, regardless of outward splendor, as in Jim or Nostromo, is a function of secret shame" ("Conrad," 32). But only Allon White elaborates it. Although his emphasis lies elsewhere and though he applies his insights only to *Heart of Darkness*, White's contention is quite similar to my own. "What fears were allayed, or what desires fulfilled," he asks, "by the evasion, equivocations, enigmas, and obliquities" of George Meredith, Henry James, and Conrad? His answer to this self-posed question is that "the obscurities are, to a certain extent, a kind of semiotic defence.... textual opacities often serve to prevent a certain kind of knowledge" (*Uses of Obscurity*, 3, 4).

White's primary interest is in the writer's need to perpetuate his text, to avoid clarity not principally for defensive or ideological reasons but to sustain the fiction given impetus by the painful secret he explores. But behind his perceptive and evocative exploration lies a hypothesis accordant with my own.

Ted Billy's study, informative and praiseworthy in its own right, is far more typical in its almost insistent missing of this link. Although Billy notices and describes at considerable length Conrad's Nietzschean commendation of evasion and illusion, he does not consider it as a possible source of the elusiveness and obscurity of these texts. Like virtually all of Conrad's critics who address this issue, he instead ascribes these exclusively to Conrad's ideological skepticism and his sense of the inherent inadequacy of language to relate experience or communicate awareness (*Wilderness of Words*, 5–7, 70–71).

50. Letter to Cunninghame Graham, January 31, 1898, in *CL* 2:30. The quotation is more powerful read in full: "Egoism is good, and altruism is good, and fidelity to nature would be the best of all, and systems could be built, and rules could be made—if we could only get rid of consciousness. What makes mankind tragic is not that they are the victims of nature, it is that they are conscious of it. To be part of the animal kingdom under the conditions of this earth is very well—but as soon as you know of your slavery the pain, the anger, the strife—the tragedy begins. We can't return to nature, since we can't change our place in it. Our refuge is in stupidity, in drunken[n]ess of all kinds, in lies, in beliefs, in murder, thieving, reforming—in negation, in contempt—each man according to the promptings of his particular devil." Conrad's particular devils, I am suggesting, were negation, evasion, obscurity, and other forms of deliberate or impelled obfuscation.

51. Letter to Helen Sanderson, August 31, 1898, in *CL* 2:90.

52. Why self-knowledge may be less than desirable is suggested by the narrator's remark that Razumov looked at his journal, "I suppose, as a man looks at himself in a mirror, with wonder, perhaps with anguish, with anger or despair" (*UWE* 214). The universalizing "as a man" extends the notion of the desperate anguish of self-perception indefinitely. But self-reflection is by no means the only thought inimical to well-being. As noted earlier, Conrad called thinking "the great enemy of perfection, profound reflection the "most pernicious" habit of civilized man (*Victory*, x–xi). It is because he has never formed this habit that Razumov's fellow student "Madcap Kostia," notable for his "elated voice and great gestures," fills "the bare academy corridors with the joy of thoughtless animal life" (79).

For Daniel Ross, who writes illuminatingly on Conrad's commitment to the saving illusion, that illusion is "a deeper truth than the surface reality reveals" ("*Lord Jim*," 45). But as this reply to Graham and a great deal more reveal, the most effective of all illusions is not the coherent principle or fiction that deceptively fills the void but the illusion that there is no void in need of filling, nothing but the job at hand to be known.

53. Warren, introduction, xvii.
54. Ibid., xviii.
55. Quoted in ibid., xvi.

56. Ibid.

57. Lenormand, "Note sur un séjour de Conrad en Corse," 666.

58. Letter to Charles Chasse, January 31, 1924, in Jean-Aubry, *Joseph Conrad*, 2:336.

59. Meyer, *Joseph Conrad*, 343–44. See also Watt, *Conrad in the Nineteenth Century*, 12, 16.

60. Edward Said is one of few who have taken note of this ambivalence. But Said restricts it to the drama within the fiction. He does not read it as the drama of the narratives themselves and therefore does not connect this dramatized vacillation with the evasiveness he explains in other terms. "This form of Conrad's tales," Said observes, "enacts the dialectic between two opposed impulses, one, that of what Nietzsche calls the man who wants knowledge, and who 'must again and again abandon the terra firma where men live and venture into the uncertain' and two, 'the impulse' which desires life [and which] must again and again grope its way toward a more or less secure place where it can find a purchase" ("Conrad and Nietzsche," 71).

61. Although I apply it more broadly, I am indebted to Daphna Erdinast-Vulcan's "Some Millennial Footnotes," 60, for this quotation and its psychological implications.

62. Conrad's novels and prefaces often carry on a cross-referential dialogue on the value of illusion and concealment, completing, exemplifying, or explaining one another. As the language teacher in *Under Western Eyes* remarks, "What all men are really after is some form or perhaps only some formula for peace" (5). Hence Conrad's observation in the author's note to *Almayer's Folly* on "the curse of facts and the blessing of illusions, the bitterness of our wisdom and the deceptive consolation of our folly" (viii). This dialogue also takes place between Razumov's journal and the enveloping narrative of the language teacher in *Under Western Eyes* and among Marlow, Kurtz, and Jim in *Heart of Darkness* and *Lord Jim*.

63. This would seem to be at least partially borne out by Conrad's attempt to trivialize this virulently serious novel. In a letter to Galsworthy on September 12, 1906, he wrote: "In such a tale one is likely to be misunderstood. After all you must not take it too seriously. The whole thing is superficial and is but a tale. I had no idea to consider anarchism politically—or to treat it seriously in its philosophical aspect: as a manifestation of human nature in its discontent and imbecility." A more serious treatment of anarchism, "if it were worth doing—would be the work of a more vigorous hand and for a mind more robust, and perhaps more honest than mine" (CL 3:354–55). Moreover, as Lissa Schneider observes, the title of the novel is "a cover-up, so to speak, that reveals even as it conceals the subversive social implications of a story that describes a wife who stabs her husband to death.... In a novel where disguise, secrecy, and masquerade are the rule, Conrad's ironic title functions as a kind of cloak or mask that disguises the story's ultimate focus. With the title *The Secret Agent*, Conrad raises readerly expectations for one type of story, only to confound those expectations by instead producing, as he repeatedly mentions in his introduction to the 1920 reprint, the story of 'Mrs. Verloc's maternal passion'" (*Conrad's Narratives of Difference*, 116–17).

64. Miller, *Poets of Reality*, 40. See also, among others, Claire Rosenfield's characterization of the novel's London as "this monstrous presence of stone and brick and darkness," an iconic "world totally devoid of meaning" (Paradise of Snakes, 90); and, portentously, Jeffrey Berman's just observation that "no novel in the English language pours as much contempt onto politics as *The Secret Agent*. . . . It is the author whose cynicism in . . . *The Secret Agent* approaches the boundaries of the dangerous 'freedom of moral Nihilism' Conrad warns against in 'Books'" (Joseph Conrad, 112).

65. Winner, *Culture and Irony*, 75.
66. Baines, *Joseph Conrad: A Critical Biography*, 340.
67. Miller, *Poets of Reality*, 44; Schwarz, *Conrad*, 83.
68. Winner, *Culture and Irony*, 91, 87, 88.
69. Stein, "*Secret Agent*," 523, 525.
70. Watt, *Conrad*, 47.
71. As Erdinast-Vulcan rightly observes, "Conrad's work has never really lent itself to de-authorizing criticism, and has only rarely been subjected to wholly intrinsic and textualist readings" (*Strange Short Fiction*, 185). Conrad himself affirmed the inevitability of an authorial presence in his productions. "A novelist lives in his work," he wrote in *A Personal Record*. "He stands there, the only reality in an invented world, among imaginary things, happenings, and people. Writing about them, he is only writing about himself. But the disclosure is not complete. He remains, to a certain extent, a figure behind a veil; a suspected rather than a seen presence—a movement and a voice behind the draperies of fiction" (xiii).

Perhaps it is because Conrad so unabashedly insisted on the autobiographical nature of fiction, his own in particular, and because he does typically veil himself quite effectively within his works, that critics ride off in such eager pursuit of traces, and the claims of discovery are everywhere in the literature. Signs of Conrad's history and character have been noted not only in Marlow but also in Jim, Decoud, Razumov, Renouard, and a long list of others. David Smith remarks that "one of the most striking aspects of Conrad's writing is the intensity of his presence in it" and declares *Under Western Eyes* the most autobiographical of his novels ("Hidden Narrative," 39–40). Keith Carabine seeks the authorial figure behind the narrative veil in "The Figure behind the Veil: Conrad and Razumov in *Under Western Eyes*," chapter 3 in his *Life and the Art*, 97–127.

Perhaps the richest studies of autobiographical presence in these fictions, fixing more on attitude, psyche, or ideology than on shared experience, are Said's *Joseph Conrad and the Fiction of Autobiography*, Meyer's *Joseph Conrad*, and Erdinast-Vulcan's *Strange Short Fiction* and *Joseph Conrad and the Modern Temper*. Zdzisław Najdar, Conrad's authoritative biographer, exaggerates somewhat when he remarks that "scholars have shown beyond doubt that his literary works are mostly based on material drawn from real life or from reading, with his imagination playing a lesser part" (*Joseph Conrad*, 39). In a letter to Sir Sidney Colvin, Conrad, speaking of *The Shadow Line*, admitted that "there can be no possible objection to your recognizing the autobiographical character of that piece of writing—let us call it. It is so much so that I shrink from calling it a Tale. If you will notice I call it *A Confession* on the title page. For, from a certain point of view," he begins to complicate, "it is that—and essentially as sincere as any confession can be. The more perfectly so, perhaps, because its object is not the usual one of self-revelation" (letter to Sir Sidney Colvin, March 18, 1917, in Jean-Aubry, *Joseph Conrad*, 2:184). It is this sort of biographical pressure I am interested in and attempt to measure in this study: not the usual one of self-revelation but, more unusually, the self-revelation all but inevitably entailed in the effort to avoid or conceal it.

Chapter 2. The Lie of Fiction

1. Glassman, *Language and Being*, 250.
2. Rank, *Will Therapy*, 252.
3. Becker, *Denial of Death*, 182.
4. That there is no real difference in this regard between women and the rest of us is apparent in the similarity between the vacuous inhabitants of the sepulchral city—men and women alike—of *Heart of Darkness* and the girls of "the old French families" described in "A Smile of Fortune." "The girls are almost always pretty, ignorant of the world, kind and agreeable and generally bilingual; they prattle innocently both in French and English. The emptiness of their existence passes belief" (*'Twixt Land and Sea*, 34–35). It surfaces more overtly in a letter Conrad wrote to his friend Cunninghame Graham. "We, living, are out of life," he wrote, "—utterly out of it . . . we don't know even our own thoughts. Half the words we use have no meaning whatever and of the other half each man understands each word after the fashion of his own folly and conceit" (*CL* 2:16–17). Not only women are out of it, have to be out of it, and probably should be. We all are.
5. Marianna Torgovnick locates in Conrad "an axiomatic identification of 'primitive' landscape with the female body" and an equation of the grave and death with that same body. "The nexus of associations," she observes, "is one we have seen before in Western conceptions of the primitive—women, sex, death, mortality—and women, as a result are, collectively, seductive, dangerous, deadly" (*Gone Primitive*, 156). Like the elusive and threatening truth or knowledge they and the wilderness embody and consequently like the fictions that contain them, they attract and repel, promise and betray, momentarily reveal and ultimately mystify and obscure.
6. Conrad's belief in the inadequacy of language to communicate experience is, of course, one of the causes cited most frequently to explain the indeterminacy of his fictions. "Where something is too deep for words," remarks Jeremy Hawthorn, "then you leave them out. . . . It is not too outrageous to suggest that Conrad is using a comparable technique in his 'adjectival insistence,'" that is, his tendency to resort at crucial junctures to vacantly evasive adjectives such as *inscrutable, mysterious, inconceivable,* and *unspeakable.* (*Language and Fictional Self-Consciousness*, 10). Speaking, with Hawthorn, for many who subscribe to this account of the Conrad's evasiveness, Ted Billy infers that Conrad "recognized too well the gulf separating word from thing to place his wholehearted trust in arbitrary and provisional verbal counters. . . . Using words to emphasize the duplicities of language, he seems to engage in what postmodern critics might call a deconstruction of the art of fiction" (*Wilderness of Words*, 1).

My point throughout is that often, in the fiction and perhaps elsewhere, Conrad offers up the alleged inadequacies of language to obscure a lack or failure of will. Certain experiences or glimpsed revelations are deemed "unspeakable" not because they cannot be described but because, rattling necessary defenses, they should not be.

7. Hyland, "Little Woman," 9.

8. As all these complementarities and interlocking identifications imply, the self he protects here includes the vulnerable feminine self that weakens and may unravel self-possession. All-inclusive in this narrative, Marlow contains within him not only Kurtz but also the savage woman and the Intended as well, two aspects of the woman within, both identified with "the horror" that, like both women, cannot or will not be named. In his iconoclastic essay "An Image of Africa: Racism in Conrad's *Heart of Darkness*," Chinua Achebe famously identified Conrad's Africa as the repressed dark side of the racist mind of Europe. His assaultive formulation, at least partially justified, offers a geographical extension of the image of woman presented here as man's rejected but menacingly latent and internal other. Speaking of the Thames and Congo Rivers, representative of the two worlds, Western and African, Achebe asks:

> Is Conrad saying then that these two rivers are very different, one good, the other bad? Yes, but that is not the real point. *It is not the differentness that worries Conrad but the lurking hint of kinship,* of common ancestry. For the Thames, too, "has been one of the dark places of the earth." It conquered its darkness, of course, and is now in daylight and is now at peace. But if it were to visit its primordial relative, the Congo, it would run the terrible risk of hearing grotesque, suggestive echoes of its own forgotten darkness, and of falling victim to an avenging recrudescence of the mindless frenzy of the first beginnings. (783–84, emphasis mine)

With a degree of taming modification and the recognition that for Conrad man never lives in daylight and at peace, one might substitute *Man* for *Thames*, *Woman* for *Congo* here. Similarly when Achebe concludes that "consequently Africa is something to be avoided just as the picture [of Dorian Gray] has to be hidden away to safeguard the man's jeopardous integrity. Keep away from Africa, or else!" (792). Africa is an "other" name for Woman.

9. Henry James is said to have objected to the elusive vagueness of Kurtz in *Heart of Darkness*, complaining that readers never really get hold of Kurtz after all the talk about him (cited in Moser, "From Olive Garnett's Diary," 525). James's discontent and Kurtz's perpetually anticipated but hardly realized presence point to Conrad's personal sense of the trace of the author in his fiction. "In his very vagueness of appearance, the writer seen through the leaves of his book becomes a fascinating companion in a land of fascination" (*NLL* 59).

10. In a book of a certain kind, writes Conrad, "the author's personality ... shapes itself before one in the ring of sentences, it is seen between the lines—like the progress of a traveller in the jungle that may be traced by the sound of the *parang* chopping the swaying creepers" (*NLL* 59). "The man," as Marlow says, "presented himself as a voice." He is a "gifted creature" whose preeminent gift "was his ability to talk, his words—the

gift of expression" (*HD* 113). For other references to Kurtz as a voice, see *HD* 108, 122, 131, 133.

11. In its detachment from the surface facts of life that keep men ethical and sane and that are at the core of Conrad's moral aesthetic, Kurtz's report differs markedly from the *Inquiry into Some Points of Seamanship* Marlow happens on. It was "not a very enthralling book; but at the first glance you could see there a singleness of intention, an honest concern for the right way of going to work, which made these humble pages, thought out so many years ago, luminous with another than a professional light.... [It was] something unmistakably real" (99).

12. Martin Ray observes that "Carlyle's preference for 'good work with lips closed' ... is characteristic of the Victorian disdain for mere eloquence, a contempt which Conrad shared" ("Language and Silence," 20).

13. Regueiro, *Limits of Imagination*. See particularly, pp. 9–15, 23–42.

14. Mayoux, *Vivants piliers*, 127.

15. "I saw him open his mouth wide," recalls Marlow; "—it gave him a weirdly voracious aspect, as though he had wanted to swallow all the air, all the earth, all the men before him" (134). And later: "I had a vision of him on the stretcher, opening his mouth voraciously, as if to devour all the earth with all its mankind" (155). Romanticism, Aaron Fogel suggests, is for Conrad the literary expression of imperialism in its dialogical disproportions. Its "overheardedness," its half dialogues, its language, cries, ambiguous speech acts, prophecies, even its sense of adventure, grow out of the dramatic conditions of colonialism (*Coercion to Speak*, 58). For Henry Staten, "Kurtz is a large-scale entrepreneur who seeks to satisfy his rage for being by appropriating as much as he can of the world" ("Conrad's Mortal World," 731). My own view is that Kurtz is no ordinary imperialist, colonialist, or appropriating entrepreneur but a specifically literary and artistic one as well, a Romantic imperialist and colonialist who appropriates and incorporates his world.

16. Rank, *Will Therapy*, 146–47. For Ernest Becker, who adopts a variant of Conrad's oral metaphor, this kind of creative individual takes in "too large a chunk of the world" and is "constantly biting off "more than [he] ... can chew" (*Denial of Death*, 182).

17. Glassman, *Language and Being*, 234.

18. Renouard in "The Planter of Malata," the Captain in "A Smile of Fortune," Captain Falk in the story that bears his name, Willems in *An Outcast of the Islands*, Ossipon in *The Secret Agent*, Ortega in *The Arrow of Gold*, Lingard in *The Rescue*, and a number of others.

19. See Watt, *Conrad in the Nineteenth Century*, 32.

20. Or as Conrad writes in his preface to *The Nigger of the "Narcissus,"* "Confronted by the ... enigmatical spectacle [truth] the artist descends within himself, and in that lonely region of stress and strife, if he be deserving and fortunate, he finds the terms of his appeal" (xi–xii).

21. Guerard, introduction, 15.

22. Andrew Gibson makes this point effectively in his "Ethics and Unrepresentability in *Heart of Darkness*."

23. Erdinast-Vulcan, "Some Millennial Footnotes," 57.

24. For an informative discussion of Conrad's attitude toward nihilistic skepticism, see Kertzer, "'Bitterness of Our Wisdom.'"

25. See discussions of this contradiction in, for example, Hampson, *Joseph Conrad*, 181, and Hawthorn, *Narrative Technique*, 180–81.

Chapter 3. The Soft Spot

1. Stape, "*Lord Jim*," 63. "Marlow's persistent interrogation of motives and the metaphor of inquiry itself," writes Stape, "have by the novel's conclusion educated the reader into epistemological scepticism, a doubting of the adequacy of any means of apprehension and analysis. This encourages an open verdict in the face of absent, or in the presence of conflicting and unreliable, evidence" (77).

2. Miller, *Fiction and Repetition*, 31.

3. The resistance to coherent interpretation originates in the proliferation of viable but incompatible explanations and the impossibility of justifying one in preference to the others. Andrzej Gasiorek agrees, finding in *Lord Jim* "a plethora of competing perspectives that remain mutually incommensurable." Their purpose, for Gasiorek, is to "disclose that there is no escape from incertitude. Its refusal of closure supports Marlow's claim that he is involved 'in a dispute impossible of decision if one had to be fair to all the phantoms in possession'" ("To Season," 107–8).

4. Armstrong, *Challenge of Bewilderment*, 133, 118. Offering a somewhat less avant-garde reading of the novel's perplexities, Suresh Raval attributes the indeterminacy of *Lord Jim* less to a postmodern refusal of meaning than to Conrad's fascination with contradictions in human affairs and to "a disturbing ambivalence that seems to show the inadequacy of language." Marlow's narrative, Raval argues, reveals a knot of complications. Language is problematical, Marlow's understanding of Jim is unclear, and Jim himself is misleading (*Art of Failure*, 47). See also Tanner, "Butterflies and Beetles," and Cox, *Joseph Conrad*, 19–44. Fredric Jameson remarks that "the existential investigation has been rigorously prosecuted, but ends up in neither truth nor metaphysics, but in philosophical paradox" (*Political Unconscious*, 264).

5. Glassman, "Intelligible Picture," 35, 50.

6. As Marlow observes, Jim "loved these dreams and the success of his imaginary achievements. They were the best parts of life, its secret truth, its hidden reality. They had a gorgeous virility, the charm of vagueness, they passed before him with a heroic tread; they carried his soul away with them and made it drunk with the divine philtre of an unbounded confidence in itself. There was nothing he could not face" (20). Stein concurs: "He wants to be a saint, and he wants to be a devil—and every time he shuts his eyes he sees himself as a very fine fellow—so fine as he can never be" (*LJ* 213).

7. See Becker, *Denial of Death*, 172, 185.

8. Gose, "Truth in the Well," 10. See also *LJ* 330. That Robert Hampson and Agnes S. K. Yeow argue persuasively for the accuracy of Conrad's representation of Malay culture in *Lord Jim* and elsewhere does not, of course, negate Patusan's metaphoric

rendering as a world of art. Under Conrad's pen they prove eminently compatible (Hampson, *Cross-Cultural Encounters*, and Yeow, *Conrad's Eastern Vision*).

9. Becker, *Denial of Death*, 172, 182.
10. Erdinast-Vulcan, *Joseph Conrad*, 355. See also 34–47.
11. For an essay-length study of the identification of woman with truth in Conrad and the origins of this topos in religious literature, mythology, philosophy, and psychology, see my "Conrad's 'Woman as Truth' Topos: 'Supposing Truth Is a Woman—What Then?" and the appendix to this volume.
12. Gose, "Truth in the Well," 25.
13. Cited in ibid., 23.
14. Miller, *Fiction and Repetition*, 29.
15. Gasiorek, "To Season," 108.
16. See also *LJ* 35, 51, 129, 138, 177, 179–80, 182, 221, 241, 307, 308, 393, 410, 414–17.
17. In this he (in)curiously resembles Peter in Swift's *Tale of a Tub*, whose modern criticism, as Frank Boyle properly reads it, "is not an attempt to think critically about anything, but rather to order the world in a way that is increasingly satisfying to his narcissistic desires" (Boyle, *Swift as Nemesis*, 164).
18. Jim's feminine nature is suggested repeatedly. He blushes "like a girl," and "had he been a girl," a bachelor friend of Marlow's wrote him, "one could have said he was blooming—blooming modestly—like a violet" (187). Jim also has a young girl's "freshness" and a helpless purity about him that leads Padmini Mongia to see in him "a description of the Gothic heroine" ("'Ghosts of the Gothic,'" 12). He is incurably romantic, physically attractive to many who know him, including Marlow, and, as one reader noted, he "assumes the position of a woman in relation to a succession of older men," Marlow among them (McCracken, "'Hard and Absolute Condition,'" 27). Since Jim is, as Marlow repeatedly remarks, "one of us," the threat of recognition is magnified, the urgency of concealment intensified. Unsurprisingly like almost all Conrad's women and the knowledge they embody, Jim is elusive, inscrutable, and enigmatic.
19. Brierly is also still more dependently committed than Marlow to protective denial, the habit of letting contradictory facts and ideas be hanged, on which the principle of fidelity relies. For Linda Dryden, who takes a more negative and political view of this code, Jim's real crime is, for Brierly, "the betrayal of the idea of gentlemanly honour and heroism, the empty rhetoric of imperialism and imperialist *Romance* fiction upon which Brierly's conduct is based" (*Joseph Conrad*, 148).
20. Letter to Charles Chasse, January 31, 1924, in Jean-Aubry, *Joseph Conrad*, 2:336. Later in *Lord Jim*, Marlow offers a similar observation about the universality of artful dodging or brightening self-delusion. "For a moment," he confesses, "I had a view of a world that seemed to wear a vast and dismal aspect of disorder, while, in truth, thanks to our unwearied efforts, it is as sunny an arrangement of small conveniences as the mind of man can conceive" (313).
21. Like the evocative "blessed stiffness," the "poisoned shaft" Marlow speaks of here seems sexually laden. But the plainer reference is to his pen, which he seems to acknowledge here is dipped in lies subtler than any found on earth. Conrad does,

by implication, seem to place himself among those writers for whom, as Gilbert and Gubar claim, the pen is analogous to the phallus, imposing its will on the blank page that is the woman's body. The claim seems somewhat far-fetched, but if we apply it here, Conrad's pen, I am claiming, repeatedly wilts at the prospect (3–16).

22. A similar acknowledgement that we have knowledge we choose not to speak appears later in the novel, in a passage quoted in part in chapter 1 above. The statement is seminal and worth quoting in full. Insisting, as he does repeatedly, that Jim defies revelation and description, Marlow wanders toward an anomalous but significant confession. "The last word," he adds,

> is not said,—probably shall never be said. Are not our lives too short for that full utterance which through all our stammerings is of course our only and abiding intention? I have given up expecting those last words, whose ring, if they could only be pronounced, would shake both heaven and earth. There is never time to say our last word—the last word of our love, of our desire, faith, remorse, submissions, revolt. The heaven and the earth must not be shaken, I suppose—at least, not by us who know so many truths about either. My last words about Jim shall be few. I affirm he had achieved greatness; but the thing would be dwarfed in the telling, or rather in the hearing. Frankly, it is not my words that I mistrust but your minds. I could be eloquent were I not afraid you fellows had starved your imaginations to feed your bodies. I do not mean to be offensive; it is respectable to have no illusions—and safe—and profitable—and dull. Yet you, too, in your time must have known the intensity of life, that light of glamour created in the shock of trifles, as amazing as the glow of sparks struck from a gold stone—and as short-lived, alas! (225)

As is often the case, the revelation presents itself as though by forced extrusion in a parenthetical, in the "not by us who know so many truths about either." Here too Marlow—and by strong implication Conrad—admits to the knowledge of a truth that will remain unspoken. That the last words will not be said because there is no time for them is less persuasive than that they will be suppressed because they would shake both heaven and earth, which must not be shaken. In this passage, having admitted to a terrible knowledge, Marlow takes sudden refuge in the inability of his audience to absorb his message. Arguing in *Heart of Darkness* for the failure of language as the source of noncommunication—as does the narrator of *Under Western Eyes*—here Marlow shifts the blame to the starved imaginations of his audience. Yet his last words about Jim will be few and will insist on Jim's ultimate mystery and inscrutability, not for either of these reasons but because heaven and earth, an externalizing metaphor for the fearful self, must not be shaken. The erosion of this attempt to transfer responsibility to language and audience has, I believe, implications for similar indictments in other Conrad novels.

23. See my "Conrad's 'Woman as Truth' Topos," 67–68.

24. A comparable statement, in which the epistemological haze blankets morality as well, likewise trips over anguished recognitions and the appeal of their occlusion.

Listening to Jim's painful recounting of his leap, Marlow senses the "mists . . . closing again." The image carries him to recollections of the "magnificent vagueness" and "glorious indefiniteness" that obscure the treacheries of the sea. And when his attention returns to Jim, he discerns in his discourse a belief "that age and wisdom can find a remedy against the pain of truth." It is at this point that Jim, speaking words of self-defense that have been routinely quoted as though Conrad spoke them, blurs the distinction between right and wrong, whether cognitively or morally construed. "That wretched story they made up," he stumbles. "It was not a lie—but it wasn't truth all the same. It was something. . . . One knows a downright lie. There was not the thickness of a sheet of paper between the right and wrong of this affair" (128–30).

25. Mongia, "'Ghosts of the Gothic,'" 6–7. See also Torgovnick, *Gone Primitive*, 156.
26. Watt, *Conrad in the Nineteenth Century*, 308; Batchelor, *Edwardian Novel*, 46.
27. Raval, *Art of Failure*, 63; Hampson, *Joseph Conrad*, 117.
28. Letter to Garnett, November 12, 1900: "Yes!" exclaimed Conrad with some distress; "you've put your finger on the plague spot. The division of the book into two parts" (*CL*, 2:302).

Chapter 4. A More Dangerous Revolution

1. Keith Carabine is especially thorough in detailing the autobiographical underpinnings of *Under Western Eyes* and their profound influence on the novel, particularly on the covert relationship between Conrad's desire, announced in a letter to Galsworthy, "to capture the very soul of things Russian" and the psychological developments leading to Razumov's betrayal and confession, which he identifies as "the real subject of the story" (*CL* 4:8–9). The key, for Carabine, is Conrad's eager flight from Poland, "the land his ancestors 'had bedewed with their blood' 'pro patria!'"—an act others, and subsequently Conrad himself, would perceive as a faithless betrayal and desertion. See chapter 3, "The Figure behind the Veil": Conrad and Razumov in *Under Western Eyes*," in Carabine's *Life and the Art*, 97–197.
2. Szittya, "Metafiction," 835, 838.
3. Berman, *Joseph Conrad*, 132.
4. For Berman, "Never does Conrad's language assume a more exclamatory quality as when he dramatizes the exact moment of Razumov's entry into confessional art. . . . Nowhere in the novel is Conrad closer to his protagonist than when Razumov expresses his determination to write—and his fear of being unable to write" (ibid., 138, 139–40).
5. To cite but two more examples, he "indulge[s] his wounded spirit in a feeling of immense moral and mental remoteness," and he entertains the notion that he "might have been the chosen instrument of Providence" (249, 301).
6. See *UWE* 117, 177, and 192.
7. Tanner, "Nightmare and Complacency," 213.
8. Berman, *Joseph Conrad*, 142–43.
9. See Penn R. Szittya's account of this transformation ("Metafiction," 822, 830–31).

10. Winner, *Culture and Irony*, 96, 100. Winner's chapter on *Under Western Eyes* offers a rich and insightful reading, parts of which coincide with my own. See especially his emphasis on the centrality of the role of women in what he identifies as the most feminine of Conrad's major novels. Fixing principally on the novel's inviting but deceptive silences, Yael Levin likewise perceives the novel as a hermeneutic minefield and trap. "Both to the readers of the novel and the characters within," she argues, "the novel presents a series of ideas, key words, and citations, all of which are immersed in a deceitful silence that inevitably carries the interpreter into a mistaken path of understanding" (*Tracing the Aesthetic Principle*, 74–75).

11. This disclaimer, as several critics have remarked, itself marks a transition between the first and second parts of the novel. As Guerard remarks, "The teacher of languages again protests, at the outset of the second part, his lack of professional skill . . . while accomplishing with ease the major transition from Councillor Mikulin's 'Where to?' to the society of Nathalie Haldin and her mother" (*Conrad the Novelist*, 251). See also *UWE* 24, 34, 161–62, 363, 364, 370–71.

12. See, for example, Erdinast-Vulcan, *Strange Short Fiction*, 18, 23.

13. Meyer, *Joseph Conrad*, 211–12.

14. See also his observation that Razumov's wish for an honored name, for distinction, was "nothing strange," since "[a] man's real life is that accorded to him in the thoughts of other men by reason of respect or natural love" (14). Again the teacher finds nothing surprising or unusual in the behavior of a people he offers as impenetrably other.

15. Letter to Charles Chasse, January 31, 1924, in Jean-Aubry, *Joseph Conrad*, 2:336–37.

16. Guerard, *Conrad the Novelist*, 248.

17. Szittya, "Metafiction," 822.

18. Berman, *Joseph Conrad*, 130.

19. See, for example, Lewitter, "Conrad, Dostoyevsky"; Jeffrey Berman, "Introduction to Conrad"; Meyer, "Conrad and the Russians"; Wheeler, "Russia and Russians"; Erdinast-Vulcan, *Strange Short Fiction*, esp. 11–29; and Crankshaw, "Conrad and Russia."

20. See Berman, "Introduction to Conrad," 3.

21. Lewitter, "Conrad, Dostoyevsky," 654. See also Meyer, "Conrad and the Russians," 13–20; Najder, *Conrad's Polish Background*, 13; Hewitt, *Conrad*, 127; Karl, *Joseph Conrad*, 91.

22. Letter to Sidney Colvin, November 12, 1917, in Jean-Aubry, *Joseph Conrad*, 2:198.

23. Crankshaw, "Conrad and Russia," 99. Najder is more explicit about the extent of Russian persecution of Conrad's family: in addition to the arrest of Conrad's father and the exile of his parents, Apollo and Ewa Korzeniowski. Apollo's "brother Hilary had been under arrest since 23 January [1863]. . . . Robert was killed in May. Stefan Bobrowski was killed on 12 April in a duel provoked by his right-wing opponents. His brother Kazimierz was put in prison. And while both families were suffering heavy losses, [Apollo] Korzeniowski felt helpless. . . . His health was visibly

deteriorating, and Ewa's condition was daily growing more serious" (Najder, *Joseph Conrad*, 18).

24. Berman, "Introduction to Conrad," 6. Conrad attacked Dostoyevsky so violently, Hewitt agrees, not because they were so different, "but because Dostoyevsky keeps always in the forefront of his works elements similar to those in Conrad's sensibility which he had thrust to the back and any suggestion of which he repudiated" (*Conrad*, 127).

25. Letter to George Keating, December 14, 1922, in Jean-Aubry, *Joseph Conrad*, 2:289.

26. For references to the revolution and its adherents in these precise terms, see *UWE* 16, 124, 213, 380 (pity and compassion); 19–20, 50, 121, 148 ("noble ardor of service"); 121 ("spiritual superiority"); 360 ("truth itself"); 22, 279, 302, 377 (utopian promise); 116, 250 ("unappeasable passion"); 294 ("a physical intoxication, a sort of hysteria"); 21, 66, 308 ("disruption" and a "horrible discord"); 140 ("indefinite promises").

27. Even, a classical Freudian might suggest, between a cruelly oppressive superego (the autocracy), the revolutionary id forces that rise against it, and the timid narrating ego—appropriately a teacher of languages—that attempts a nervous negotiation between them.

28. Berman, "Introduction to Conrad," 8–9.

29. Threatened by his denied attraction, the narrator expresses gratitude to Miss Haldin "for not embarrassing me by an outward display of deep feeling," admires her for that "wonderful command over herself," and is conspicuously anxious that it might "suddenly snap" (112). He also finds her, predictably, incomprehensible: "My concern [for her] was reduced to silence by my ignorance of her modes of feeling. Difference of nationality is a terrible obstacle for our complex Western natures" (116). Textual signals of the narrator's repressed attraction for Miss Haldin are numerous, and they are presented in the familiar sequence. "The grip of her strong, shapely hand had a seductive frankness," the linguist notices, "a sort of exquisite virility." And no sooner is the sensation noted than it is wrapped in a securing claim of ignorance and noncomprehension. "I do not know why she should have felt so friendly to me," he muses. "It may be that she thought I understood her much better than I was able to do. The most precise of her sayings seemed always to me to have enigmatical prolongations vanishing somewhere beyond my reach" (118). A seductive touch of the hand yields to disingenuous questions about friendship, these to confessions of ignorance followed by a sense of enigma and a vanishing (of that warmly threatening hand) "beyond my reach."

30. Jessie Conrad, *Joseph Conrad*, 143; letter from Jessie Conrad to David Meldrum, February 6, 1910, in *Joseph Conrad: Letters to William Blackwood and David S. Meldrum*, 192 (qtd. in Berman, *Joseph Conrad*, 146).

Chapter 5. Drowning in the Romance of the Shallows

1. Karl, *Reader's Guide*, 282; Schwarz, *Later Fiction*, 105; Knowles and Moore, *Oxford Reader's Companion*, 308.

2. Quoted in Karl, *Reader's Guide*, 282. The complaints were frequent and anguished. On March 29 of that year he wrote to Garnett: "I ask myself sometimes whether I am bewitched, whether I am the victim of an evil eye? . . . Sometimes it takes all my resolution and power of self control to refrain from butting my head against the wall. I want to howl and foam at the mouth but I daren't do it for fear of waking that baby and alarming my wife. . . . After such crises of despair I doze for hours till half conscious that there is that story I am unable to write" (*CL* 2:49). Again to Garnett on June 7: "This *Rescue* makes me miserable—frightens me—and I shall not abandon it—even temporarily—I must get on with it, and it will destroy my reputation. Sure!" (*CL* 2:66). And then on August 3: "I am writing hopelessly—but still I am writing. . . . pages accumulate and the story stands still. I feel suicidal. . . . I am utterly out of touch with my work—and I can't get in touch" (*CL* 2:83). At some point not long after, he abandoned it. See John Dozier Gordan's careful history of the novel's aborted gestation in *Joseph Conrad: The Making of a Novelist*, 198–219.

3. Moser, *Joseph Conrad*, 63–69; Meyer, *Joseph Conrad*, 118–19. "Some time in 1899," Moser concludes, "Conrad completely gave up 'The Rescuer'. He appears to have quit at a point in the story between the time when Edith Travers moved to Lingard's brig, and the time when she and Lingard sailed together to the mainland. In other words, Conrad gave up when the heroine was completely in the hero's hands. Yet it matters little precisely where Conrad stopped. All the evidence indicates that after an initial burst of enthusiasm, when the time came for Conrad to create the gentleman and the lady, he became acutely uncomfortable. Conrad's initial disaster with 'The Rescuer' thus follows the same pattern as that of *The Sisters*. The sympathetic treatment of love between a white man and woman is not congenial to Conrad's creativity; an examination of a few scenes between Lingard and Edith Travers in 'The Rescuer' makes this quite clear. Whether Conrad was consciously aware of it or not, he felt the relation between hero and heroine to be a powerfully sexual one" ("'Rescuer' Manuscript," 330).

4. Glassman, *Language and Being*, 143.
5. Baxter, "Rescuer Synopsis," Caserio, "Rescue," 126.
6. Gordan, *Joseph Conrad*, 217–18.
7. Erdinast-Vulcan, *Joseph Conrad*, 47–67, esp. 66.
8. Schwarz, *Later Fiction*, 105–24.
9. Roussel, *Metaphysics of Darkness*, 56–71 (quote on 71). An interesting exception to this prevailing view is Zdzisław Najder's tentative speculation that the problem lay in the conflicting loyalties the book's plot hinges on and the troubling associations they may have summoned. Captain Lingard "is torn by conflicting loyalties, and his Malay friends end up as losers. Consciously or subconsciously Conrad may have associated this situation with his own duties toward his own country—duties that he brushed aside, attracted [as Lingard is] by a different kind of life" (Najder, *Joseph Conrad*, 227).

10. Schwarz, *Later Fiction*, 119.
11. The mortal danger to masculine self-possession by the female gaze is replicated in *An Outcast of the Islands*, in which Aïssa gives Willems "the look that was

like a stab, not of anger but of desire; of the intense, over-powering desire to see in, to see through, to understand everything: every thought, emotion, purpose; every impulse, every hesitation inside that man . . . all their good or evil shut up within the breast of that man; of that man who could be persuaded, cajoled, entreated, perhaps touched, worried, frightened . . . if only first he could be understood!" (247–48). Willems confirms the paralyzing success of her invasive enterprise shortly after: "She is a ferocious creature . . . she took me as if I did not belong to myself . . . she is a savage. . . . She found out something in me. She found it out, and I was lost" (269). As the feminized jungle in *The Heart of Darkness* did to Kurtz, she peered into man's heart and saw that he was hollow at the core. In *Nostromo* Martin Decoud, who seems to speak for Conrad, argues that friendship between a man and a woman is impossible, except between brother and sister. By friendship Decoud means "the frank unreserve, as before another human being, of thoughts and sensations; all the objectless and necessary sincerity of one's innermost life, tying to re-act upon the profound sympathies of another existence" (223). The implication, it seems, is that where sexual attraction is part of the relationship, the unreserved exposure of one's thoughts, sensations, and innermost life, trying to react, which Lingard naively permits himself in this telling, is impossible, which is to say, too dangerous to one's self-possession to justify the risk.

12. Roussel, *Metaphysics of Darkness,* esp. 51–71, for a richly persuasive account of these parallels.

13. Quoted in Moser, *Joseph Conrad,* 146–47.

14. Also, as the second of the suppressed passages from *The Rescue* indicates, with his mother, whose early death left a residual legacy of feared loss, betrayal, and abandonment. As is often and most menacingly because least resistibly the case, here the betrayal is from within.

15. See *R,* 190–92 and note 2 above. It is my belief, based principally on these mirroring revelations, that Conrad abandoned the novel very near this point. But if, as is conceivable, they were written after he undertook the revision twenty years later, they occur near the point of prior exit and serve as retroactive explanations of his earlier plight. In either case there is, to my mind, little doubt of their reflexive application, conscious or otherwise, to the author's battle with his text.

16. Erdinast-Vulcan, *Joseph Conrad,* 53.

17. Nadelhaft, *Joseph Conrad,* 132–33. There is, of course, as we will see, considerable danger for Conrad in such a feminized identification.

18. Expressing revealingly vehement and injured objection to André Gide's assigning the translation of *The Arrow of Gold* to a woman translator, Conrad ranted: "If my writings have a distinct character it lies in their virility—in their spirit and method of expression. No one has denied me that. And you throw me to women! One would think that you're taking me for a fool" (qtd. in Najder, *Joseph Conrad,* 447).

19. An expanded version of this supplement, "Joseph Conrad's Tormented *Rescue* (Fantasy)," appeared in *Psychoanalytic Review* 101 (February 2014).

20. Bernard Meyer notes that the rescue theme occupies a conspicuous position in Conrad's individual creations and in his collaborative efforts with Ford Madox Hueffer. *The Nature of a Crime* (1924), a work in which Hueffer had the heavier hand

but to which Conrad contributed, describes a rescue fantasy that shares important elements with *The Rescue*. The book, not quite a novel, is a series of letters written to a married woman by a "writer" who has long been in love with her. The writer not only abstains from "that which one most desired" but also—like Lingard and like Arveragus in Geoffrey Chaucer's Franklin's Tale, lines from which Conrad used as his inscription to the novel—sacrificially rescues her husband as proof of his love and in exchange for her surrender. The true identity of the beloved woman is clear, Meyer affirms. "As the 'loved woman of the first cry that broke the silence,' she is a symbolic mother with whom the 'writer' aspires to attain an 'eventual and incomprehensible union'" (*Joseph Conrad*, 143–44).

21. Freud, "Contributions to the Psychology," 167.

22. "On the anniversary of her death, writes Baines, he [Apollo] would sit motionless before her portrait, saying nothing and eating nothing all day" (Meyer, *Joseph Conrad*, 28). Korzeniowski's letter to his friend Kazimierz Kaszewski about the consuming effect of her death upon their son is poignant and revealing: "Poor child: he does not know what a contemporary playmate is; he looks at the decrepitude of my sadness, and who knows if that sight does not make his young heart wrinkled or his wakening soul grizzled. These are important reasons forcing me to tear this poor child away from my dejected heart" (September 18, 1865, qtd. in Najder, *Joseph Conrad*, 21).

23. Sigmund Freud, "Contributions to the Psychology," 175.

24. Berman, "Ferenczi, Rescue, and Utopia," 431.

25. See, for example, *R* 183, 208, 214, 215, 242, 255, 282, 288, 300, 431, 433.

26. Freud, "Contributions to the Psychology," 168–69. An alternative explanation might suggest that the rescue of the father is an expression of compensatory guilt, a need to disguise the guilty desire for the mother by including the father, however hostile and unsavory his character, in the rescue.

27. Berman, "Ferenczi, Rescue," 431–32.

28. For additional examples of Lingard's self-idealizing romanticism, see also *R* 11–12, 73, 80, 100, 115, 121, 130, 164, 215, and 219.

Appendix

1. This appendix is a revised version of my essay "Conrad's 'Woman as Truth' Topos: 'Supposing Truth Is a Woman—What Then?'" which first appeared in *Partial Answers: Journal of Literature and the History of Ideas* 8 (2010): 67–90.

2. Merchant, *Death of Nature*, xv.

3. For a studious elaboration of this identification, see Merchant, *Death of Nature*, xv–xx, 1–41, 127–48.

4. I am indebted for my discussion of *aletheia* to Page du Bois, *Torture and Truth*, 75–91.

5. Qtd. in ibid., 81.

6. Campbell, *Hero with a Thousand Faces*, 291.

7. Du Bois, *Torture and Truth*, 78.

8. Merchant, *Death of Nature*, 29–41.

9. Qtd. in ibid., 28.

10. Qtd. in ibid., 30.

11. Lloyd, *Man of Reason*, 3. My discussion of this distinction is indebted to Lloyd's; see 3–37.

12. Nietzsche opens *Beyond Good and Evil* with the question "Supposing Truth is a woman—what then?" and the answer has assumed a surprising consistency. Woman/truth is deceptive or elusive, resistant and illusory. If woman is truth, it is, like her, undefinable, unattainable, ultimately not quite there. "Certainly," remarked Nietzsche, "she has not let herself be won" (*Beyond Good and Evil*, 2), and it is no wonder. For as Derrida, interpreting his forerunner, observes, "woman" is a beguiler. "There is no such thing as the essence of woman because woman averts, she is averted herself. Out of the depths, endless and unfathomable, she engulfs and distorts all vestige of essentiality, of identity, of property." Woman "bestows the idea. And the idea withdraws, becomes transcendent, inaccessible, seductive. It beckons from afar," but it is never possessed, for "there is no such thing as the truth of woman. . . . Woman is but one name for that untruth of truth" (Derrida, *Spurs/Eperons* 51, 87–89, 51).

13. Lloyd, *Man of Reason*, 3.

14. Schiebinger, "Feminine Icons," 663.

15. These figures were often nude to emphasize the principally physical foundation of the nature-woman analogy.

16. Lloyd, *Man of Reason*, 9.

17. Bacon, "Masculine Birth of Time," 62.

18. Ibid., 72.

19. Cited in Hodge, "Subject, Body," 159.

20. Qtd. in Fox Keller, *Reflections on Gender*, 51.

21. Cited by Walker, "Locke Minding Women," 261.

22. Ibid.

23. Easlea, *Science and Sexual Oppression*. Cited in Fox Keller, *Reflections on Gender*, 51. As Easlea observes, Bacon did not see nature as "Mother Nature" but as a female nature that could not in the long run resist a sufficiently virile male conqueror (84). And again, Bacon and other natural philosophers of the seventeenth century "viewed the scientific quest as a masculine penetration into a female nature basically deprived of creative maternal status (and certainly of the possibility of any dangerous 'sexual' response). They saw nature as a woman passively awaiting the display of male virility. . . . that would conquer and subdue her, . . . [even] shake her to her foundations" (86).

24. Cited in Fox Keller, *Reflections on Gender*, 51.

25. Jordanova, *Sexual Visions*, 89.

26. Ibid., 88.

27. Stone, *When God Was a Woman*, 220.

28. Ibid., 199. Stone cites Langdon's assertion in 1915 that "the Goddess known as Nina, another, perhaps earlier form of the name Ianna, was a serpent goddess in the most ancient Sumerian periods. As Nina, she was revered as an oracular deity and an interpreter of dreams, to whom the following prayer was addressed: 'O Nina of priestly rites, Lady of precious decrees, Prophetess of Deities art Thou.' 'The evidence,' suggested Langdon, 'points to an original serpent goddess as the interpreter of dreams

of the unrevealed future'" (Stone, *When God Was a Woman*, 199). Statues and reliefs of the ancient goddess, Stone adds, often show serpents in the background or entwined around the goddesses themselves.

29. See Nina Auerbach's study of the woman, the serpent, and demonic power as a central theme in Victorian thought and writing. The iconographic invasion "of mermaids, serpent-women, and lamias who proliferate in the Victorian imagination ... may typify the restoration of an earlier serpent woman, the Greek Medusa" (*Women and the Demon*, 80–81).

30. Beauvoir, *Second Sex*, 160.
31. Lederer, *Fear of Women*, 20.
32. See, for example, Noddings, *Women and Evil*, 10.
33. See, for example, Horney, "Dread of Women."
34. Winnicott, *Playing and Reality*, 130–38.
35. Dinnerstein, *Mermaid and the Minotaur*, 93.
36. Winnicott, *Playing and Reality*, 14–15.

37. The condition, of course, extends well beyond the earliest stages of infancy. "The temptation is strong in all of us," writes Dinnerstein, "to melt back into that from which we have carved ourselves out. The mother supports the active project, but she is also on hand to be melted into when it is abandoned. She may, indeed, even encourage the child's lapses from selfhood, for she as well as the child has mixed feelings about its increasing separation from her. There is of course no such thing as a wholly benevolent mother, with no antagonism whatsoever to the child as an autonomous being. But even if there were, she would be experienced by the child, in its struggle to become such a being, both as an interfering influence and as a lure back into non-being" (*Mermaid and the Minotaur*, 111).

38. Lederer, *Fear of Women*, 97.
39. Fox Keller, *Reflections on Gender*, 94.
40. Fox Keller, "Gender and Science," 202.

WORKS CITED

Achebe, Chinua. "An Image of Africa: Racism in Conrad's *Heart of Darkness*." *Massachusetts Review* 18 (1977): 782–94.
Armstrong, Paul B. *The Challenge of Bewilderment: Understanding and Representation in James, Conrad, and Ford*. Ithaca, N.Y.: Cornell University Press, 1992.
Auerbach, Nina. *Women and the Demon: The Life of a Victorian Myth*. Cambridge, Mass.: Harvard University Press, 1982.
Bacon, Francis. "The Masculine Birth of Time" (1653). In *The Philosophy of Francis Bacon: An Essay on Its Development from 1603 to 1609 with New Translations of Fundamental Texts*, 60–72. Translated by Benjamin Farrington. Liverpool: Liverpool University Press, 1964.
Baines, Jocelyn. *Joseph Conrad: A Critical Biography*. New York: McGraw-Hill, 1960.
Batchelor, John. *The Edwardian Novel*. London: Duckworth, 1982.
———. *The Life of Joseph Conrad: A Critical Biography*. Oxford & Cambridge, Mass.: Blackwell, 1994.
Baxter, Katherine. "The Rescuer Synopsis: Transcription and Commentary." *Conradian* 31 (2006): 117–27.
Beauvoir, Simone de. *The Second Sex*. New York: Knopf, 1953.
Becker, Ernest. *The Denial of Death*. New York: Free Press, 1973.
Berman, Emanuel. "Ferenczi, Rescue, and Utopia." *American Imago* 60 (2003): 429–44.
Berman, Jeffrey. "Introduction to Conrad and the Russians." *Conradiana* 12 (1980): 3–12.
———. *Joseph Conrad: Writing as Rescue*. New York: Astra Books, 1977.
Billy, Ted. *A Wilderness of Words: Closure and Disclosure in Conrad's Short Fiction*. Lubbock: Texas Tech University Press, 1997.
Bloom, Harold. Introduction to *Joseph Conrad's "Lord Jim": Modern Critical Interpretations*, edited by Harold Bloom, 1–6. New York: Chelsea House, 1987.
Boyle, Frank. *Swift as Nemesis: Modernity and Its Satirist*. Stanford: Stanford University Press, 2000.
Bronfen, Elisabeth. "death-drive [Freud]." In *Feminism and Psychoanalysis: A Critical Dictionary*, edited by Elizabeth Wright, 52–57. Oxford & Cambridge, Mass.: Blackwell, 1991.
Campbell, Joseph. *The Hero with a Thousand Faces*. Cleveland: World, 1956.
Carabine, Keith. *The Life and the Art: A Study of Conrad's "Under Western Eyes."* Amsterdam & Atlanta: Rodopi, 1996.

Caserio, Robert. "The Rescue and the Ring of Meaning." In *Conrad Revisited: Essays for the Eighties*, edited by Ross C. Murfin, 125–50. University: University of Alabama Press, 1985.

Cave, Terence. "Joseph Conrad: The Revenge of the Unknown." In *Joseph Conrad*, edited by Andrew Michael Roberts, 47–70. London & New York: Longman, 1998.

Chon, Sooyoung. "*Nostromo*: A Postmodern Conrad?" *Conradian* 20 (1995): 57–76.

Conrad, Jessie. *Joseph Conrad and His Circle*. New York: Dutton, 1935.

Conrad, Joseph. *The Collected Letters of Joseph Conrad*. Edited by Frederick Karl and Laurence Davies. 9 vols. London & New York: Cambridge University Press, 1983–2008.

———. *The Works of Joseph Conrad*. Uniform Edition. 22 vols. London: Dent, 1923—1: *Almayer's Folly. Tales of Unrest;* 2: *The Arrow of Gold;* 3: *Chance;* 4: *The Inheritors*, by Conrad and F. M. Hueffer [Ford Madox Ford]; 5: *Lord Jim;* 6: *The Mirror of the Sea. A Personal Record;* 7: *The Nigger of the "Narcissus." Typhoon;* 8: *Nostromo;* 9: *Notes on Life and Letters;* 10: *An Outcast of the Islands;* 11: *The Rescue;* 12: *Romance*, by Conrad and Hueffer; 13: *The Rover;* 14: *The Secret Agent;* 15: *A Set of Six;* 16: *The Shadow-Line. Within the Tides;* 17: *Suspense;* 18: *Tales of Hearsay. Last Essays;* 19: *'Twixt Land and Sea, Tales;* 20: *Under Western Eyes;* 21: *Victory;* 22: *Youth, A Narrative, and Two Other Stories.*

Cox, C. B. *Joseph Conrad: The Modern Imagination*. London: Dent, 1974.

Crankshaw, Edward. "Conrad and Russia." In *Joseph Conrad: A Commemoration*, edited by Norman Sherry, 91–104. London: Macmillan, 1976.

Curle, Richard. *The Last Twelve Years of Joseph Conrad*. London: Sampson, Low & Marston, 1928.

Daleski, H. M. *Joseph Conrad: The Way of Dispossession*. New York: Holmes & Meier, 1977.

Derrida, Jacques. *Spurs: Nietzsche's Styles / Eperons: Les styles de Nietzsche*. Chicago & London: University of Chicago Press, 1979.

Dinnerstein, Dorothy. *The Mermaid and the Minotaur: Sexual Arrangements and Human Malaise*. New York: Harper & Row, 1976.

Dodson, Sandra. "Conrad and the Politics of the Sublime." *Conradian* 22 (1997): 6–38.

Dryden, Linda. *Joseph Conrad and the Imperial Romance*. Houndmills, Basingstoke, Hampshire: Macmillan / New York: St. Martin's, 2000.

Du Bois, Page. *Torture and Truth*. New York & London: Routledge, 1991.

Easlea, Brian. *Science and Sexual Oppression: Patriarchy's Confrontation with Woman and Nature*. London: Weidenfeld & Nicolson, 1981.

Erdinast-Vulcan, Daphna. *Joseph Conrad and the Modern Temper*. Oxford: Clarendon, 1991.

———. "'The Planter of Malata': A Case of Creative Pathology." *Conradiana* 26 (1994): 187–200.

———. "Some Millennial Footnotes on *Heart of Darkness*." In *Conrad in the Twenty-First Century: Contemporary Approaches and Perspectives*, edited by Carola M. Kaplan, Peter Lancelot Mallios, and Andrea White, 55–65. New York: Routledge, 2005.

———. *The Strange Short Fiction of Joseph Conrad*. Oxford: Oxford University Press, 1999.

Fogel, Aaron. *Coercion to Speak: Conrad's Poetics of Dialogue*. Cambridge, Mass.: Harvard University Press, 1985.

Forster, E. M. "Joseph Conrad: A Note." In *Abinger Harvest*, 159–64. London: Arnold, 1936.

Foucault, Michel. *The History of Sexuality*. Vol. 1, *An Introduction*. Translated by Robert Hurley. New York: Vintage Books, 1980.

Fox Keller, Evelyn. "Gender and Science." In *Discovering Reality: Feminist Perspectives on Epistemology, Metaphysics, Methodology, and Philosophy of Science*, edited by Sandra Harding and Merrill B. Hintikka, 187–206. Dordrecht, Holland & Boston: Reidel, 1983.

———. *Reflections on Gender and Science*. New Haven: Yale University Press, 1985.

Freedman, William. "Conrad and the Anxiety of Knowledge." *Conradian* 35 (2010): 1–12.

———. "Conrad's 'Woman as Truth' Topos: 'Supposing Truth Is a Woman—What Then?'" *Partial Answers: Journal of Literature and the History of Ideas* 8 (2010): 67–90.

———. "Joseph Conrad's Tormented *Rescue* (Fantasy)." *Psychoanalytic Review* 101 (February 2014).

———. *The Porous Sanctuary: Art and Anxiety in Poe's Short Fiction*. New York: Lang, 2002.

Freud, Anna. *The Ego and the Mechanisms of Defense*. Rev. ed. New York: International Universities Press, 1966.

Freud, Sigmund. "Contributions to the Psychology of Love: A Special Type of Choice of Object Made by Men." In *Standard Edition of the Complete Psychological Works of Sigmund Freud*, vol. 11, edited by James Strachey, 165–75. London: Hogarth, 1953.

Garnett, Edward. *Letters from Conrad, 1895 to 1924*. Indianapolis: Bobbs-Merrill, 1928.

Gasiorek, Andrzej. "To Season with a Pinch of Romance: Ethics and Politics in *Lord Jim*." *Conradian* 22 (1997): 75–112.

Gibson, Andrew. "Ethics and Unrepresentability in *Heart of Darkness*." *Conradian* 22 (1997): 113–37.

Gilbert, Sandra, and Susan Gubar. *The Madwoman in the Attic: The Woman Writer and the Nineteenth-Century Literary Imagination*. New Haven: Yale University Press, 1979.

Glassman, Peter J. "An Intelligible Picture: *Lord Jim*." In *Joseph Conrad's "Lord Jim": Modern Critical Interpretations*, edited by Harold Bloom, 33–52. New York: Chelsea House, 1987.

———. *Language and Being: Joseph Conrad and the Literature of Personality*. New York: Columbia University Press, 1976.

Gordan, John Dozier. *Joseph Conrad: The Making of a Novelist*. New York: Russell & Russell, 1963.

Gose, Elliott B., Jr. "The Truth in the Well." In *Joseph Conrad's "Lord Jim": Modern Critical Interpretations*, edited by Harold Bloom, 7–31. New York: Chelsea House, 1987.

Graham, Kenneth. "Conrad and Modernism." In *The Cambridge Companion to Joseph Conrad*, edited by J. H. Stape, 203–22. Cambridge: Cambridge University Press, 1996.

Graver, Lawrence. *Conrad's Short Fiction*. Berkeley: University of California Press, 1969.

Guerard, Albert. *Conrad the Novelist*. New York: Atheneum, 1958.

———. Introduction to *Heart of Darkness*. Signet edition. New York: Penguin Books, 1950.

Guetti, James. "'Heart of Darkness' and the Failure of the Imagination." *Sewanee Review* 3 (1965): 488–504.

Hampson, Robert. *Cross-Cultural Encounters in Joseph Conrad's Malay Fiction*. Houndmills, Basingstoke, Hampshire & New York: Palgrave, 2000.

———. *Joseph Conrad: Betrayal and Identity*. New York: St. Martin's, 1992.

Hartmann, Heinz. *Essays in Ego Psychology: Selected Problems in Psychoanalytic Theory.* New York: International Universities Press, 1964.

Hawthorn, Jeremy. *Joseph Conrad: Language and Fictional Self-Consciousness.* Lincoln: University of Nebraska Press, 1979.

———. *Joseph Conrad: Narrative Technique and Ideological Commitment.* London & New York: Arnold, 1990.

Hewitt, Douglas. *Conrad: A Reassessment.* Cambridge: Bowes & Bowes, 1952.

Hodge, Joanna. "Subject, Body, and the Exclusion of Women from Philosophy." In *Feminist Perspectives in Philosophy,* edited by Morwenna Griffiths and Margaret Whitford, 152–68. Bloomington: Indiana University Press, 1988.

Horney, Karen. "Observations on a Specific Difference in the Dread Felt by Men and by Women Respectively for the Opposite Sex." *International Journal of Psychoanalysis* 13 (1932): 348–60.

Hyland, Peter. "The Little Woman in the *Heart of Darkness.*" *Conradiana* 20 (1988): 3–11.

Jameson, Fredric. *The Political Unconscious: Narrative as a Socially Symbolic Act.* London: Methuen, 1981.

Jay, Martin. *Downcast Eyes: The Denigration of Vision in Twentieth-Century French Thought.* Berkeley: University of California Press, 1993.

Jean-Aubry, G., ed. *Joseph Conrad: Life and Letters.* Vol. 2. Garden City, N.Y.: Doubleday, Page, 1927.

Johnson, Bruce. "Conrad's Impressionism and Watt's 'Delayed Decoding.'" In *Conrad Revisited: Essays for the Eighties,* edited by Ross C. Murfin, 51–70. University: University of Alabama Press, 1983.

Jordanova, Ludmilla. *Sexual Visions: Images of Gender in Science and Medicine between the Eighteenth and Twentieth Centuries.* Madison: University of Wisconsin Press, 1989.

Joseph Conrad: Letters to William Blackwood and David S. Meldrum. Durham, NC: Duke University Press, 1958.

Kaplan, Carola M. "No Refuge: The Duplicity of Domestic Safety in Conrad's Fiction." *Conradian* 22 (1997): 138–46.

Karl, Frederick R. *Joseph Conrad: The Three Lives.* New York: Farrar, Straus & Giroux, 1979.

———. *A Reader's Guide to Joseph Conrad.* New York: Noonday, 1960.

Kermode, Frank. *The Art of Telling.* Cambridge, Mass.: Harvard University Press, 1983.

Kertzer, J. M. "The Bitterness of Our Wisdom: Cynicism, Skepticism, and Joseph Conrad." *Novel: A Forum of Fiction* 16 (1983): 121–40.

———. "Watt on Conrad: Heroes of the Wars of the Mind." *Ariel* 12 (1981): 81–93.

Knowles, Owen, and Gene M. Moore. *The Oxford Reader's Companion to Conrad.* Oxford: Oxford University Press, 2000.

Leavis, F. R. *The Great Tradition.* New York: New York University Press, 1963.

Lederer, Wolfgang. *The Fear of Women.* New York: Grune & Stratton, 1968.

Lenormand, H. R. "Note sur un séjour de Conrad en Corse." *Nouvelle Revue Française,* December 1, 1924, 666–71.

Levin, Yael. *Tracing the Aesthetic Principle in Conrad's Novels.* New York: Palgrave Macmillan, 2008.

Lloyd, Genevieve. *The Man of Reason: "Male" and "Female" in Western Philosophy*. Minneapolis: University of Minnesota Press, 1984.

Lewitter, L. R. "Conrad, Dostoyevsky and the Russo-Polish Antagonism." *Modern Language Review* 79 (1984): 653–63.

Mayoux, Jean-Jacques. *Vivants piliers: Le roman anglo-saxon et les symbols*. Paris: Julliard, 1960.

McCracken, Scott. "'A Hard and Absolute Condition of Existence': Reading Masculinity in *Lord Jim*." In *Conrad and Gender*, edited by Andrew Michael Roberts, 17–38. Amsterdam & Atlanta: Rodopi, 1993.

Mencken, H. L. *A Book of Prefaces*. New York: Knopf, 1917.

Merchant, Carolyn. *The Death of Nature: Women, Ecology, and the Scientific Revolution*. New York: Harper & Row, 1980.

Meyer, Bernard C. *Joseph Conrad: A Psychoanalytic Biography*. Princeton: Princeton University Press, 1967.

———. "Conrad and the Russians." *Conradiana* 12 (1980); 13–21.

Miller, J. Hillis. *Fiction and Repetition: Seven English Novels*. Cambridge, Mass.: Harvard University Press, 1983.

———. *Poets of Reality*. New York: Atheneum, 1969.

Mongia, Padmini. "'Ghosts of the Gothic': Spectral Women and Colonized Spaces in *Lord Jim*." In *Conrad and Gender*, edited by Andrew Michael Roberts, 1–16. Amsterdam & Atlanta: Rodopi, 1993.

Morf, Gustav. *The Polish Heritage of Joseph Conrad*. London: Sampson Low, 1930.

Moser, Thomas. "From Olive Garnett's Diary: Impressions of Ford Madox Ford and His Friends, 1980–1906." *Texas Studies in Literature and Language* 16 (1974): 511–33.

———. *Joseph Conrad: Achievement and Decline*. Hamden, Conn.: Archon Books, 1966.

———. "'The Rescuer' Manuscript: A Key to Conrad's Development—and Decline." *Harvard Library Bulletin* 10 (1956): 325–56.

Nadelhaft, Ruth. *Joseph Conrad*. Atlantic Highlands, N.J.: Humanities Press International, 1991.

Najder, Zdzisław. *Conrad under Familial Eyes*. Cambridge: Cambridge University Press, 1983.

———. *Conrad's Polish Background: Letters to and from Polish Friends*. London & New York: Oxford University Press, 1964.

———. *Joseph Conrad: A Chronicle*. New Brunswick, N.J.: Rutgers University Press, 1983.

Newhouse, Neville H. *Joseph Conrad*. London: Evans, 1966.

Nietzsche, Friedrich. *Beyond Good and Evil*. Translated by Walter Kaufmann. New York: Vintage Books, 1966.

Noddings, Nell. *Women and Evil*. Berkeley: University of California Press, 1989.

Peters, John. *Conrad and Impressionism*. Cambridge: Cambridge University Press, 2001.

Rank, Otto. *Will Therapy and Truth and Reality*. New York: Knopf, 1945.

Raval, Suresh. *The Art of Failure: Conrad's Fiction*. Boston: Allen & Unwin, 1986.

Ray, Martin. "Language and Silence in the Novels of Joseph Conrad." *Conradiana* 16 (1984): 19–40.

Regueiro, Helen. *The Limits of Imagination: Wordsworth, Yeats, and Stevens.* Ithaca, N.Y.: Cornell University Press, 1976.

Ricouer, Paul. "'Original Sin': A Study in Meaning." In *The Conflict of Interpretations*, 265–283. Evanston, Ill.: Northwestern University Press, 1974.

Roberts, Andrew Michael. *Conrad and Masculinity.* Houndmills, Basingstoke, Hampshire: Macmillan, 2000.

Rosenfield, Claire. *Paradise of Snakes: An Archetypal Analysis of Conrad's Political Novels.* Chicago: University of Chicago Press, 1969.

Ross, Daniel. "*Lord Jim* and the Saving Illusion." *Conradiana* 20 (1988): 45–69.

Rousseau, Jean-Jacques. "A Dissertation on the Effects of Cultivating the Arts and Sciences." In *Miscellaneous Works of J. J. Rousseau*, vol. 1, 3–134. London: Becket & DeHondt, 1767; rpt., New York: Franklin, 1972.

Roussel, Royal. *The Metaphysics of Darkness: A Study in the Unity and Development of Conrad's Fiction.* Baltimore: Johns Hopkins University Press, 1971.

Said, Edward. "Conrad: The Presentation of Narrative." In *Critical Essays on Joseph Conrad*, edited by Ted Billy, 28–46. Boston: Hall, 1987.

———. "Conrad and Nietzsche." In *Joseph Conrad: A Commemoration*, edited by Norman Sherry, 65–76. New York: Macmillan, 1976.

———. *Joseph Conrad and the Fiction of Autobiography.* Cambridge, Mass.: Harvard University Press, 1966.

Schiebinger, Londa. "Feminine Icons: The Face of Early Modern Science." *Critical Inquiry* 14 (1988): 661–91.

Schneider, Lissa. *Conrad's Narratives of Difference: Not Exactly Tales for Boys.* New York & London: Routledge, 2003.

Schwarz, Daniel. *Conrad: The Later Fiction.* London: Macmillan, 1982.

Sedgwick, Eve Kosofsky. *Epistemology of the Closet.* New York: Harvester Wheatsheaf, 1991.

Senn, Werner. *Conrad's Narrative Voice.* Bern: Francke, 1980.

Shattuck, Roger. *Forbidden Knowledge from Prometheus to Pornography.* New York: St. Martin's, 1996.

Smith, David R. "The Hidden Narrative: The K in Conrad." In *Joseph Conrad's "Under Western Eyes": Beginnings, Revisions, Final Forms*, edited by David R. Smith, 1–37. Hamden, Conn.: Archon Books, 1991.

Stape, J. H. Introduction to *An Outcast of the Islands*, edited by J. H. Stape and Hans van Marle, xi–xxiii. Oxford & New York: Oxford University Press, 1992.

———. "*Lord Jim.*" In *The Cambridge Companion to Joseph Conrad*, edited by J. H. Stape, 63–80. Cambridge: Cambridge University Press, 1996.

Staten, Henry. "Conrad's Mortal World." *Critical Inquiry* 12 (1986): 720–40.

Stein, William Bysshe. "*The Secret Agent:* The Agon(ies) of the Word." *Boundary 2* 6 (1978): 521–540.

Stone, Merlin. *When God Was a Woman.* New York & London: Harcourt Brace Jovanovich, 1976.

Szittya, Penn R. "Metafiction: The Double Narration in *Under Western Eyes.*" *ELH* 48 (1981): 817–40.

Tanner, Tony. "Butterflies and Beetles—Conrad's Two Truths." *Chicago Review* 16 (1963): 123–40.

———. "Nightmare and Complacency: Razumov and the Western Eye." *Critical Quarterly* 43 (1962): 197–214.

Thorburn, David. *Conrad's Romanticism*. New Haven, Conn.: Yale University Press, 1974.

Torgovnick, Marianna. *Gone Primitive: Savage Intellects, Modern Lives*. Chicago: University of Chicago Press, 1991.

Walker, William. "Locke Minding Women: Literary History, Gender and *The Essay*." *Eighteenth Century Studies* 23 (1990): 245–68.

Warren, Robert Penn. Introduction to *Nostromo*, vii–xxxix. New York: Modern Library, 1951.

Wasserman, Jerry. "Narrative Presence: The Illusion of Language in *Heart of Darkness*." In *Critical Essays on Joseph Conrad*, edited by Ted Billy, 102–13. Boston: Hall, 1987.

Watt, Ian. *Conrad in the Nineteenth Century*. Berkeley: University of California Press, 1979.

———. "Impressionism and Symbolism in 'Heart of Darkness.'" In *Joseph Conrad: A Commemoration*, edited by Norman Sherry, 37–53. London: Macmillan, 1976.

Watt, Ian, ed. *Conrad: "The Secret Agent," a Casebook*. London: Macmillan, 1973.

Watts, Cedric. *The Deceptive Text: An Introduction to Covert Plots*. Sussex: Harvester, 1984.

———. *A Preface to Conrad*. Harlow: Longman, 1982.

Wheeler, Marcus. "Russia and Russians in the Works of Conrad." *Conradiana* 12 (1980): 23–36.

White, Allon. *The Uses of Obscurity: The Fiction of Early Modernism*. London: Routledge & Kegan Paul, 1981.

Wilson, Donald S. "The Beast in the Congo: How Victorian Homophobia Inflects Marlow's *Heart of Darkness*." *Conradiana* 32 (2000): 96–118.

Winner, Anthony. *Culture and Irony: Studies in Joseph Conrad's Major Novels*. Charlottesville: University Press of Virginia, 1988.

Winnicott, D. W. *Playing and Reality*. Harmondsworth, U.K.: Penguin Books, 1971.

Wollaeger, Mark. *Joseph Conrad and the Fictions of Skepticism*. Stanford: Stanford University Press, 1990.

Yeow, Agnes S. K. *Conrad's Eastern Vision*. New York: Palgrave Macmillan, 2009.

INDEX

Achebe, Chinua, 152, 165
Almayer's Folly, 7, 149, 166
Armstrong, Paul B., 61, 141, 154, 165
Arrow of Gold, 7, 33, 68, 116, 153, 161, 166
Auerbach, Nina, 164–65

Bacon, Francis, 134–36, 163, 165
Baines, Jocelyn, 30, 122, 150, 162, 165
Baxter, Katherine, 106, 160, 165
Beauvoir, Simone de, 137–38, 143, 164–65
Becker, Ernest, 5, 65, 142, 144, 151, 153–55, 165
Berman, Emanuel, 122–23
Berman, Jeffrey, 88, 91, 98, 150, 157–59, 162
Billy, Ted, 13, 144, 146, 148, 151, 165
Bloom, Harold, 142, 165
Boyle, Frank, 155, 165
Bronfen, Elisabeth, 143, 165

Campbell, Joseph, 133, 162, 165
Carabine, Keith, 150, 157, 165
Casement, Roger, 25
Caserio, Robert, 106, 160, 166
Cave, Terence, 7, 18, 143, 147, 166
Chance, 26, 100, 166
Chaucer, Geoffrey, 122–23, 126, 162
Chon, Sooyoung, 142, 166
Chrysostom, John, 139
Conrad, Jessie, 103, 159, 166
Conrad, Joseph, 122; attitudes toward art and the role of the artist, 2, 18, 20, 33–34, 43–44, 46–57, 60, 62–67, 69, 74, 78, 85–90, 92, 108–17, 119–20; attitudes toward truth and knowledge, 9–35, 144–48, 153; autobiographical elements in, 150, 152; childhood, 122, 127–28; dangerous and forbidden knowledge in, 2–4,143, 148–49, 151; obscurity of writing, 1–4, 33, 141–42, 144, 147–48, 151; personality, 2, 9–13, 15, 17, 19, 21–25, 34,105–20, 127, 128, 144; saving illusion in, 19–35, 149; view of woman and the female, 7–8, 18, 30, 33, 110–20, 143, 151–52; woman and truth in, 7–8, 15, 18, 30, 32–33
Cowley, Abraham, 136
Cox, C. B., 144–45, 154, 166
Crane, Stephen, 9–10
Crankshaw, Edward, 100, 158, 166
Curle, Richard, 10, 107, 144, 166

Daleski, H. M., 2, 13, 142, 144, 147, 166
dangerous and forbidden knowledge, 5–9, 134, 137–40, 163
Derrida, Jacques, 135, 163, 166
Descartes, René, 136
Dinnerstein, Dorothy, 139, 164, 166
Dodson, Sandra, 141, 146, 166
Dostoevsky, Dostoyevsky, 99–100, 158–59, 169
Dryden, Linda, 155, 166
Du Bois, Page, 133, 162, 166

Easlea, Brian, 137, 163, 166
End of the Tether, 18
Erdinast-Vulcan, Daphna, 55, 66, 108, 116, 146–47, 149–50, 154–55, 158, 160–61, 166

"Falk," 7, 20, 68
Fogel, Aaron, 153, 167
Forster, E. M., 1, 37, 54, 80, 141, 167
Foucault, Michel, 7–8, 143, 167
Fox Keller, Evelyn, 140, 163–64, 167
Freedman, William, 142–43, 155–56, 167
Freud, Anna, 5, 167
Freud, Sigmund, 162, 167

Galsworthy, John, 17, 47, 52, 69, 92, 149, 157
Garnett, Edward, 106–8, 113, 115, 117, 147, 157, 160, 167
Gasiorek, Andrzej, 70, 154–55, 167
Gibson, Andrew, 153, 167
Gilbert, Sandra, and Susan Gubar, 156, 167
Glassman, Peter J., 36, 62, 106, 151, 153–54, 160, 167
Gordan, John Dozier, 106, 160, 167
Gose, Elliott B., Jr., 69, 154–55, 167
Graham, Cunninghame, vi, 11, 17, 20, 25, 64–65, 148, 151
Graham, Kenneth, 141, 167
Graver, Lawrence, 144, 167
Guerard, Albert, 53, 97, 153, 158, 167
Guetti, James, 11, 144, 167

Hampson, Robert, 142, 154–55, 157, 168
Hartmann, Heinz, 5, 142, 168
Hawthorn, Jeremy, 144, 151, 154, 168
Hawthorne, Nathaniel, 6, 52
Heart of Darkness, 1, 3–4, 8, 10–11, 16, 18–19, 27, 36–61, 64, 70, 72–75, 78–79, 97, 101, 103, 106–7, 109–10, 116, 121, 129–30, 141–42, 144, 146–47, 149, 151–53, 156, 161, 165–68, 171; artist's obligation in, 46–57, 60; avoidance in, 39–60; Congo, 16, 25, 49, 51, 55, 57, 101, 152, 171; doppelganger in, 44–46; imagination in, 46–53; obscurity of, 37–60 ; saving illusion in, 44–46, 56–57; woman in, 40–41, 44–46, 53
Hewitt, Douglas, 142, 158–59, 168
Hodge, Joanna, 163, 168
Horney, Karen, 164, 168

Hudson, W.H., 52
Hyland, Peter, 44, 152, 168

Inheritors, 166

James, Henry, 56, 147, 152
Jameson, Fredric, 141, 154, 168
Jay, Martin, 142, 168
Jean-Aubry, G., 149, 151, 155, 158, 159, 168
Johnson, Bruce, 31, 145, 168
Jordanova, Ludmilla, 137, 163, 168

Kaplan, Carola M., 166, 168
Karl, Frederick R., 105, 121, 158, 159, 166, 168
Kermode, Frank, 141, 168
Kertzer, J. M., 145, 154, 168
Knowles, Owen, and Gene M. Moore, 105, 159, 168

Leavis, F. R., 141, 146, 168
Lederer, Wolfgang, 138, 140, 143, 164, 168
Lenormand, H. R., 24, 149, 169
Levin, Yael, 158, 169
Lewitter, L. R., 158, 169
Lloyd, Genevieve, 135–36, 163, 169
Locke, John, 136, 137
Lord Jim, 3–4, 7, 12, 16–17, 21, 36, 43–44, 51, 61–87, 97, 103, 106–8, 110, 129–30, 142, 146, 148–49, 154–55, 165–71; art and imagination in, 62, 65–70, 74, 84–87; avoidance in, 61–87, 155; dangerous and forbidden knowledge in, 61–87, 156–57; doppelganger in, 73–74; obscurity of, 61–62, 69–71, 78–79, 83–87, 154; woman in, 68–70, 81, 84, 87, 155

Mayoux, Jean-Jacques, 49, 153, 169
McCracken, Scott, 155, 169
Mencken, H. L., 1, 141, 169
Merchant, Carolyn, 2, 22, 133–34, 162, 169
Meyer, Bernard C., 25, 93, 106, 147, 149–50, 158, 160–62, 169

Miller, J. Hillis, 13, 16, 20, 29–30, 61, 63, 70, 142, 144, 147, 150, 154–55, 169
Mirror of the Sea, 166
Mongia, Padmini, 84, 155, 157, 169
Montaigne, Michel de, 6
Moser, Thomas, 106, 152, 160–61, 169

Nadelhaft, Ruth, 116–17, 161, 169
Najder, Zdzisław, 144, 146, 158–62, 169
Newhouse, Neville H., 144, 169
Nietzsche, Friedrich, 135–36, 144, 146, 148–49, 163, 166, 169
Nigger of the "Narcissus," viii, 13, 19–20, 26, 47, 56, 72, 106, 109, 118, 121, 146, 153, 166
Noddings, Nell, 143, 164, 169
Nostromo, 21, 24–25, 142, 161, 166, 171
Notes on Life and Letters, viii, 166

Outcast of the Islands, 19, 106, 153, 160, 166, 170

Patusan, 26, 37, 43, 49, 52, 56, 64–68, 70, 76, 80, 83–87, 154
Personal Record, viii, 48, 69, 98, 150, 166
Peters, John, 14, 145, 169
"Planter of Malata," 7, 68, 82, 147, 153, 166
Poe, Edgar Allen, 52

Rank, Otto, vi, 5, 36, 49, 65, 142, 151, 153, 170
Raval, Suresh, 144–46, 154, 157, 170
Ray, Martin, 163, 170
Regueiro, Helen, 153, 170
Rescue, viii, 3–4, 105–11, 114–16, 118–22, 127, 130–31, 147, 153, 160–61, 166; art and artist in, 108–117, 120, 128; autobiography in, 109, 116–17, 119, 122, 127; Conrad's difficulty with, 105–10, 120–21, 128, 160–61; rescue fantasy in, 120–128; woman in, 109–120, 121, 126–28, 160–62
"Rescuer," 105, 111, 121, 160
"Return," 7, 18, 68, 147
Ricouer, Paul, 143, 170

Roberts, Andrew Michael, 2, 142, 166, 169–70
Romance, 155, 166
Rosenfield, Claire, 150, 170
Ross, Daniel, 148, 170
Rousseau, Jean-Jacques, 6, 143, 170
Roussel, Royal, 13, 108, 110, 144, 160–61, 170
Rover, 166

Said, Edward, 1, 13, 146–47, 149, 170
Schiebinger, Londa, 136, 163, 170
Schneider, Lissa, 149, 170
Schwarz, Daniel, 30, 105, 108, 150, 159–60, 170
Secret Agent, 1, 14, 27–30, 32, 147, 149–50, 153, 166, 170; Avoidance in, 27–32; Dangerous and forbidden knowledge in, 27–32; Obscurity of, 27, 29–30; Woman in, 30
Secret Sharer, 110
Sedgwick, Eve Kosofsky, 145, 170
Set of Six, 166
Shadow Line, 33, 150, 166
Shattuck, Roger, 6, 142–43, 170
"Smile of Fortune," 19, 151, 153
Smith, David R., 150, 170
Stape, J. H., 154, 167, 170
Staten, Henry, 153, 170
Stein, William Bysshe, 6, 16, 30, 56, 64, 68, 75–76, 84, 129, 150, 154, 170
Stone, Merlin, 137, 171
Suspense, 166
Swift, Jonathan, 6, 22, 141, 155
Szittya, Penn R., 88, 98, 157–58, 171

Tales of Hearsay and Last Essays, 18, 33, 166
Tales of Unrest, 7, 166
Tanner, Tony, 91, 154, 157, 171
Tertullian, 6
Thorburn, David, 146, 171
Torgovnick, Marianna, 151, 157, 171
'Twixt Land and Sea, 19, 151, 166
Typhoon, 20, 23, 166

Under Western Eyes, 3–4, 7, 29, 34, 88–104, 130, 141, 149–50, 156–58, 165–66, 170–71; Art and Artist in, 88–90, 157; Autobiography in, 88, 98–99, 104, 157; Avoidance in, 88–104; Dangerous and forbidden knowledge in, 88–104; Dostoevsky in, 100; Narrator in, 92–104; Poland and Polish in, 3, 95, 98–99, 102–3; Revolution in, 99, 101–2; Russia and Russian in, 3, 46, 88, 92–94, 96–104, 130, 157–58, 165–66, 169, 171; Woman in, 101–3, 158
Victory, 17, 20, 27, 34, 54, 81, 142, 148, 166

Walker, William, 137, 163, 171
Warren, Robert Penn, 14, 21–22, 145, 148, 171
Wasserman, Jerry, 144, 171
Watt, Ian, 85, 145, 149–50, 153, 157, 171
Watts, Cedric, 141, 171
Wheeler, Marcus, 158, 171
White, Allon, 147, 171
Wilson, Donald S., 1, 171
Winner, Anthony, 29–30, 92, 142, 145, 150, 158, 171
Winnicott, D. W., 139, 164, 171
Within the Tides, 7, 10, 49, 166
Wollaeger, Mark, 14, 145, 171
Woman and Truth: 12, 133–140, 155, 162–64
Yeow, Agnes S. K., 154, 171

"Youth," 18, 121
Youth, A Narrative, and Two Other Stories, 166

CPSIA information can be obtained at www.ICGtesting.com
Printed in the USA
LVOW06*0417280314

379268LV00003B/5/P